JSTL

Practical Guide for JSP Programmers

The Morgan Kaufmann Practical Guides Series
Series Editor, Michael J. Donahoo

JSTL: Practical Guide for JSP Programmers
Sue Spielman

JSP: Practical Guide for Java Programmers
Robert J. Brunner

Java: Practical Guide for Programmers
Zbigniew M. Sikora

The Struts Framework: Practical Guide for Java Programmers
Sue Spielman

Multicast Sockets: Practical Guide for Programmers
David Makofske and Kevin Almeroth

TCP/IP Sockets in Java: Practical Guide for Programmers
Kenneth L. Calvert and Michael J. Donahoo

TCP/IP Sockets in C: Practical Guide for Programmers
Michael J. Donahoo and Kenneth L. Calvert

JDBC: Practical Guide for Java Programmers
Gregory D. Speegle

For further information on these books and for a list of forthcoming titles, please visit our website at *http://www.mkp.com/practical*

JSTL

Practical Guide for JSP Programmers

Sue Spielman

Switchback Software LLC

AMSTERDAM • BOSTON • HEIDELBERG • LONDON
NEW YORK • OXFORD • PARIS • SAN DIEGO
SAN FRANCISCO • SINGAPORE • SYDNEY • TOKYO

This book is printed on acid-free paper.

Senior Editor:	Rick Adams
Developmental Editor:	Karyn Johnson
Publishing Services Manager:	Simon Crump
Senior Project Manager:	Angela G. Dooley
Project Management:	Keyword
Composition:	CEPHA
Cover Design:	Cate Barr
Printer:	Maple-Vail

Morgan Kaufmann
An imprint of Elsevier Science
340 Pine Street, Sixth Floor, San Francisco, California 94104-3205, USA
http://www.mkp.com

Library of Congress Catalog Card Number: 2003107479
International Standard Book Number: 0-12-656755-7

Printed in the United States of America
03 1 2 3 4 5

Act mindfully
Accept entirely
Move strongly
Think softly
Speak beautifully
Live simply
Love completely

Anonymous

Dedicated to my family

Mommasita, Papar, Liz, Ken, Randi, Ryan, Christopher, Bev, and Sid

Contents

Preface

As a JSP developer, you are probably always looking for ways to improve your JSP page authoring. The JSP Standard Tag Library (JSTL) will provide you with a plethora of useful actions that you can start taking advantage of today. It will allow you to focus on the true presentation features of your pages, while providing a comprehensive cover for common tasks that page authors continually run into. My goal in writing this book is to get you up to speed as quickly as possible on all that is available in the JSTL and how to apply that knowledge to your daily page authoring. You'll be amazed at how much cleaner your pages will appear and how much better you'll feel about them. Just like when you finally clean out of your closet the 10-year-old t-shirts that you thought you couldn't live without.

What's to Come

First we'll look at how we arrived at the need for the JSTL and what it can provide. In the introduction chapters, I'll provide answers to some initial questions about what custom tags are and what custom tag libraries look like and what types of actions are available in the JSTL. The next few chapters include JSTL basics, the JSTL layout and how to work with the expression language. We'll then go into each of the functional areas, and the custom actions provided by each, and work through detailed samples for each and every action. We will focus on the details of using each of the various tags as well as the various situations that each tag can be applied to. Plenty of code samples are included.

I hope that, provided with the quick reference for all of the tags and attributes contained in JSTL 1.0, you'll be able to use this reference during your JSP development and flip to the appropriate page for specific tag information. I take the "practical" in the title of this book seriously.

The Code Samples

All of the code samples you will encounter in this book are provided in a sample download. I wanted to cover all of the attributes and features of each action. Each and every action has an accompanying sample file that you can reference according to the chapter in which it appears. These samples should give you an excellent reference for how to use the actions so that you can go off and utilize them in your applications.

You can access the download from *http://www.mkp.com/practical/jstl* or from *http://www.switchbacksoftware.com*. I am utilizing the reference implementation of the JSTL from the Jakarta Tablib standard project. The .jar files required for the JSTL are provided with the download; however, you can visit the Jakarta site at *http://jakarta.apache.org/taglibs/doc/standard-doc/intro.html* for the latest information on the available reference implementation. This book uses the JSTL 1.0.3 reference implementation along with Tomcat 5.0.

Tomcat 5.0 is the next major release of Tomcat. It builds on the Tomcat 3.3 and Tomcat 4.1.x code base. The 5.0 release implements the JSP 2.0 and Servlet 2.4 specifications that will be available in the next major release of the J2EE 1.4 platform. At the time of this writing, Tomcat 5.0 is still in Alpha. Taking that into consideration, I have also run the code samples on Tomcat 4.1.20, so if you are on that version, you should have no problem. The Tomcat 4.1.x release implements the JSP 1.2 and the Servlet 2.3 specifications.

When J2EE 1.4 is released there should be some minor enhancements to the JSTL and the revision will become v1.1. These enhancements include support for some of the functionality that will be available in the expression language in JSP 2.0. However, by reading this book, you will be ahead of the game because you'll already have a full understanding of the expression language (EL) and how to use it. I suggest that, if you are going to be working with JSP 2.0, you take a few minutes to examine the small changes in the expression language so that you can take full advantage of it.

Specifications to Be Familiar With

Like any of the web technologies that developers work with, there is always an overabundance of additional specifications with which we must become familiar. Since the JSTL covers different areas of functionality, there are more than a few specs that you probably want to be aware of, or explore, in more detail. Don't worry; you don't have to be an expert on any of them. However, this book assumes that you are at least familiar at a high level with the topics covered in the specifications listed in Table 0.1.

Acknowledgments

This project seemed to take on a life of its own, but I am glad that it found its roots. Each time I take on a new book project, I conveniently forget how much time, energy, thought,

Specification	Location
JavaServer Pages (JSP)	http://java.sun.com/jsp
Java Servlet Technology	http://java.sun.com/servlet
Java 2 Platform, Standard Edition	http://java.sun.com/j2se
Java 2 Platform, Enterprise Edition	http://java.sun.com/j2ee
JavaBeans	http://java.sun.com/beans
JDBC	http://java.sun.com/jdbc
Java Technology and XML	http://java.sun.com/xml
XPath specification	http://www.w3.org/TR/xpath
XML home page at W3C	http://www.w3.org/XML
HTML home page at W3C	http://www.w3.org/MarkUp
XML.org home page	http://www.xml.org

Table 0.1: Related specifications.

and debugging go into it. Similarly to what I do when I'm riding my bike up a long steep mountain pass, I typically say "How hard can it be?", and then just start. It is only when you start that it all comes back at you. It's then that you realize that not only does it take a major time commitment on your own part, but also that it relies on a number of people whose support and work bring the project to life.

Thanks (again) to Karyn Johnson and Rick Adams for bringing me on board for another book in the Practical Guide Series. My sincere thanks to all of the proposal and technical reviewers who were an absolute stellar bunch. They include: Thomas Paul, Anthony Ikeda, Tom Marrs, John Raley, Matt Houser, Pierre Delisle, Ireno Marchenko, and Grandin Hammell. The technical review comments inspired me to completely reorganize this book from its orginial form. As I said, this project has a life of its own and you just have to go with it sometimes. The comments and suggestions that I received as input from the reviewers were invaluable and raised the bar on the book for all readers.

Thank you to the production staff at Morgan Kaufmann and Keyword who really are industry top notch. They include: Maureen Allen and Angela Dooley.

Thanks (again) to Pierre Delisle, the JSTL specification lead at Sun Microsystems, for always promptly answering my email questions.

I'd like to acknowledge my grandparents, for while they aren't physically on this planet any more, they are in my thoughts every day. I know that they'd be beaming holding this book. I miss you both.

And last, but certainly not least, thank you to Elizabeth for just about everything. Your assistance, patience, and understanding are never overlooked or under-appreciated.

chapter 1

Introduction

The fact that you are holding this book in your hands indicates that you are not only intrigued by the world of the web, but you are actually shaping it. As a developer you either have built, or are about to build, some form of web application. This book is focused on how to get the most out of the JSP Standard Tag Library, also referred to as the JSTL, when you are building your web applications.

This first, introductory chapter answers the basic questions surrounding what the JSTL is, why using it will make your life easier, how it deals with dynamic content, and why a JSTL is needed. I make no bones about it, when you're done with this chapter you should be raring to start using the JSTL.

1.1 What Exactly Is the JSTL?

JSTL is the JSP Standard Tag Library. The JSTL came about under JSR-52 of the Java Community Process (JCP). The specification can be found at *http://jcp.org/jsr/detail/52.jsp*. JSR-52 covers the creation of a standard tag library for JavaServer Pages and allows this library to be available to all compliant JSP containers. These tag libraries provide a wide range of custom action functionality that most JSP authors have found themselves in need of in the past. Having a defined specification for how the functionality is implemented means that a page author can learn these custom actions once and then use and reuse them on all future products on all application containers that support the specification. Using the JSTL will not only make your JSPs more readable and maintainable, but will allow you to concentrate on good design and implementation practices in your pages. We can finally take the "custom" out of custom action and replace it with "standard." No more creating your own iteration action for the tenth time. Additionally, your favorite Integrated Development Environment (IDE) that supports JSP authoring will now support these standard actions and can assist the JSP page author in rapid development.

So to sum up how the JSTL got here, an expert group was tasked with creating custom actions that are valuable to a range of JSP authors and developers, and that is exactly what they created.

1.2 Why a JSP Standard Tag Library?

We have answered the "what is the JSTL" question, but let's answer the "why" question. Why a JSP standard tag library and, for that matter, why now? The answer to both is quite simple: because writing your own custom actions is a time consuming pain.

With the introduction of JSP 1.1, there existed a standard mechanism for the creation of tag libraries. Initially, we all referred to this mechanism as custom tags, now we refer to it as custom actions. That's why we still see the collection of actions called Tag Libraries as opposed to Action Libraries. Otherwise, we'd be referring to the JSAL instead of the JSTL. JSTL just sounds better. Both terms, custom tags and custom actions, refer to the same exact technology.

1.3 Why Now?

While custom tags were a big improvement in functionality over the JSP 1.0 specification, they still left room for the "reinventing the wheel" syndrome. How many times is it really necessary to create a custom tag for formatting a date for different customers? Apparently the answer was "a lot." JSP page authors saw the same custom tag functionality being required over and over again. Out of this need grew the start of open source projects to provide numerous tag libraries. Granted, the Jakarta taglib project helped and provides hundreds of custom tags within the various libraries. But there still was no standard, no way to just learn the tag once and be done with it. The lack of a standard tag library helped fuel the fire for the JSTL.

Many of the features of the expression language supported in the standard tag library have been folded into the next release of the JSP specification—which is JSP 2.0 or JSR-152. But the JSTL remains a separate entity. Having a separate expert group ensures that the basic mechanisms in JSP 1.2 are applicable to any tag library. It also allows for the possibility of supporting both JSP 1.2 and JSP 1.1 containers. While many members of the expert group sit on both the JSP specification and the JSTL, having different expert groups allows for different interests to be served. Probably the biggest reason to have two separate JSRs is that the release schedules are therefore not dependent on one another, or on the J2EE release for that matter.

1.4 Why You *Really* Want to Use the JSTL

Although the mechanism of custom tags enabled the creation of libraries to be shared across many different user communities, there are direct benefits to engineers and page authors that can be realized through the use of a standard tag library:

- It is easy to learn and provides a wide range of functionality.
- JSP authors and JSP authoring tools can easily generate pages on all compliant JSP containers using standard tags.
- Standard tags created by the expert group will meet the needs of a wide variety of communities.
- The tags will already be well tested and ready for use.
- There will be reduced training costs by providing targeted training materials and simplified portability and maintainability of JSP pages and applications.
- Specialized implementations of the library will be available so that containers can provide both portability and higher performance.

With all the time you save using the JSTL, you'll be able to concentrate on making the core value of your application even greater.

Aside from the development process benefits that will be realized by using the JSTL, the functionality contained in the JSTL is impressive. Since this book is dedicated entirely to the JSTL, we will be going over all of the available actions in detail.

1.5 The Need for Encapsulation

Most JSP 1.1 (or higher) containers are already providing a tag library that is being used by their customers. It was clear in the JSP authoring community that there was a need for encapsulation of functionality. The reasons are quite simple. If functionality is encapsulated, JSP authors can use the custom tags without much knowledge of Java or by making any other coding effort. Encapsulation also allows for reuse of common functionality within an application and across applications. With each custom tag written, the testing and debugging of that tag only has to take place once. Once it has been tested, debugged, and used, the return on investment in the developer as well as the source code becomes greatly increased.

1.6 Functional Overview

The JSTL encapsulates common functionality that a typical JSP author would encounter. This set of common functionality has come about through the input of the various members of the expert group. Since this expert group has a good cross section of JSP authors and users, the actions provided in the JSTL should suit a wide audience.

The JSTL is a set of custom actions that is based on the JSP 1.2 and Servlet 2.3 specifications. While the JSTL is commonly referred to as a single tag library, it is actually composed of four separate tag libraries:

- Core
- XML manipulation
- SQL
- Internationalization and formatting

These libraries are defined by the Tag Library Descriptor files. Using separate TLDs to expose the tags, the functionality for each set of actions is apparent and makes more sense. Using separate TLDs also allows each library to have its own namespace.

To sum up for now, the layout of the JSTL is straightforward. The overriding theme throughout the JSTL is simplifying the life of the page author. The page author is the person who builds the JSP pages. There has always been a need (although not a requirement) that the page authors have some understanding of a programming language (usually Java) in order to create complex pages. This dilemma is what has hampered the true role separation between the JSP page author and the Java programmer. Using the tags provided in the JSTL, we are closer to reaching that clean division of labor. The functional areas in the JSTL help page authors identify what type of functionality they need and where they can find it.

To give you an idea of what's to come, let's briefly describe the four tag libraries that are provided in the JSTL.

1.7 JSTL Tag Libraries

The Core library provides general-purpose actions that get and set scoped variables, write to the `JspWriter`, and handle catching exceptions. The actions in Core library also take advantage of the expression language features. Also included in the Core library are those actions related to conditional processing, handling iterations, and dealing with URL resources. Writing a message to the `JspWriter` is as simple as Example 1.1.

Example 1.1 My First JSTL Tag

```
<c:out value="Hello my friend" />
```

The XML library addresses the basic needs of a page author as it relates to supporting XML manipulation in pages. The actions in this library have to do with parsing and writing XML content, handling flow control, and doing transformations. Example 1.2 shows how we can import an XML document, parse it, set the DOM object in a variable called doc, access information from that document using XPath, and then set an additional variable based on data for further use. Not bad for four lines of JSP code.

Example 1.2 Easy XML Parsing

```
<!-- parse an XML document -->
<c:import url="http://www.mkp.com/booklist.xml" var="xml"/>
<x:parse source=${xml}" var="doc"/>
<!-- access XML data via XPath expressions -->
<x:out select="$doc/title"/>
<!-- set a scoped variable -->
<x:set var="bookTitle" scope="request" select="$doc/title"/>
```

The SQL library provides the capabilities to interact with databases. This includes dealing with data sources, doing queries, updates, and transactions. Using the SQL actions in combination with iteration actions makes it very easy to loop through result sets, as shown in Example 1.3.

Example 1.3 Displaying Result Sets

```
<sql:query var="bookList" dataSource="${datasource}">
      SELECT * FROM books WHERE title = 'JSTL' ORDER BY author
</sql:query>
<table>
<c:forEach var="book" items="${bookList.row}">
      <tr>
            <td><c:out value="${book.title}" /></td>
            <td><c:out value="${book.author}" /></td>
      </tr>
</c:forEach>
</table>
```

The International and Formatting library is concerned with actions that deal with assisting page authors in internationalizing their application. This includes actions related to locales and resource bundles, date, time and timezone issues. In Example 1.4, we are using a default Locale and doing a key lookup on the default ResourceBundle for that application. Also shown is how easy it is to provide parametric content to your message resources.

Example 1.4 Using International Messages

```
<fmt:message key="welcome">
      <fmt:param value="${visitCount}" />
<fmt:message/>
```

This is just the tip of the iceberg as far as the international and formatting features are concerned.

1.8 Getting Ready to Use the JSTL

Before you can use the JSTL, you need to have an environment set up correctly. This is done easily (and quickly) by following the download and installation directions that are on the Jakarta site at *http://jakarta.apache.org/taglibs/doc/standard-doc/intro.html*. The Jakarta site hosts the reference implementation of JSTL 1.0 under the Taglibs project. The reference implementation (RI) is called the "standard" project and can be used in conjunction with a JSP 1.2 or higher enabled container. Apache Tomcat 4.x server fits the bill nicely if you are looking for JSP 1.2 support. All of the samples in this book are built and tested against the standard project 1.0.3 and Tomcat 4.1.20, which is the current production release at the time of this writing. I have also run all the samples against Tomcat 5.0, which might or might not be to your liking. Tomcat 5.0 has support for JSP 2.0 as well as the Servlet 2.4 specifications. You can download and install Tomcat from *http://jakarta.apache.org/tomcat/*.[1] All of the screen shots used in this book are from Tomcat 5.0.

1.9 The Road to the JSTL

It is always good to have an understanding of the evolution of a technology. This helps to put architectural decisions into perspective as well as to provide an understanding of how our development lives have changed. They've changed for the better, we hope. Everything in web application development starts with our need to get content to the user. Since the JSTL is firmly focused on dealing with dynamic content, let's start there.

1.9.1 Dynamic vs. Static Content

While this might be review for some, let's get the difference of dynamic content and static content clear from the get-go. Dynamic content is that which is generated based on program parameters, HTTP requests and responses, database queries, transformations, and possibly remote procedure calls. In other words, dynamic content is that which changes based on the needs of the current situation.

Static content, on the other hand, is, well ... static. Regardless of what else is happening in the application, the output produced for the consumer is the same. This is your

[1] When this book is published it is probable that Tomcat 5.0 will be available in production release. Tomcat 5.0 has the support for JSP 2.0 and Servlet 2.4 specification. I have run all of the JSTL samples against Tomcat 5.0 while it was still in Alpha.

typical HTML that contains nothing more than HTML. No forms, no cookie information, just plain ordinary HTML. As you can easily see, the processing of information to produce dynamic content is where anything interesting in application development lies.

1.9.2 Using Dynamic Content

Not all websites need dynamic content. Many content-based sites don't require user-specific actions or database results: they just display information. However, many other sites—these days, maybe most sites—need to work with data in some way. "Working with data" could mean something as simple as using a cookie that allows users to customize the pages they see, or it could be something as complex as taking orders and processing payment information in a highly secure way. Utilizing dynamic content also allows for content to be specific to the consumer of that information; whether that is a web browser, a handheld, or some other type of device.

To summarize, using dynamic content:

- Allows for a personalized experience.
- Provides content based on user requests.
- Provides the right information at the right time.
- Allows for display of that content as appropriate for that consumer.

1.9.3 Using Dynamic Web Features

Generating dynamic content can consist of using of both client-side and server-side technologies. Examples of technologies used on the client side include Java, JavaScript, DHTML, and VBScript. Server-side examples include Servlets, JSP, ASP, CGI (Common Gateway Interface), PERL, Shell scripting, Java, and database queries. The evolution of these technologies grew out of the Darwinian needs of programmers. We'll take a brief walkthrough of the server side by example of the evolution of the Java related technologies so that you have a full appreciation for where the JSTL fits into the bigger picture.

1.9.4 Server-Side Processing

Server-side processing is where things start getting interesting. OK, so I'm biased since most of this book will revolve around server-side aspects. Server-side indicates that there is backend interaction going on. The term "backend" usually refers to any processing logic that takes place behind the presentation tier. Samples of backend technologies are Servlets, transformations, EJBs and databases.

Usually the majority of application processing is done on the server side; either in the web server or in the application server. These are two different types of servers. The web server is used for processing HTTP requests, while the application server acts as a container for specific technologies. Sometimes you can have web servers running within application servers, but it is more common to have them as separate processes for a number of reasons—security and performance being two of them.

The term middleware[2] is sometimes used to refer to everything between the web server and the actual physical data store. The middleware layer takes incoming requests from the web server, or sometimes through a Remote Procedure Call (RPC), and performs most of the business logic provided in an application. Middleware layers interact with all sorts of resources including data stores, other applications, business objects, operating system resources, and authentication services such as a Lightweight Directory Access Protocol (LDAP) server.

The mechanism in Java that allows for server-side processing is Servlets.

1.10 Servlets to the Rescue

Servlets are a Java technology-based solution that run inside a Java Virtual Machine (JVM). As a result, servlets are portable. Servlets are generic server extensions that can be dynamically loaded when needed by the web server. Their advantage over earlier server-side technologies like CGI (and FastCGI) is that servlets are handled by threads within the web server. This is a much more efficient approach than having separate processes and allows for a better story when it comes to scalability for an application. Being written in Java, Servlets are portable between operating systems as well as between web servers that support servlets.

Servlet technology is supported by Sun, and it is part of the `javax` packages. Using the Java classes and a servlet container, you can write servlets to your heart's content.

Tomcat has a built-in servlet container[3] so there is nothing special you need to do to run servlets. There are many web servers and add-on servlet engines available from vendors. For a complete listing of supported servlet containers reference *http://java.sun.com/products/servlet/industry.html*. Since all servlet containers are not created equal, make sure to investigate what APIs from the Servlet specification are included and that they meet the needs of your application.

Being written in Java, servlets are able to take full advantage of all of the Java APIs (minus Abstract Window Toolkit (AWT) which, in my humble opinion, we'd all like to forget anyway). Since there is no process spawning that goes on with servlets, and except for the performance hit the first time the servlet is loaded,[4] the servlet invocation is extremely fast. A servlet will stay in memory once it's loaded, allowing for state management of other resources like database connections. The servlet model is shown in Figure 1.1.

---

[2]Middleware is an overloaded term these days. It can be a component, set of components, or a complete tier layer. I use it to mean a set of components that might span multiple tier layers.

[3]Catalina is the servlet container portion of Tomcat. Just in case you ever see the package name in a stack trace and were wondering.

[4]It's possible to use `<load-on-startup>` in the `web.xml` to pre-load servlets.

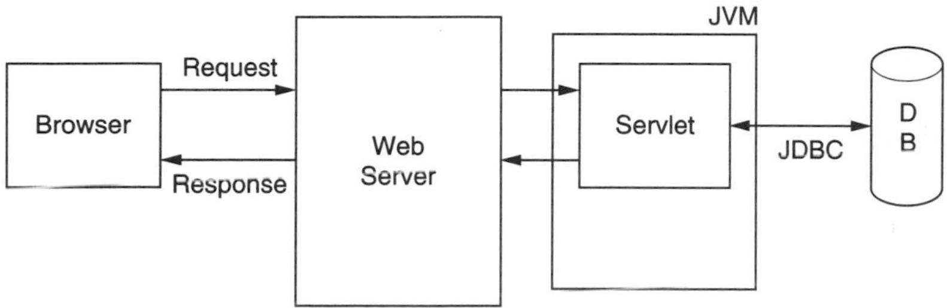

Figure 1.1: Servlet model.

The final draft version of the Servlet 2.3 specification can be found at *http://jcp.org/jsr/detail/53.jsp* for downloading.[5] The JSTL 1.0 is based on the Servlet 2.3 specification. This version includes among other things: applications lifecycle events, a filtering mechanism, internationalization support, and a number of other enhancements.

Servlets can be used for basically anything that needs to be accomplished on the backend as far as business logic is concerned.

1.11 Hello My Friend Servlet

Writing a servlet is relatively painless. That is assuming you know how to code Java and after you've learned the various Objects associated with the `javax.servlet` and `javax.servlet.http` packages, which is not exactly a five-minute adventure. Then you can sit down and code yourself a simple servlet. Say we want to say hello to our friend, and do it in a servlet. The code shown in Example 1.5 is a servlet that will read a parameter value and output it so that a browser can render the HTML file correctly. This code was actually generated for us by the Tomcat servlet container based on the JSP that we will use in our next example. If you really wanted to write it totally from scratch, you certainly could. I'm not going to walk through step-by-step what is being accomplished by the servlet objects. I'm cheating here because we are going to be more interested in the JSP aspects. Primarily this is to get the thought into your head of "*I can't believe it takes this much code to say hello.*" OK, here we go.

Example 1.5 Hello My Friend, Servlet Style

```
package org.apache.jsp;

import javax.servlet.*;
import javax.servlet.http.*;
```

[5] Servlet 2.4 will be the current version included in the J2EE 1.4 release.

```
import javax.servlet.jsp.*;
import org.apache.jasper.runtime.*;

public class hello$jsp extends HttpJspBase {

      static {
      }
      public hello$jsp( ) {
      }

      private static boolean _jspx_inited = false;

      public final void _jspx_init() throws
      org.apache.jasper.runtime.JspException {
      }

      public void _jspService(HttpServletRequest request,
      HttpServletResponse, response)
            throws java.io.IOException, ServletException {

            JspFactory _jspxFactory = null;
            PageContext pageContext = null;
            HttpSession session = null;
            ServletContext application = null;
            ServletConfig config = null;
            JspWriter out = null;
            Object page = this;
            String _value = null;
            try {

                  if (_jspx_inited == false) {
                        synchronized (this) {
                              if (_jspx_inited == false) {
                                    _jspx_init();
                                    _jspx_inited = true;
                              }
                        }
                  }
                  _jspxFactory = JspFactory.getDefaultFactory();
                  response.setContentType("text/html;
                  charset=UTF-8");
                  pageContext = _jspxFactory.getPageContext(this, request,
                              response, "", true, 8192, true);

                  application = pageContext.getServletContext();
                  config = pageContext.getServletConfig();
```

```
                session = pageContext.getSession();
                out = pageContext.getOut();

                // HTML // begin [file="/hello.jsp";from=(0,50);to=(9,0)]
                    out.write("\r\n<html>\r\n<head>\r\n<title>\r\nHello
Sample\r\n</title>\r\n</head>\r\n<body>\r\n<h1>\r\n");

                // end
                // begin [file="/hello.jsp";from=(9,2);to=(18,0)]

                    String myFriend = request.getParamcter ("name");

                    if (myFriend == null){
                        out.println("Hello my friend");
                    } else {
                        out.println("Hello " + myFriend);
                    }

                // end
                // HTML // begin [file="/hello.jsp";from=(18,2);to=(22,7)]
                    out.write("\r\n\r\n</h1>\r\n</body>\r\n</html>");

                // end

            } catch (Throwable t) {
                if (out != null && out.getBufferSize() != 0)
                    out.clearBuffer();
                if (pageContext != null) pageContext.handlePageException(t);
            } finally {
                if (_jspxFactory != null)
                _jspxFactory.releasePageContext(pageContext);
            }
        }
}
```

As we can see in this simple sample, just because you can write a servlet doesn't mean you should. Servlets definitely serve a purpose in the J2EE architecture and there are very good reasons for using them in certain situations. Using servlets as the controller in an MVC architecture is a perfect example.[6] However, we are going to move quickly to a step higher up on the J2EE presentation ladder, to the JSP technology. If you are interested

[6]For a complete description and understanding of how to use and work with MVC, refer to *The Struts Framework: Practical Guide for Java Programmers*.

in knowing all of the goodies that surround servlets, check out the servlet tutorial on the Sun site located at *http://java.sun.com/j2ee/tutorial/1_3-fcs/doc/Servlets.html.*

So now we can move on to JavaServer Pages, which are the next step in the Java evolution.

1.12 JavaServer Pages

When one talks about the J2EE presentation tier, the first thing that comes to mind (or should come to mind) is JavaServer Pages (JSP). In fact, JSPs *are* the presentation for most J2EE applications. If you are building dynamic web applications, then chances are that you have both come across and used JSP technology.

The correct use of JSP allows for a clean implementation of the Model-View-Controller design pattern, allowing the presentation to be clearly separated from the business logic. The technology also allows for readable, reusable, and maintainable pages. Basically, we have something that is much more readable to a page author than the sample servlet we just saw. This book assumes a solid familiarity with the workings of the JSP technology, so we won't spend a lot of time going into JSP basics. If you feel that you need to have a more thorough understanding of JSP in general, pick up the latest edition of *JSP: Practical Guide for Java Programmers* (Morgan Kaufmann).

JSPs allow for code to be utilized within markup content. This, as we will see, has been the downfall of the JSP technology. The purpose of JSP technology is to separate the content from the logic and allow non-programmers to create the necessary pages that include custom tags. That way, the JSP programmer (who might not be a programmer at all) doesn't necessarily need to be the same person who is coding the business logic. JSPs are relatively easy to build and have the full Java API set available to them. JSP and servlets are related because a JSP page actually gets translated into a Java source file that then is compiled into a servlet. This is shown in Figure 1.2.

When a JSP is first requested on the URL line, it is parsed into a Java source file and then compiled into a servlet class. While this is a performance hit the first time the page is accessed, the class doesn't need to be rebuilt each time. Viewing the source code that is produced when a JSP is parsed into its Java file gives you an appreciation for how much the JSP coder doesn't need to worry about.

Let's take a quick break before we get back to our regularly scheduled programming. A JSP file that says hello to a friend is shown in Example 1.6.

Example 1.6 Hello My Friend, JSP Style[7]

```
<%@ page contentType="text/html; charset=UTF-8" %>
<html>
```

---

[7]When checking for the existence of form parameters, it's important to check for both null and a 0 length String. getParameter() returns null only if the parameter name was not found at all. If the user simply didn't fill it in, it will be a 0 length String.

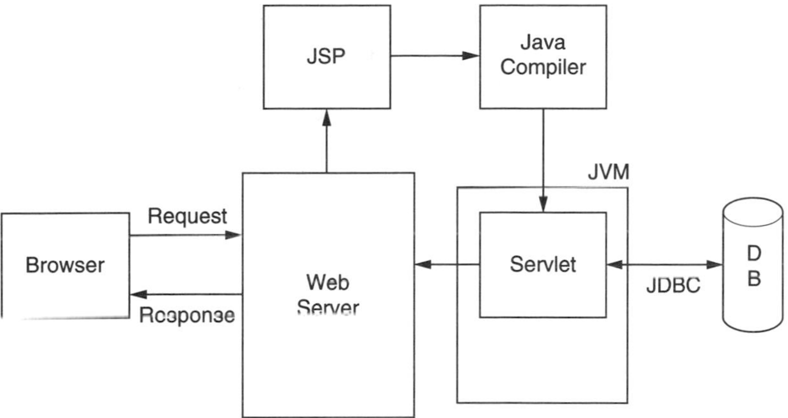

Figure 1.2: JSP model.

```
<head>
<title>
Hello Sample
</title>
</head>
<body>
<h1>
<%
      String myFriend = request.getParameter("name");

            if (myFriend == null || myFriend.length() == 0) {
%>
      Hello my friend
<%
      } else {
%>
      Hello <% = myFriend %>
<%
      }
%>
</h1>
</body>
</html>
```

This of course, is the very JSP file that was used to create the servlet code we looked at in Example 1.5. You can clearly see that the code necessary to complete exactly the same task in a JSP is far simpler than the code required to create the servlet. We have some simple HTML, followed by some relatively simple Java code. You'll notice that we are accessing a request parameter by using an object called `request` and the output stream using an object called out. These objects are just a few of the implicit objects available to a JSP page author as defined in the JSP specification.

By using these implicit objects, the page author can access all the information she needs without worrying too much about coding. Ever since JSP technology hit the streets, there has been a JSP mantra about the separation of page authoring from Java programming. While in theory this has always been the goal, in practice it has been anything but. JSTL makes a giant leap for us in that arena.

If you want to read up on the latest JSP specification, you can find it at *http://java.sun.com/products/jsp/download.html*. JSP 2.0 will be the version of the specification released with the J2EE 1.4. This is the next-generation enterprise platform. Many of the features of the JSTL are also part of JSP 2.0, so just by reading this book you'll be ahead of the game in terms of having a good understanding of the JSP 2.0 support.

1.13 When a JSP, When a Servlet?

The question becomes: when to write a JSP and when to just write a servlet? I wonder if Shakespeare had such difficulties between a play and a sonnet? But I digress. The answer is:

It really depends on the purpose.

For mostly layout concerns, it is wiser to write a JSP and access the information necessary through scriptlets, custom tags, or JavaBeans. This was usually not the case when using servlets since presentation and logic were commonly used in the infamous `out.println()`. Using JSPs, the presentation then stays (mostly) separate from the logic. Make a note of the word "mostly" in the previous sentence. The "mostly" is what JSTL tries to get rid of. JSTL makes the attempt to turn it into "completely."

When dealing with primarily code in terms of logic, it is best to create a servlet to do the work. Having a lot of logic code inside JSPs makes for some interesting (read: frustrating) debugging sessions. We will see throughout the course of this book how using JSTL can eliminate having to include logic code inside your JSP pages.

1.14 Evolving JSP

JSP is an extremely popular technology and can be used on large-scale sites successfully. While there are many good things about the JSP technology, there are a few drawbacks. JSP makes it easy, maybe too easy, to mix Java code within the JSP itself. It is possible to use custom tag libraries (which we'll talk about in a minute) to keep much of the Java code separate from the actual page. Simply using <% %> to contain code makes it convenient to just add logic into the page. The problem with this is that if you have page designers who have little or no programming background, working with the JSP can blur the line between the separation of content and logic. This can lead to maintenance issues, not to mention debugging issues.

Now, those of us in the real world who have built real *n*-tier web applications know that the JSP mantra mentioned above—"allowing the presentation to be clearly separated from the business logic"—is somewhat flawed.

Scriptlets are source code contained within the <% and %> delimiters. With the use of scriplets in JSPs, it became easy to mix Java code—which more than likely is business logic—into the presentation. It is also possible to use expressions to embed a short Java expression between the <%= and %> delimiters. Using expressions, the value of the expression can be written to the client response.

The prolific use of scriptlets and expressions in JSPs is what germinated the problems concerning readability, maintainability, and the mixture of business logic and presentation logic within the page. Even way back in about 1998 (which is like three lifetimes ago for most developers), when JSPs were becoming recognized as a preferred way to develop the presentation tier, it was already becoming apparent that the need for using JavaBeans was commonplace. And it wasn't until December of 1999, when JSP 1.1 was released, that we saw the introduction of custom actions.

1.15 Custom Actions in Action

The custom tag extension mechanism is used for encapsulating logic and provides a way to simplify the constructions of JSPs. At least it separated the role of the JSP page author from that of the Java developer. By taking advantage of custom tags, the page author was able to concentrate on presentation features, while the Java developer was able to code the necessary logic and present it back to the page author in an easy to use tag. In short, custom actions started us back on the path of readability, reusability, and maintainability.

1.15.1 Why Use a Custom Action

In the JSP technology, an action can modify and create objects. By doing so, actions usually affect the existing output stream by performing some logic. A number of standard actions were introduced in JSP v1.1 and some more were introduced in v1.2.

In addition to the standard actions, the most notable addition to the JSP specification was the introduction of the development of reusable modules called *custom actions*. A custom action is invoked by using a custom tag in a JSP page. A tag library is a collection of custom tags. Custom actions are made available to the JSP authors by using the `taglib` JSP directive. One of the advantages of using a custom tag over, for example, a JavaBean, is that when using custom tags you get access to the context and JSP scope objects. These include the request, response, session, and attributes that we are all familiar with.

There are a number of reasons to use custom actions:

- Actions can be customized by using attributes passed from the calling page.
- Custom actions have access to all the objects available to JSP pages.
- Custom actions can modify the response generated by the calling page.
- Custom actions can cooperate with each other by using variables or JavaBeans.
- Custom actions can be nested within one another, allowing for complex interactions within a JSP page.

Some examples of tasks that can be performed by custom actions include form processing, XML processing, iterating, accessing data sources, and other enterprise services such as email, security, and flow control. Before the availability of custom actions, JavaBeans components in conjunction with scriptlets were the main mechanism for performing such processing within JSPs. However, there were a couple of disadvantages to using JavaBeans. For one, the pages became more complex. It also required a working knowledge of Java coding and the JavaBean specification. Lastly, the JSPs became more difficult to maintain with scriptlet code scattered throughout the page.

Custom actions alleviated these problems by abstracting the functionality. Custom actions encapsulate recurring tasks. By doing so, they can be reused across more than one application. Custom actions also increase productivity by encouraging division of labor between library developers and library users. Java developers, and not page authors, usually create JSP tag libraries. JSP tag libraries are used by web application designers who can focus on presentation issues rather than being concerned with how to access databases and other enterprise services.

1.15.2 Hello My Friend Using Custom Actions

We have seen how our progression from Servlet coding to JSP coding made our lives easier when trying to say hello to a friend. Let's take the same sample and move it forward by using custom actions. By walking through this sample we'll see that we still have to put in a fair amount of effort to define, create, and configure custom actions. First we need to define our tag library descriptor (TLD) file, then create a tag handler, then create the tag library. However, at least we only have to do it once and then we can use our `<jstlpg:hello>` custom action from a JSP forever.

1.15.3 The TLD File

A tag library descriptor file is an XML document that describes the library. A TLD contains information about the library as a whole and about each tag contained therein. TLDs are used by a JSP container to validate the tags. TLD files have the extension `.tld` when deployed within a JAR file in the directory you specify.

There is typically some header information followed by elements used to define the tag library. Our tag library descriptor file will consist of one tag, called HelloTag. The HelloTag will print a personalized hello to the JspWriter (which is the output stream for a JSP) if an optional name attribute is provided. The <name> element (opposed to the name attribute) specifies how we will reference this tag from a JSP page. The <tag-class> is the class file that will be instantiated when this tag is encountered in a JSP. The complete TLD file is shown in Example 1.7.

Example 1.7 TLD File

```
<?xml version="1.0" encoding="ISO-8859-1" ?>
<!DOCTYPE taglib
      PUBLIC "-//Sun Microsystems, Inc.//
      DTD JSP Tag Library 1.2//EN"
      "http://java.sun.com/j2ee/dtds/web-jsptaglibrary_1_2.dtd">
<taglib>
      <tlib-version>1.0</tlib-version>
      <jsp-version>1.2</jsp-version>
      <short-name>Application Tag Library</short-name>
      <uri>http://www.mkp.com/taglibs/simple-example-1.0</uri>
      <description>
            This tag library contains one tag to demonstrate a
            TLD file as well as a tag definition
      </description>

      <tag>
            <name>hello</name>
            <tag-class>jstlpg.tags.HelloTag</tag-class>
            <body-content>empty</body-content>
            <description>
                  This tag will print a personalized hello message
                  Attributes:
                  name - Name to say hello to.
            </description >
            <attribute>
                  <name>name</name>
                  <required>false</required>
                  <rtexprvalue>true</rtexprvalue>
            </attribute>
      </tag>
</taglib>
```

As you can see, this is only step one in the custom tag process. Already you have to know, or at a minimum understand, XML to create your TLD file. The next step is to create your tag handler.

1.15.4 The Tag Handler

The tag is defined in a handler class. This would be the jstlpg.tags.HelloTag referenced in the tag definition in the <tag-class> element. It is a standard naming convention, although not required, to name your tag handler class by the name followed by Tag to indicate that it is a tag handler. TagSupport is the base class used for simple tags. It can be found in the javax.servlet.jsp.tagext package. The Tag interface defines the contract between the JSP page and a tag that might be used on that page. The Tag lifecycle is defined in the JSP specification. What your tag actually does depends on what methods of the Tag interface could potentially be called and what must be implemented. TagSupport is a utility class that supplies a default implementation for the lifecycle methods.

If we continue with our HelloTag sample, the Java file for the HelloTag looks like:

```
public final class HelloTag extends TagSupport {
      private String name = null;

      public int doStartTag() throws JspException {
            try {
                if (name == null){
                      pageContext.getOut().write
                      ("Hello!");
                } else {
                      pageContext.getOut().write
                      ("Hello " + name);
                }
            }
            catch (java.io.Exception ioe){
                  throw new JspTagException
                  (ioe.getMessage());
            }
                  return (SKIP_BODY);
            }
      public String getName() {
            return (this.name);
      }

      public void setName(String name) {
                  this.name = name;
      }

      public void release() {
            super.release();
            name = null;
      }

}
```

We must only implement the doStartTag() and release() methods from the Tag interface. We will rely on the default implementation provided in the TagSupport class for the implementation of the remainder of the interface. The container will call the setter method on any attribute encountered for the custom action. Therefore, it is required that a public setter method be present in your handler. That is why we see a setName() method in our handler. A getter is not required, but I tend to include the following standard JavaBean definition. When the JSP page encounters a start of a tag, the doStartTag() method is called on the handler. It is here that we determine if a name attribute has been set so that we know how to send output to the current JspWriter. We return SKIP_BODY to indicate that there is no evaluation required on the tag body.

It's good practice implementing the release() method in your tag handler classes. When the JSP container is finished with the tag, the last step in the lifecycle is to release any resources that might have been consumed. For example, a database connection would qualify here as a resource. It is also possible to reset any state that might be necessary. This is important since a container may recycle handler objects for the following request and you don't want to have left-over states contained in your handler.

Some of the more advanced features of tags, like using scripting variables, are made much easier through the JSTL. We'll talk about this in more detail as we come across it within the JSTL, but I wanted to at least make sure that you are familiar with the feature. Typically an attribute is passed to the tag that contains the ID of the object to be used. The usual operation is that the tag handler retrieves a scripting variable value object using pageContext.getAttribute(name), performs some processing on it, and then sets the scripting variable's value using the pageContext.setAttribute(name, object). In addition to setting the value of the variable within the tag handler, you must define a class derived from TagExtraInfo that provides information to the JSP container about the nature of the variable. That class is then listed in the <tei-class> attribute of the tag in the TLD.

One tag by itself is not very interesting. What we really want to do is combine tags that have common functionality into libraries.

1.16 The Power of Tag Libraries

As we've seen, a tag library can contain one or many custom tags. Custom tag libraries are collections of custom tags that usually fall within the same functional area. The tag library includes the two primary parts: the tag handler, and the TLD file. If we rewrite our hello.jsp file to use the custom tag library we defined, we can have a cleaner JSP file with no Java code. The new JSP file is shown in Example 1.8.

Example 1.8 Hello My Friend, Custom Tag Style

```
<%@ page contentType="text/html; charset=UTF-8" %>
<%@ taglib uri="/jstlpg/samples/SampleTaglib" prefix="jstlpg" %>
<html>
<head>
```

```
      <title>
            Hello Sample
      </title>
</head>
<body>
<h1>
      <jstlpg:hello name="Sue"/>
</h1>
</body>
</html>
```

The JSP is now more maintainable, easier to read, and bug free (we hope).

1.16.1 Need for a Tag Library

As the use and power of custom actions became more apparent, lots of custom tag libraries started popping up. Vendors began providing tag libraries for their J2EE containers, Open Source projects like the Jarkarta Taglibs project (*http://jakarta.apache.org/taglibs/index.html*) appeared. It became clear that the use of custom actions was a way to start to reuse code, keep JSPs cleaner in terms of embedded code, and preserve the MVC model better.

Throughout this evolution, JSPs have been improving at their core reason for existing. That reason is, again, the clean separation of presentation and business logic. While many (probably too many) JSPs out there in the web application world still have embedded Java code, scriplets, and a "partridge in a pear tree" included within them, many have moved toward custom tags. In my opinion, the adoption of custom tag libraries has been slower than it should have been since their introduction. The most likely reason for this is that, as we can see from our sample, it still takes a fair amount of coding effort to create a custom tag library. It would be better, more cost effective, and quicker if page authors could learn a set of custom tags once and then just reuse them. No additional engineering time would be required from the team because the TLD, tag handlers, and libraries would already have been defined, documented, and tested. Wouldn't that be great?

Now we arrive at the point where the JSP Standard Tag Library appears.

1.17 Making Life Easier, JSTL in Action

At this point, we have clearly seen the evolutionary process that has taken place in the Servlet-JSP arena. We have seen how you can write your own servlet that does the same thing that a JSP can do, assuming you are a Java programmer, and then abstract and encapsulate some of that required functionality into custom actions. Using the JSTL takes away the development requirement of writing your own TLD files and tag handlers, and creating your own tag libraries. To put it simply, JSTL provides the functionality and you provide the purpose.

Let's now create a JSP using actions from the Core tag library. Saying hello to our friend is shown in Example 1.9.

Example 1.9 Hello My Friend, JSTL Style

```
<%@ page contentType="text/html; charset=UTF-8" %>
<%@ taglib uri="http://java.sun.com/jstl/ea/core" prefix="c" %>
<html>
<head>
<title>
     Hello Sample
</title>
</head>
<body>
<h1>
Hello <c:out value="${param.name}" default="my friend" />
</h1>
</body>
</html>
```

Using the out tag provided in the Core tag library, we have pulled a value out of a parameter called name from our HTTP request to display. If this value is `null`, then the default "my friend" will automatically be used instead. This is exactly the same functionality that we previously had to code a TLD and tag handler for. Using the JSTL, we have the functionality with no more than one line's worth of effort.

If we really wanted to get crazy, we could utilize one more JSTL tag and make our simple JSP into a completely internationalized page ready for any language that our clients might be using (and we have translated strings for).

Example 1.10 Hello My Friend, Internationalized

```
<%@ page contentType="text/html; charset=UTF-8" %>
<%@ taglib uri="http://java.sun.com/jstl/ea/core" prefix="c" %>
<%@ taglib uri="http://java.sun.com/jstl/ea/fmt " prefix="fmt" %>
<html>
<head>
<title>
<fmt:message key="hellotitle">
</title>
</head>
<body>
<h1>
<fmt:message key="hello">
```

```
<c:out value="${param.name}" default="<fmt:message key='myfriend'>" />
</h1>
</body>
</html>
```

You might have noticed that we are using a syntax that probably doesn't look familiar. This is the `${}` as shown in the value attribute. This syntax is part of the new expression language support that is part of the JSTL (and JSP 2.0) and which we will look at in the next chapter. A whole new way of writing JSPs will unfold before your very eyes.

This is just the beginning of the power of the JSTL actions. Effectively, if we take out the HTML, we have accomplished quite a bit in just a handful of lines. We have declared use of the JSTL tag libraries, accessed data from a resource bundle, pulled out a parameter from the HTTP request, and determined what is the correct message to display to our output stream. Think back to the amount of servlet code we looked at to accomplish just some of this!

So without further ado, let's get started using the JSTL.

chapter 2

JSTL Basics

This chapter covers some of the JSTL basics that are common throughout the various tag libraries and actions. Reviewing these basics sets the foundation for us to talk about actions in more detail. First we'll cover basic setup and then we'll talk about some of the common ideas observed throughout the various JSTL actions. These include:

- How variables, scope, and visibility are handled
- Dynamic and static attributes
- Handling exceptions
- Action body content

After that, we'll cover configuration settings. The expression language is basic to the JSTL, but since we are going to focus the entire next chapter to it, I won't talk too much about it in this chapter. Once we get these basics under your belt, we will move ahead to looking at each of the functional areas individually and we'll also go over the tags in greater detail in upcoming chapters.

2.1 Environment Setup

As an engineer, the first thing I usually want to do while learning about new technologies is to get an environment set up so that I can play along. I'm assuming you would like the same. I also assume that you are familiar with the JSP technology referred to throughout this book, and therefore you already have the working environment for JSP development. This environment should include a Java Developers Kit installed, as well as a JSP application container. If this is *not* the case, I strongly suggest that you pick up your favorite JSP book that goes into the details of configuring your JSP environment.

The samples in the book you're reading right now have all been developed and tested with the Sun JDK 1.4.1 and Tomcat 5.0. You can use any web application server you choose, as long as it supports JSP 1.2 and Servlets 2.3 or higher. For more information about the Tomcat server, visit the Apache project at *http://jakarta.apache.org/*.

The reference implementation (RI) of the JSTL 1.0 specification is provided on the Apache site in the Jakarta Taglibs project. The Taglibs project is an open-source repository for JSP custom tag libraries and associated projects. The RI for the JSTL is located in the `standards` directory, and it can be found at *http://jakarta.apache.org/taglibs/doc/standard-doc/intro.html*.

It is possible to download either the binary distribution of the RI or the entire source for the Taglibs project. If you download the entire source, you will get source to tag libraries other than those included in the standard project. It is up to you what you want to do. If you want my advice (and obviously you do since you're reading my book), it should suffice to just get the binary version from *http://www.apache.org/dist/jakarta/taglibs/standard/* and then select either the `jakarta-taglibs-standard-current.zip` for Windows platforms or `jakarta-taglibs-standard-current.tar.gz` for Unix platforms.[8]

Once you have the downloaded file expanding into your favorite directory, you simply copy the `standards-doc.war` and `standards-examples.war` to the `webapps` directory of wherever you installed Tomcat. If you are using another web server, it should just be a matter of putting the WAR files in the correct place where the particular web server requires new web applications to be. You should be able to point your browser to your server and access the application as `standards-examples`. You should have a screen that looks similar to Figure 2.1.

2.2 Using the Book Examples

Using the book's examples is quite simple. Everything you need, including the JSTL reference implementation JARs, is included in the download. All you need to do is download the Web Archive (WAR) file from *http://www.mkp.com/practical/jstl* and put the WAR file in the `webapps` directory of your Tomcat installation. Then you can access the application by typing[9]

```
http://localhost:8080/jstlsample
```

---

[8]The location of the downloads and names of the files have changed several times, so don't be surprised if they don't match exactly to what's given here.

[9]Depending on how your machine is configured, you might need to access localhost using the IP address 127.0.0.1 if localhost does not resolve correctly.

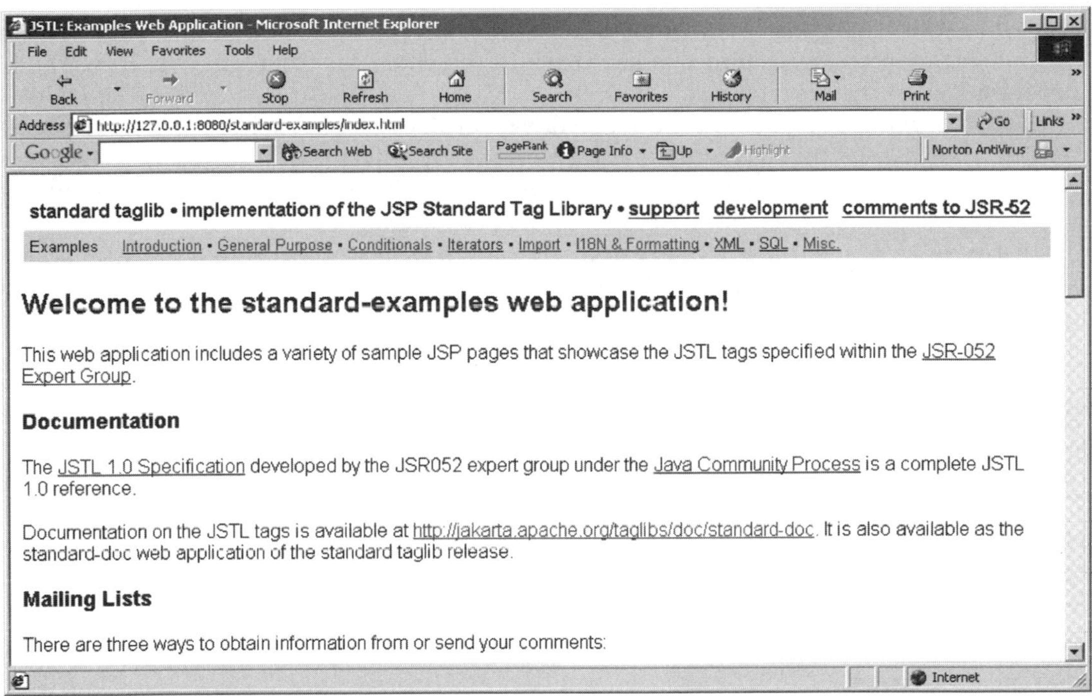

Figure 2.1: JSTL example application screenshot.

The sample application uses the MySQL database. This is an open-source (free) database that you can download from *http://www.mysql.com/*. Once you have the database downloaded, place the drivers in your classes directory of Tomcat. Follow the installation directions from the MySQL site and then create a database called `jstlbook` using the MySQLAdmin console. Then just click the `databaseinit.jsp` that is linked from the welcome page. It will create and initialize the necessary tables and data that are used throughout the book.

2.3 JSP Scopes

As I've already indicated, I'm assuming that you are already familiar with JSP development. However, since the objects and scopes defined in the JSP specification play a role in many of the JSTL actions, let's briefly review them.

A JSP page can access, create, and modify server-side objects. These objects can be made visible to standard and custom actions, as well as to scripting elements. When we talk about an object's *scope*, we are describing what entities can access the object. The available scopes are defined as `page`, `request`, `session`, and `application`.

Objects with page scope are only accessible from within the page in which they are created. As soon as the response is sent back to the client (or the request is forwarded), all references to the object are released.

Objects with request scope are accessible from all pages that are processing the same request. This means that if a request is forwarded, the object is still in scope. References to objects with request scope are stored in the request implicit object. When the request has been processed, all references to the object are released.

Objects with session scope are accessible from pages processing requests that are in the same session as the one in which they were created.[10] All references to the object are released after the associated session ends. References to objects with session scope are stored in the session object associated with the page.

Objects with application scope are accessible from pages processing requests that are in the same application as the one in which they were created. Objects with application scope can be defined (and reached) from pages that are not session-aware. References to objects with application scope are stored in the application object associated with a page activation. The application object is really the servlet context that is obtained from the servlet configuration object. All references to the object are released when the ServletContext is released.

To make this a bit more visual, think of page scope as being the innermost ring, and application scope as being the outermost ring, as shown in Figure 2.2.

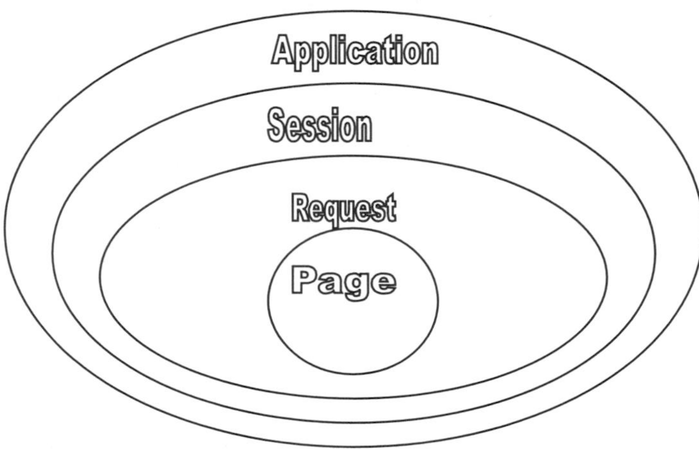

Figure 2.2: JSP object scopes.

---

[10]It is not legal to define an object with session scope from within a page that is not session-aware as defined by the page directive.

Objects are visible to the current ring they reside in or any rings that are contained within it, but not rings outer to their defined scope. Actions can access objects using a named attribute in the PageContext object. A PageContext instance is accessible through the implict object pageContext. This provides access to all the namespaces associated with a JSP page and provides access to all properties associated with the PageContext of a JSP. This includes such objects as the HttpServletRequest, HttpSession, and ServletContext objects and their properties.

An object exposed through a scripting variable has a scope within the page. As we will see, the JSTL provides many actions that have a scope attribute allowing for variables to be defined and exported to the scope specified.

2.4 JSTL Scoped Variables

Actions can collaborate with their environment in implicit ways, explicit ways, or both ways. Implicit collaboration is often done via a well-defined interface that allows nested tags to work seamlessly with the ancestor tag exposing that interface. A good example of this is the JSTL iterator tags that we'll be talking about.

Explicit collaboration happens when a tag explicitly exposes information to its environment. Traditionally, this is by exposing a scripting variable with a value assigned from a JSP scoped attribute (which was saved by the tag handler). Because JSTL supports an expression language, the need for scripting variables is significantly reduced. This is why all the JSTL tags expose information only as JSP scoped attributes (no scripting variable exposed). These exported JSP scoped attributes are referred to as *scoped variables* in the JSTL; this helps to prevent too much overloading of the term "attribute."

2.4.1 Var and Scope Attributes

Now that we understand JSP variables and scopes in general, let's see how it all applies to the JSTL. Many actions provided in the JSTL allow for variables to be exported. The convention is to use the name var for attributes that export information. We can look at <c:set>, which is one of the actions available in the Core tag library that sets the value of a scoped variable. In the sample below, we are setting a variable called name to the value "Sue" and allowing that variable to be visible in session scope.

```
<c:set var="name" value="Sue" scope="session" />
```

If we didn't specify a value for scope, page scope is the default. It is also important to note, as per the JSP specification, that specifying session scope is only allowed if the page has sessions enabled. If an action exposes more than one scoped variable, the main one uses attribute names var and scope, while secondary ones have a suffix added for unique identification. For example, in the <c:forEach> action there is both a main and a secondary variable that can be defined. The var attribute is the main variable and exposes the current item of the iteration, while the varStatus attribute is the secondary variable and exposes the current status of the iteration.

We'll see the var and scope attribute frequently used in various actions.

2.4.2 Variable Visibility

Another point to understand is how the scope attribute defines the visibility of a variable. Scoped variables exported by JSTL actions are categorized as either nested or at-end. *Nested* scoped variables are only visible within the body of the action and are stored in page scope. Since nested scoped variables are always saved in page scope, no scope attribute is associated with them. An example is the <c:forEach> action. There is a var attribute that contains the current item in the collection. This variable is considered nested because it is only visible during the execution of the <c:forEach>. This is shown in Figure 2.3.

In the JSTL 1.0 specification, scoped variables exposed by actions are considered at-end by default. If a scoped variable is nested, providing a scope attribute in the action allows the scope to be explicitly stated. *At-end* scoped variables are only visible at the end of the action. An example of an at-end variable is shown in Figure 2.4.

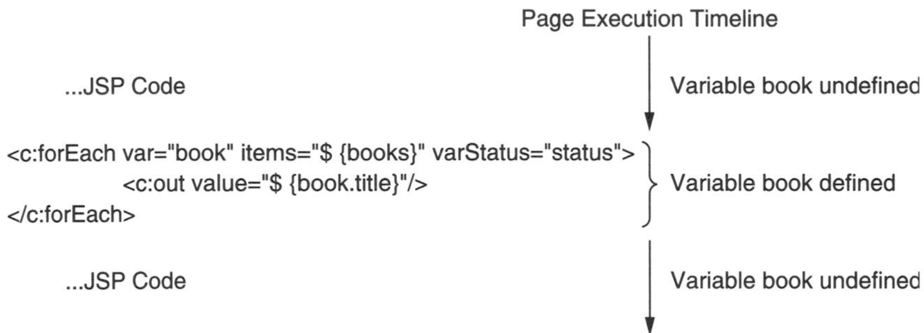

Figure 2.3: Nested visibility.

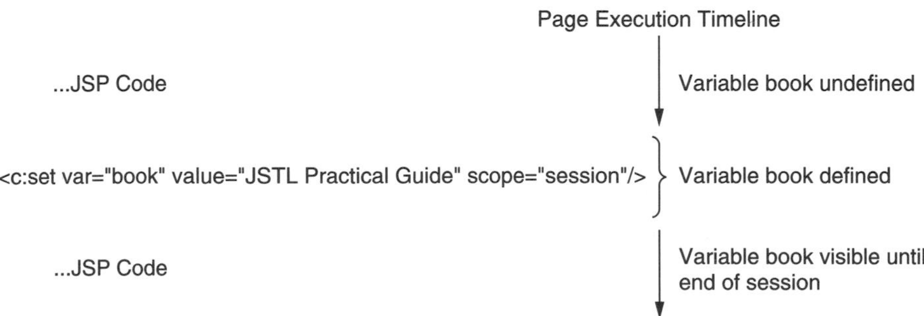

Figure 2.4: At-end visibility.

2.5 Dynamic and Static Attributes

Attribute values of JSTL actions can almost always be specified dynamically by using a request-time expression value, such as the scripting language of the page, or by using an expression language expression value. You'll learn all about the expression language in Chapter 3, aptly titled "Using the Expression Language." I said "almost always" above because there are two exceptions to when JSTL actions can be specified dynamically via a request-time expression value. The first exception to this convention is for the `select` attribute of XML actions. The `select` attribute is defined to specify a `String` literal that represents an expression in the XPath language. The second exception is for attributes that define the `name` and `scope` of scoped variables exported by JSTL actions.

2.6 Handling Errors and Exceptions

Obviously, when dealing with dynamic data, we must have a mechanism in place for handling errors and exceptions. When using JSTL actions, the syntax varies from action to action. We'll discuss the specific syntax of each action as we encounter it. If a syntax error in an action is found, then it is reported at translation time. Any constraints on the action, such as required attributes or conflicts when using certain attributes, are also reported at translation time. The exception to this is if the attribute value is dynamic, such as an expression. Since there is no way to validate whether the value is correct until runtime, these types of errors are reported then. When using the RT-based libraries, the conversion from a `String` value to the expected type of an attribute is handled according to the rules defined in the JSP 1.2 specification Section 2.4.

In general, handling exceptions on a JSP has been, to be polite about it, a pain. JSTL tries to make it easier from this point forward. JSTL doesn't try to replace the `errorpage` mechanism we are familiar with in JSP 1.2, but instead tries to improve when and how errors are thrown and handled. There are a number of conventions in place to try to avoid having runtime exceptions constantly being thrown. These conventions are described in Table 2.1.

The `<c:catch>` action is provided to enable page authors to catch exceptions. `<c:catch>` exposes the exception through its `var` attribute. The `var` is removed if no exception has occurred. We'll be going into more detail on the `<c:catch>` action in the chapter on the Core library but here's a quick sample to illustrate. In Example 2.1 we are setting up a catch block so that if anything bad happens we will save the exception into a variable called `fileError`. If nothing bad happens, this variable will be empty. It so happens that trying to import an empty URL causes an exception to be thrown. Instead of this exception immediately going to the `errorPage` that might be defined for this page, we have the opportunity to address the problem ourselves. By checking for the existence of the `fileError` variable we can tell if an exception was thrown and handle it accordingly.

Error or Exception	How or When it is Handled
Invalid value on scope attribute	Translation time validation error
Empty var attribute	Translation time validation error
Dynamic attributes *with* a fixed set of valid String values containing a null value	Use the default value
Dynamic attributes *with* a fixed set of valid String values containing an invalid value	Throw an exception
Dynamic attributes *without* a fixed set of valid values with a null value	Behavior specific to the action
Dynamic attributes *with* a fixed set of valid values with an invalid type	Throw an exception
Dynamic attributes *without* a fixed set of valid values with an invalid value	Throw an exception
Exceptions caused by the body content	Always propagate, possibly after handling them
Exceptions caused by the action itself	Always propagate, possibly after handling them
Exceptions caused by the EL	Always propagate
Exceptions caused by XPath	Always propagate

Table 2.1: JSTL error and exception conventions.

Example 2.1 Handling an Exception

```
<c:catch var="fileError">
      <c:import url=""/>
</c:catch>

<c:if test="${not empty fileError}">
      <b> Your file was not found!</b>
      Here's more information on the error:
      <br><font color="#FF0000"> <c:out value="${fileError}" /></font>
</c:if>
```

When a JSTL action throws an exception, it is an instance of javax.servlet.jsp.JspException or a subclass. Sometimes it might be the case where the action catches an exception that occurred in its body. In that case, its tag handler will provide the caught exception as the root cause of the JspException it re-throws. By default, JSTL actions do not catch or otherwise handle exceptions that occur during evaluation of their body content.

2.7 Action Body Content

When we talk about the body content of an action, what we are speaking of is the content between the start and end tags of the action. We can rewrite our <c:set> example as:

```
<c:set var="name" scope="session" >
      Sue
</c:set>
```

where "Sue" becomes the body content of the action.

How an action handles the body content is defined by using the <body-content> element in the TLD file. There are three choices that an action has for defining body content. It can be defined as empty, JSP, or tagdependent.

For example, body content is defined in the <c:set> action as taken from the c.tld file:

```
<tag>
     <name>set</name>
     <tag-class>org.apache.taglibs.standard.tag.el.core.SetTag
     </tag-class>
     <body-content>JSP</body-content>
     <description>
          Sets the result of an expression evaluation in a
          'scope'
     </description>
...
</tag>
```

The <body-content> element is optional in the TLD file, so if it is not defined, the default value is JSP. If the body content is defined as empty, this means that there can be no body content for the action. Having an empty body also allows for the tag to be written using either the long or short format like <jstlpg:tag></jstlpg:tag> or <jstlpg:tag/>.

Defining the body content to be JSP means that the body of the tag may contain standard JSP elements. This could include markup, content, scriptlets, and expressions. Using body content type JSP also means that the body content can be empty. When the body content is defined as JSP, the content such as scriptlets, expressions, and escape characters are all processed or evaluated as usual. This also means that tags can be nested within each other and they will still be evaluated correctly. Many of the JSTL actions are of body content type JSP.

The third type of body content is tagdependent. This means that the JSP container will not process the content in any way. It will be left to the tag to handle how it wants to process or evaluate the content.

If a JSTL action accepts body content, an empty body is always valid unless it's explicitly stated otherwise. If there is nothing in the body content, it is considered empty. If the body content is used to set the value of an attribute, then an empty body content sets the attribute value to an empty string. So the following example would set the var name to be an empty string:

```
<c:set var="name" scope="session" >
</c:set>
```

It is good practice, if you have simple strings or expressions, to set these values in the attribute. In JSTL 1.0, expressions are only valid in attributes, not template text. Therefore, you cannot use the expression lanauge in the body content.[11] If you are using other JSP elements that you want the container to interpret, then you'd use the body content approach.

2.8 Configuration Settings

Most web applications require some type of configuration setup. Typically this is accomplished in the deployment descriptor file. As defined in the Servlet 2.3 specification, this file is the web.xml file and describes necessary context initialization parameters. There are a number of initialization parameters that can be defined for the JSTL.

The JSTL provides what are called configuration variables. The configuration variables are used to provide default settings for various actions at deployment time. These variables allow for data to be overridden dynamically for a particular JSP scope (page, request, session application) by using a scoped variable. This is extremely useful because the JSTL tag libraries can use default values for attributes that are not explicitly defined in the particular action usage. An example of this is a default locale used for the internationalization (I18N[12]) actions. The term *configuration setting* is used for data that can be set either by using a context initialization in a descriptor file or dynamically with a *configuration variable*. You can set these configuration settings in the application's web.xml deployment descriptor through a context parameter. This would then be used as an appropriate default for your application. For example, if we want our default locale to be English, then we can set the locale configuration parameter to be en_US. This is shown in the web.xml snippet below:

```
<web-app>
...
        <context-param>
                <param-name>
                        javax.servlet.jsp.jstl.fmt.locale
                </param-name>
                <param-value>
                        en_US
```

[11]If you are using Tomcat 5.0 and/or working with a JSP 2.0 container, the EL can be used in both attributes and template text.

[12]I18N is a common shorthand for the 18 letters between I and N in internationalization.

```
            </param-value>
        </context-param>
    ...
    </web-app>
```

In the JSTL, there is configuration data associated with internationalization, formatting, and SQL actions. This allows for ways to specify the locale to be used by internationalization and formatting actions, as well as defining default datasource parameters. We'll talk about each of the available configuration data variables in the chapters that contain the actions that use the settings.

The configuration variables are considered scoped variables and, because of this, fall under the definition of how scoped variables names work according to the JSP specification. We already talked about this in the previous section on JSP Scopes and Objects. The JSP specification states that "*A scoped variable name should refer to a unique object at all points in the execution.*" This means that all the different scopes (page, request, session, and application) that exist within a PageContext really should behave as a single name space.

So what does this mean for our JSTL configuration settings? It means that if we allowed for the standard JSP scoping implementation to work, setting a scoped variable in any one scope overrides it in any of the other scopes. Since it is possible to specify the scope of a variable during an action, this becomes problematic because the value of the configuration setting might be overwritten for a scope that we didn't intend. To prevent this type of scoping problem from happening when actions set the configuration variables, the JSTL provides a class called `javax.servlet.jsp.jstl.core.Config`.

2.9 The Config Class

The `javax.servlet.jsp.jstl.core.Config` class is used to manage the configuration variables as if scopes had their own private name space. This allows actions to set variables for any scope that they need. The Config class provides a number of constants that can be conveniently used to refer to the various configuration settings. These are shown in Table 2.2.

The Config class also provides a number of methods that are used to manage the various configuration settings. These include various flavors of get, set, and remove to handle the setting of configuration settings in each of the types of scopes. There is also a `find()` method provided so that you can locate a particular configuration setting as defined by its context initialization name. The `find()` method will search each of the scopes in order and return the first occurrence it finds as an `Object`. If nothing is found, then a `null` is returned. For a complete listing of the available settings for Config, refer to the JSTL reference section.

The Config class is typically instantiated in some backend code of the application. This can be a servlet, a tag handler, or a listener class. It provides a way to dynamically

```
public static final String FMT_LOCALE
  = "javax.servlet.jsp.jstl.fmt.locale";
public static final String FMT_FALLBACK_LOCALE
  = "javax.servlet.jsp.jstl.fmt.fallbackLocale";
public static final String FMT_LOCALIZATION_CONTEXT
  = "javax.servlet.jsp.jstl.fmt.localizationContext";
public static final String FMT_TIME_ZONE
  = "javax.servlet.jsp.jstl.fmt.timeZone";
public static final String SQL_DATA_SOURCE
  = "javax.servlet.jsp.jstl.sql.dataSource";
public static final String SQL_MAX_ROWS
  = "javax.servlet.jsp.jstl.sql.maxRows";
```

Table 2.2: Configuration setting constants.

change the configuration settings of the JSTL. We won't spend too much time on Config because it is primarily used in backend code, but here is a quick sample of how you would dynamically set the FMT_LOCALE configuration variable to US English for a particular session:

```
import javax.servlet.jsp.jstl.core.Config;
...
Config.set(session,Config.FMT_LOCALE, "en_US");
```

2.10 Summary

This chapter talked about the common themes that we find used by many actions throughout the JSTL. If you want to try out the samples as we proceed, we talked about how to get your environment set up so that you can run the samples.

The concepts involved with JSP scopes are important when dealing with JSTL actions, so we spent some time making sure everyone has a complete understand of the available scopes: page, request, session, and application and what they mean in terms of an object's accessibility. We also talked about how the var and scope attributes, used by many actions, follow these JSP concepts. Exceptions and errors can happen just about anywhere, so we looked at some of the rules that are applied to handling exceptions within actions. The use of an action's body content was also discussed so we can see the difference of when to use attribute and when to use body content appropriately. Lastly, we saw how configuration settings can be used by the JSTL to set defaults for an application as well as how to change settings dynamically.

chapter 3

Using the Expression Language

Before we dive into the various functional areas in the JSTL, we should start with the expression language. As touched on briefly in the first chapter, this is one of the most important features of the JSTL and is a prominent feature of the JSP 2.0 specification. The expression language (EL) allows for a much simpler syntax for doing application data manipulation for the page author. Currently the EL in the JSTL can only be used with tag attribute values, primarily in actions that reside in the Core tag library. It is possible to use the EL within template text if you are working with the JSP 2.0 specification. Expressions in template text are not supported if you are using JSTL 1.0 with JSP 1.2. What it means to use EL in attributes can be shown in the following example:

```
<c:if test="${book.orderQuantity > book.inStock}">
The book <c:out value="${book.title}"/> is currently
out of stock.
</c:if>
```

Using the <c:if> conditional tag (which we'll talk about in detail shortly), we can use the EL in the test attribute to determine if we can order a book that is currently in stock. If the book is not in stock, we can access the book Object by using the EL and assigning that to the value attribute. Anyone who has worked with JSPs before can certainly appreciate the ease-of-use and coding simplification possible with the EL.

If you are working with JSP 2.0, this sample could also be written using the expression in the template text like:

```
<c:if test="${book.orderQuantity > book.inStock}">
The book ${book.title} is currently out of stock.
</c:if>
```

Keep in mind that when using an identifier (like book, for example) with the EL, it is the same thing as if you had done PageContext.findAttribute(*identifier*). The identifier itself can reside in any of the known JSP scopes. This includes page, request, session, or application scope. If the identifier isn't found in any scope, then a null value is returned.

3.1 Implicit Objects Available in the EL

There are quite a few implicit objects exposed through the EL. These objects allow for access to any variables that are held in the particular JSP scopes. Objects include pageScope, requestScope, sessionScope, and applicationScope. All of these xScope objects are Maps that map the respective scope attribute names to their values. Using the implicit objects param and paramValues, it is also possible to access HTTP request parameters. This holds true for request header information as well as for using the implicit objects header and headerValues.

The param and header objects are Maps that map the parameter or header name to a String. This is similar to doing a ServletRequest.getParameter(String name) or ServletRequest.getHeader(String name). The paramValues and headerValues are Maps that map parameter and header names to a String[] of all values for that parameter or header. Again, this is as if you had made ServletRequest.getParameterValues(String name) or ServletRequest.getHeaders(String) calls.

The initParam gives access to context initialization parameters, while cookie exposes cookies received in the request. The implicit object pageContext gives access to all properties associated with the PageContext of a JSP page such as the HttpServletRequest, ServletContext, and HttpSession objects and their properties. Table 3.1 summarizes the available implicit objects.

Object Name	Description
pageScope	Collection of all variables in page scope
requestScope	Collection of all variables in request scope
sessionScope	Collection of all variables in session scope
applicationScope	Collection of all variables in application scope
param	Request parameters for this page
paramValues	All parameter values for a parameter
header	Headers sent by the web browser
headerValues	All values for a particular header
initParam	A context initialization parameter
cookie	Value of a cookie
pageContext	Allows access to page information

Table 3.1: EL implicit objects.

Let's look at a couple of samples to drive the usage of the objects home:

- `${pageContext.request.servletPath}` will return the Servlet path obtained from the `HttpServletRequest`.
- `${sessionScope.loginId}` will return the session-scoped attribute named "loginId," or `null` if the attribute is not found.
- `${param.bookId}` will return the String value of the "bookId" parameter, or `null` if it's not found.
- `${paramValues.bookId}` will return the `String[]` containing all values of the `bookId` parameter, or `null` if it's not found. Using `paramValues` is particularly useful if you have a form with check boxes or for some other reason a parameter might have multiple values like a multiselect box.

3.2 Accessing Data Structures

When a page author accesses data in a JSP, it's usually done by accessing objects. Actually, for the most part these objects have been JavaBeans or collections. There are two ways provided by the EL to access data structures. The operators are `.` and `[]`. Using these operators makes it easy to access encapsulated data. If fact, we've already seen this access in the example above using the conditional `if` tag. Using the `.` (also called dot) notation is a shortcut for accessing an object's property.

Taking a brief look at our previous sample:

```
The book <c:out value="${book.title}"/> is currently out of stock.
```

We access the value of `title`, which is a property of the book object. The `[]` is used for accessing collections. This includes lists, maps, and arrays. For example, the following `Map` object can be accessed like so:

```
Book Description: <c:out value="${bookDesc[book.isbn]}"/>
```

Being able to index by a value or by a String is very convenient; depending on what type of collection is being referenced.

We have seen the use of the dot notation to access a member of an unordered collection. For example, to get the title property of the book variable, we used `${book.title}`. It's also possible to access properties of unordered collections using the `[]` syntax, just as with ordered collections. When a collection isn't ordered, you need to use a string in order to index it. For example, the expression `${pageScope.book["title"]}` is equivalent to `${pageScope.book.title}`.

The reason why the JSTL supports two syntaxes to do the same thing is largely because JavaScript does so. The other reason is that if the name contains a special character—like . or - (or any other valid character that isn't a number or letter)—it's not possible to use the dot notation with it. You have to use `[]`. For example, if a property is named `current-price`, you'd want to access it like this: `${book["current-price"]}`. You also need to use quotes around the name of the property in this case.

3.3 EL Operators

The EL operations are necessary to handle data manipulations. All of the standard and common operators are available. Functionality is included in the EL for relational, arithmetic, and logical operators.

3.3.1 Relational Operators

These operators include: ==, !=, <, >, <=, >=, `eq`, `ne`, `lt`, `gt`, `le`, and `ge`. The last six operators are made available to avoid having to use entity references in XML syntax. Entity references are sometimes required because, if you place a character like < inside an XML element, the parser will throw an error due to its thinking that it's the start of a new element.

All illegal XML characters have to be replaced by entity references. For example, if we had an XML element that looked like:

```
<book>if price < 50 then </book>
```

we would have to replace the < with `<` so it looked like:

```
<book>if price &lt; 50 then </book>
```

and could be parsed correctly. If you need to brush up on XML info or how to deal with entity references, visit the tutorial at *http://www.w3schools.com/xml/*.

The `empty` prefix operator is also provided for testing whether a value is `null` or empty meaning "". For example:

```
<c:if test="${empty param.bookId}">
    A book must be selected to process the order
</c:if>
```

3.3.2 Other Operators

In addition to the relational and prefix operators, there are also arithmetic and logical operators that can be used with the EL. Arithmetic operators consist of addition (+), subtraction (-), multiplication (*), division (/ or `div`), and remainder/modulo (% or `mod`). Logical operators consist of &&, ||, and !. These represent `and`, `or`, and `not`, respectively.

3.3.3 Using Operators

Some examples of how to use the various operators in expressions are shown in Table 3.2. All of these expressions listed in the table are being shown as they would be used in a `test`

<table>
<tr><th>Expression</th><th>Description</th><th>Boolean Result</th></tr>
<tr><td>${1 == 1}</td><td>Equals operator</td><td>True</td></tr>
<tr><td>${1 != 1}</td><td>Not equals operator</td><td>False</td></tr>
<tr><td>${1 <= 1}</td><td>Less than or equals</td><td>True</td></tr>
<tr><td>${1 le 1}</td><td>Less than or equals using entity reference</td><td>True</td></tr>
<tr><td>${1 == 1 || 2 > 3}</td><td>Compound comparison results in (true || false) evaluation</td><td>True</td></tr>
<tr><td>${1 == 1 and 2 > 3}</td><td>Compound comparison results in (true and false)</td><td>False</td></tr>
<tr><td>${6 * 5 == 30}</td><td>Multiplication used in comparison results in (30 == 30)</td><td>True</td></tr>
<tr><td>${param.name == 'Sue'}</td><td>Check that request parameter called name is equal to the string Sue. Note the use of single quote around value.</td><td>True, because our JSP is being called with a query string of operators.jsp?name=Sue</td></tr>
<tr><td>${empty param.name}</td><td>Check for a value of the request parameter called name. If the value is null or "", empty will result in true.</td><td>False, because our JSP is being called with a query string of operators.jsp?name=Sue</td></tr>
<tr><td>${(not empty param.name && param.name == \"Sue\") and (param.month == 9)}</td><td>More complex sample of using logical, prefix, and compound expression with parenthesis. If the request parameter called name exists and the value is Sue, and the parameter called month equals 9, then the expression results in true. Note the use of the escape character "\" prior to using double quotes on the param.name comparison. This is an alternative to using single quotes.</td><td>False, because our JSP is being called with a query string of operators.jsp?name=Sue so the expression evaluates to (true && true) and (false) which results in a final value of false.</td></tr>
</table>

Table 3.2: Using operators in expressions.

attribute, like:

```
<c:if test="${1 == 1}">
     <b> Equals operator</b>
</c:if>
```

The evaluation of each expression will result in a Boolean value. For brevity, I only include the expressions (everything between the attribute's quotes) in the table.

Let's make a couple of quick points about working with expressions:

- The ${} syntax is used for the entire expression, not individual components. This is why we write ${1 == 1 || 2 > 3} not ${1 == 1} || ${2 > 3} or ${ ${1 == 1} or ${2 > 3} }.
- If you are using && keep in mind that for strict XML documents you need to do &&.
- String concatenations do not require the + operator. For example (${param.areacode})-${param.number} x(${param.ext}) would print a string like (303)-5551212 x(11) given the appropriate parameter values.

3.4 Automatic Type Conversion

The automatic type conversion is a very convenient feature of the EL in that a full set of coercion between various object and primitive types is supported. Coercion means that the page author isn't responsible for converting parameters into the appropriate objects or primitives. The JSTL defines appropriate conversions and default values. For example, a String parameter from a request will be coerced to the appropriate object or primitive. If we are dealing with A, which is an item or object, the coercion rules supplied by the JSTL will be applied for each given type. These coercions are done under the covers for you by the implementation, but it is always a good idea to understand how, and in what order, the rules are being applied. For this reason, I'm including the coercion rules from the JSTL 1.0 specification in JSTL Reference section so that you can review them if you want.

Let's look at Example 3.1. If we have a variable called myInteger and want to use the value in an expression as a number, we simply declare a variable with the value using <c:set>. If a parameter that represents the month is passed in the request as a String, the value of the month variable will be correct because the String will be coerced to the correct type when used. If the value of the parameter does not parse correctly to a number (say, the value is "September" instead of 9) at that point an exception will be thrown. Having automatic type conversions can save unnecessary exceptions from happening.

Example 3.1 Performing a Coercion

```
<c:set var="myInteger" value="${param.month}"/>
<p>
The value of myInteger is: <c:out value="${myInteger}" />
Perform a multiplication operation to show that the type is correct:
<c:out value="${myInteger * 2}" />
```

If the coercion is not possible, the exception might look something like:

```
javax.servlet.ServletException: An error occurred while
evaluating custom action attribute "value" with value
"${myInteger * 2}": An exception occured trying to convert
String "September" to type "java.lang.Double" (null)
```

Keep in mind that it's possible to use <c:catch> to prevent a complete exception stack from being displayed to the user. The page author can handle an unexpected value more in a user-friendly way, perhaps informing the user of the type of data that is expected or providing a sample of the format of data required by the user. A more graceful handling of an error is shown in Example 3.2.

Example 3.2 Friendly Handling of a Coercion Error

```
<c:catch var="coercionError">
The value of myInteger is: <c:out value="${myInteger}" />
Perform a multiplication operation to show that the type is
correct: <c:out value="${myInteger * 2}" />
</c:catch>

<c:if test="${not empty coercionError}">
      <b> The value of month is supposed to be a number.</b>
      Here's more information on the error:
      <br><font color="#FF0000"> <c:out value="${coercionError}" />
      </font>
</c:if>
```

3.5 Default Values

Another valuable feature of the JSTL is that it supports default values for expressions. This is very handy for allowing JSPs to handle simple errors gracefully instead of throwing a dreaded `NullPointerException`. Using default values allows for a better flow within the JSP and allows the user to have a better experience. Most common error situations can be avoided, thereby allowing the users to continue on their merry way without having an error page displayed. The default values are type correct according to what the EL indicates and they allow the JSP to recover from what would have been an error.

Let's look at an example. The expression `${book.title}` evaluates to `null` if there is no title associated with the book object. Even if the book object itself is `null`, we will not get a `NullPointerException` thrown due to the fact that we are trying to access a property of a `null` value. By evaluating to `null`, the specified default value is used without creating a worry about a NullPointerException being thrown by the JSP. The full expression would look like:

```
<c:out value="${book.title}" default="N/A">
```

When doing iterations, if a value is not found, it will default to 0. So, for example, when using the <c:forEach> tag, a begin, end, and step attribute can be specified. If the value of the begin uses a parameter that isn't defined, it will default to zero. In the example below, if the start parameter was not defined, then we would start iterating at 0 and end after 10 iterations.

```
<c:forEach items="${bookCatalog}"
           begin="${param.start}"
           end="{$param.start + 10}">
...
</c:forEach>
```

3.6 Summary

The most important point of this chapter concerns the details about what the expression language is, when to use it, and how to use it. The introduction of the expression language is one of the main features in the JSTL. While the expression language currently lives in the JSTL specification, it is also incorporated into the JSP 2.0 specification.

Finally, we saw various examples on how to use the EL, the operators available, and how the type coercion is done. We'll be using these basics as the foundation for all of the chapters to come.

chapter 4

Working with the Core Actions

The set of tags that are available in the Core tag library come into play for probably most anything you will be doing in your JSPs. Let's walk through code samples to see how we use each of the tags provided in this library.

The Core area comprises four distinct functional sections:

- General-purpose actions that are used to manipulate the scoped variables that might be found within a JSP. These general-purpose actions also encompass error handling.
- Conditional actions used for doing conditional processing within a JSP.
- Iterator actions that make it easy to iterate through collections of Objects.
- URL-related actions for dealing with URL resources in a JSP.

Let's look at each functional section in the Core tag library a bit more closely.

4.1 Writing Output to the JspWriter

There are four general-purpose tags. The `<c:out>` tag is probably the tag that you will see the most. It is used to output to the current `JspWriter`. This is similar to using the JSP expression `<%= scripting language expression %>` to write dynamic data to the client. The value to be written to the `JspWriter` is specified as a value attribute. You can use expressions in the value attribute. This allows for the resulting evaluation to be sent to the `JspWriter`. The `<c:out>` tag can perform XML character entity encoding for <, >, &, ", and '. This means that a < will be automatically encoded to `<`. The XML entity values that are used for encoding the characters are shown in Table 4.1.

Character	Entity Code
<	<
>	>
&	&
'	'
"	"

Table 4.1: XML entity values.

Therefore it's possible also to use this encoding capability to encode any HTML, like <br>, so that the angle brackets appear correctly. This capability is controlled by the escapeXml attribute. It defaults to true.

It should be obvious that:

```
The title of the book you just purchased is
<c:out value="${sessionScope.bookInfo.title}">
```

is much easier to read (and write) than:

```
<%@ page import="com.mk.jstl.bookInfo" %>
<% BookInfo bookInfo = (BookInfo)session.getAttribute"
                         ("bookInfo");
%>
The title of the book you just purchased is
  <%= bookInfo.getTitle() %>
```

In another example, we might want to output some data values that have been stored in a scoped variable called myData. The value of myData is "<b>I love to ride my bicycle</b>". There are HTML tags included in the string that we want to make sure are rendered correctly with the string bolded. To ensure that the data is displayed to the user correctly we would use:

```
<c:out value=${myData} escapeXml="false" />
```

With escapeXml set to false, our users see the correct display with the text bolded. Otherwise, they just see the characters <b> displayed with the text as shown in Figure 4.1.

The two displays are shown as they would appear if you were to view the source of the resulting file in your browser. The first output is using the default value of escapeXml, while the second output shows the result of using the esacpeXml set to false.

With escapeXml defaulting to true:

```
&lt;b&gt;I love to ride my bicycle&lt;/b&gt;
```

With escapeXml set to false:

```
<b>I love to ride my bicycle</b>
```

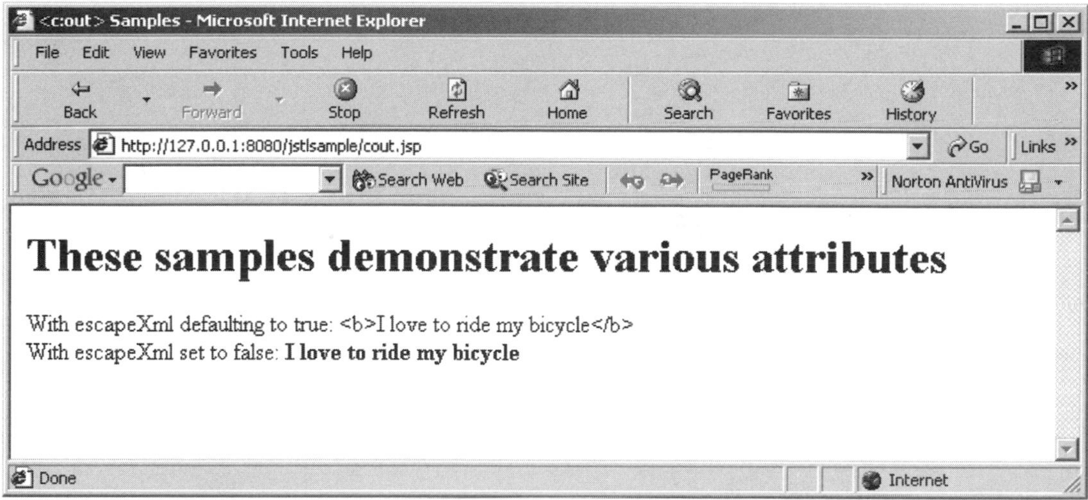

Figure 4.1: EscapeXML sample.

The other attribute of interest when using <c:out> to write to the JspWriter is the default attribute. This attribute is used to specify user-defined default values. This is the only tag that allows for a specific default value to be set. For JSTL 1.0, it was decided that for other tags the default mechanism that is handled by the coercions to empty values would suffice.

For example, we can use the expression language to determine if a value is present or set. If it is not defined, then the user-defined default value will appear in the JspWriter. Let's look at the following code statement:

```
Hello <c:out value="${param.name}" default="my friend"/>
```

If no parameter is specified called name, then the default value of "my friend" will appear as shown in Figure 4.2. Otherwise, we'll see the value of the parameter name as shown in Figure 4.3.

4.2 Setting Variables

The <c:set> tag is used to set the value of a scoped variable in any JSP scope, or is used to set a property of a specified target object. It is possible to set the value attribute using the EL or to set the value by using the body content of the tag. A common task is that of setting variables so that they can be used by other actions on pages. <c:set> can also be used to set a property of a target object. If using a target object, the target must evaluate to a JavaBean or java.util.Map object. If the target is a JavaBean, it must contain the appropriate getter/setter methods. If the target is null, and the object is other than a Map

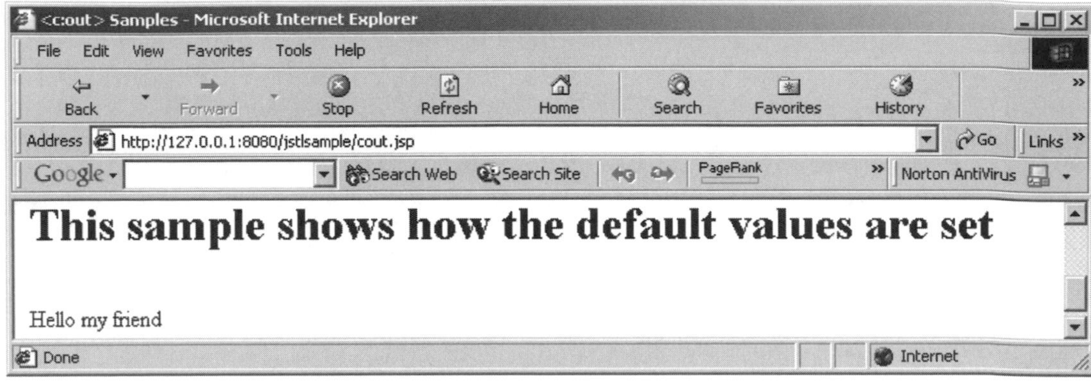

Figure 4.2: Using a default value.

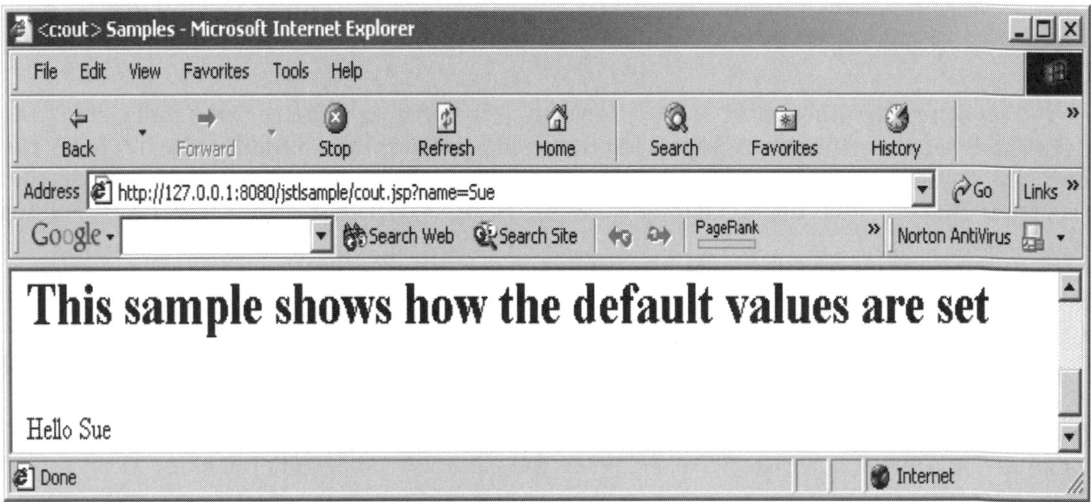

Figure 4.3: Using a parameter value.

or JavaBean, or the JavaBean doesn't have the correct property getter/setter methods, an exception will be thrown. Using the value attribute, an expression can be evaluated. This value is then set in the variable name defined by the var attribute. The scope of the var will default to page, but can easily be changed.

Let's look at a couple of samples. We've actually already used a sample of `<c:set>` that was in a previous `<c:out>` sample. The code that set the `myData` variable looks like:

```
<c:set value="<b>I love to ride my bicycle</b>" var="myData"/>
```

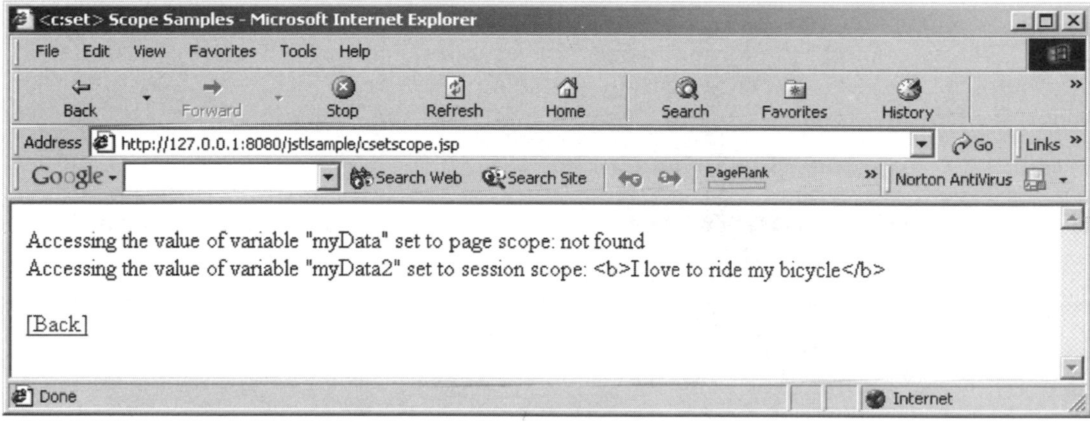

Figure 4.4: Accessing a variable from another page using Session scope.

We could also have expressed this by providing the value in the body content of the action:

```
<c:set var="myData2" scope="session" >
<b>I love to ride my bicycle</b>
</c:set>
```

If you have template text, you can put it in the body if it makes it easier to read. If you are using any EL, then the value needs to be defined in the attribute. In the body content sample, the scope attribute is set to session. This allows access to the variable `myData2` defined by `var` on other pages. The result of setting the scope attribute to session is shown in Figure 4.4.

It is worth pointing out that not everything is updatable just because you are using the `<c:set>` action. For example, it's possible to access a parameter using

```
<c:out value="${param.name}" />
```

but if you want to update the value using

```
<c:set var="param.name" value="some new value" />
```

subsequent uses of `${param.name}` seem to have the old value, not the new one. This is, according to the Servlet specification, because you cannot change parameter values since there is no `ServletRequest.setParameter()` method call. The values of parameters are intentionally immutable. If you need mutable values, it's probably best to create a new scoped attribute variable and set the value from a parameter like:

```
<c:set var="newVar" value="${param.name}" />
Value of initial parameter name: <c:out value="${newVar}"/>
<c:set var="newVar" value="another value" />
Value after an update: <c:out value="${newVar}"/>
```

It is also possible to set the value of variables based on a concatenation of EL expression values. While one might think you can use the + operator common in String concatenation, this is not the case. To do concatenation, you simply access the values you are interested in and include them with static text if you like, as shown in Example 4.1.

Example 4.1 Concatenating Strings in the EL

```
<c:set var="phone" value="(${param.areacode})-${param.number} x(${param.ext})"/>
The phone number is: <c:out value="${phone}" />
```

This produces the following output:

```
The phone number is: (303)-555-1212 x(2066)
```

It is also possible to use a target attribute that specifies an Object, and to set a specific property. Let's say that we want to provide a sorted list for display. A convenient way to do this is to use a java.util.TreeMap Object since it will keep the list sorted for us automatically. We first need to make this Object available to us as an Object on our page like:

```
<jsp:useBean id="list" class="java.util.TreeMap" />
```

Next, we use that Object by referencing it by its ID list in the target attribute and set the key value to be the parameter name in the <c:set> action.

```
<c:set target="${list}" property="${param.name}" value="1" />
```

We're using the value here to demonstrate that the list will hold the correct value when the key is outputed. We add a number of key/value pairs in this manner. Then we can loop through the TreeMap and print the key/value pairs. The full source is shown in Example 4.2.

Example 4.2 Using <c:set> with Target Objects

```
<jsp:useBean id="list" class="java.util.TreeMap" />
<c:set target="${list}" property="${param.name}" value="1" />
<c:set target="${list}" property="Zuni" value="2" />
<c:set target="${list}" property="Amy" value="3" />
<c:set target="${list}" property="Liz" value="4" />
<c:set target="${list}" property="Les" value="5" />
<%-- Print out the list of keys to see the sort --%>
<c:forEach var="item" items="${list}" >
      <c:out value="${item.key}" />,<c:out value="${item.value}" />
      <br>
</c:forEach>
```

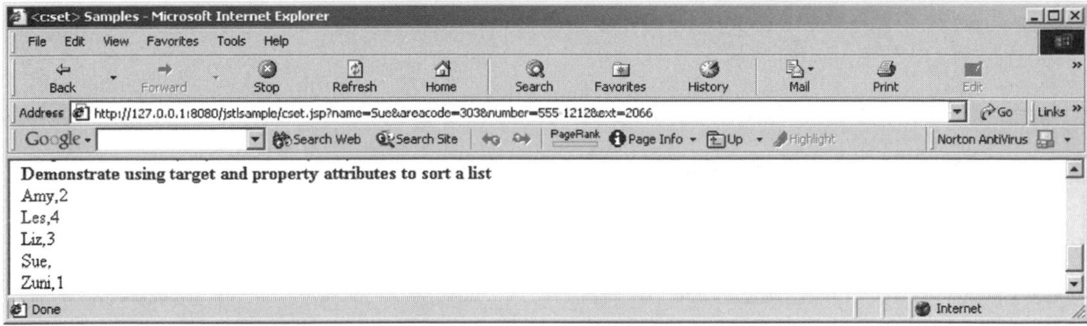

Figure 4.5: <c:set> to show a sorted list.

As you can see, we've added the properties in an unsorted order but the output appears as shown in Figure 4.5.

4.3 Removing Variables

Removing variables that have been set in any scope using <c:set> is done with the <c:remove> action. Removing variables is not all that interesting. Basically, you just need to specify the variable name in the var attribute and the scope. If the scope is not specified, then it's the same as doing:

```
PageContext.removeAttribute(var)
```

Otherwise, the specific scope is searched for the variable name. As an example, let's look at a couple of variables set into different scopes. The code is shown in Example 4.3.

Example 4.3 Setting Variables into Different Scopes

```
<c:set value="<b>I love to ride my bicycle</b>" var="myData"
       scope="application"/>
<c:set value="<b>I love to ride my bicycle</b>" var="myData2"
       scope="session" />
```

We can remove these variables in various ways—either by specifically indicating the scope, or by just letting the container locate the variable. Example 4.4 shows the various remove actions:

Example 4.4 Removing variables

```
<c:remove var="myData" scope="session" />
```

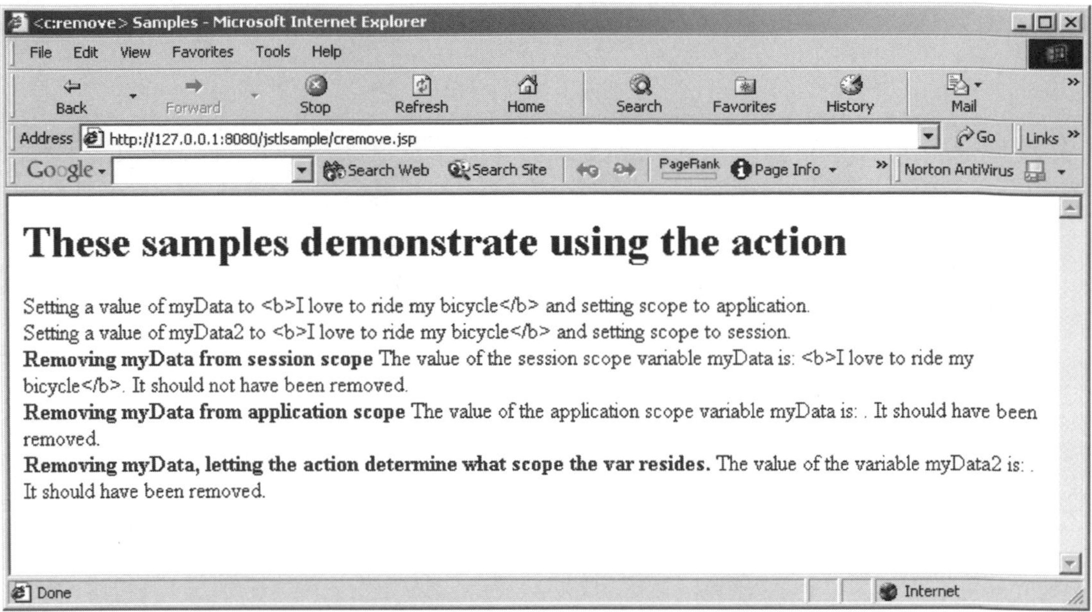

Figure 4.6: Output from cremove.jsp.

```
<c:remove var="myData" scope="application" />
<c:remove var="myData2" />
```

You'll notice from the output in Figure 4.6 that the removal of the `myData` variable from the session scope did not actually remove the variable. This is because the container did not specifically find the variable in that scope.

4.4 Using <c:catch>

The `<c:catch>` action is a new way to handle exceptions. It can handle errors from any action as well as from multiple actions at once by nesting those actions within `<c:catch>`. It is not meant to be a replacement for the JSP error page, but rather a way to fine-tune how your exceptions are handled. If you have an exception that is germane to the JSP, then it is best to let it propagate to the error page specified for the JSP. Exceptions that aren't really critical can be caught by the `<c:catch>` tag and so can be better handled for the user.

When an exception is thrown, it is stored in a page-scoped variable that is identified by the `var` attribute of the tag. If there is no exception, the scoped variable is removed if it already exists. Specifying a var is not mandatory, and if one isn't specified, the exception is caught—but not saved—anywhere. Let's look at how to use <c:catch> in more detail.

4.4.1 Handling Exceptions

The <c:catch> action is used to handle exceptions within a JSP. It catches a java.lang.Throwable thrown by any of its nested actions. Using <c:catch> is handy for dealing with errors that you might not want to send along to a defined error page. There might be some errors that the page author would prefer to handle on the page. For example, say you want to import a file but the file is not found. A ServletException will be thrown. However, it would be much more pleasant for the user not to see a stack trace from a ServletException. So you might want to display a more friendly error message to the user. This is shown in Example 4.5.

Example 4.5 Catching an Exception

```
<c:catch var="urlError">
      <c:import url="" />
</c:catch>

<c:if test="${not empty urlError}">
      <b>Your file was not found.</b>
            <br>
            Here's more information on the error:
            <br><font color="#FF0000">
                <c:out value="${urlError}" /></font>
</c:if>
```

The scope of var will always be page. If no error is thrown, then the var is removed from the scope when the </c:catch> is encountered. Using the expression ${not empty urlError} we can determine whether or not an error occurred. If we did have some kind of error, then we could let the user know in a user-friendly message, and we could even include the exception message by just writing the variable to the JspWriter. The difference between using a catch and not using a catch can be seen in Figure 4.7 and Figure 4.8. Keep in mind that it is possible to have the exception sent to an errorPage that could handle the output more nicely then the stack trace I'm showing. But I'm sure you get the picture. Which do you think your user would rather see?

<c:catch> actions are not meant to replace the errorpage mechanism that already exists in the JSP specification. These actions are meant to handle the less-than-critical errors that might occur so that the page author can decide how he or she wants to deal with them.

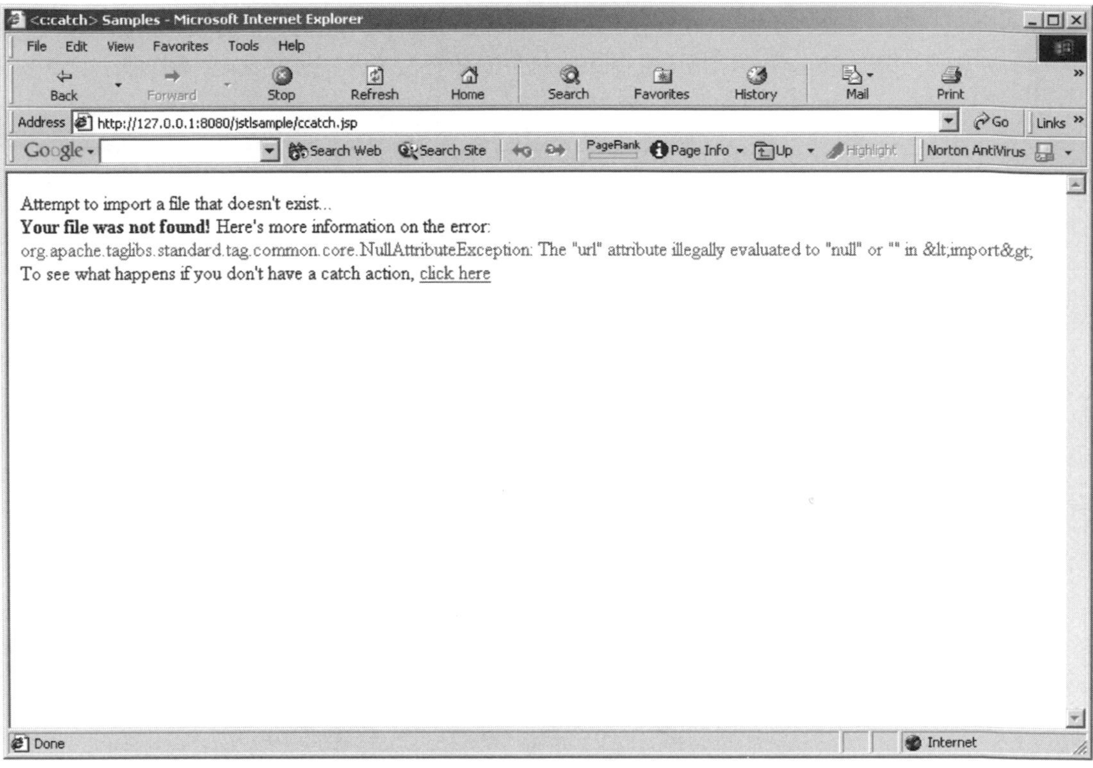

Figure 4.7: Display to the user with a <c:catch> around an exception.

4.5 Decisions, Decisions, Decisions—Conditional Actions

The JSTL supports both simple and mutually exclusive conditional actions. Using simple conditions and mutually exclusive ones, we can create some sophisticated, yet simple, pages. There are many, probably hundreds, of ways to use the various conditionals in the JSTL. It's common to have dynamic data that is used to determine what needs to happen on the JSP page. Using scriplets has been the most common way to accomplish this, but using scriplet code is what we are trying to get away from doing by using the EL. Not to mention that the JSP pages quickly start to look like a mess and become difficult to read when using scriplets. The JSTL conditional actions make it easy (and cleaner) to do conditional processing in a JSP page.

The actions that are used to do conditional processing are the `<c:if>` for simple conditions, and a combination of `<c:choose>`, `<c:when>`, and `<c:otherwise>` for handling mutually exclusive conditions. The `<c:if>` and `<c:when>` both have the `test` attribute in common.

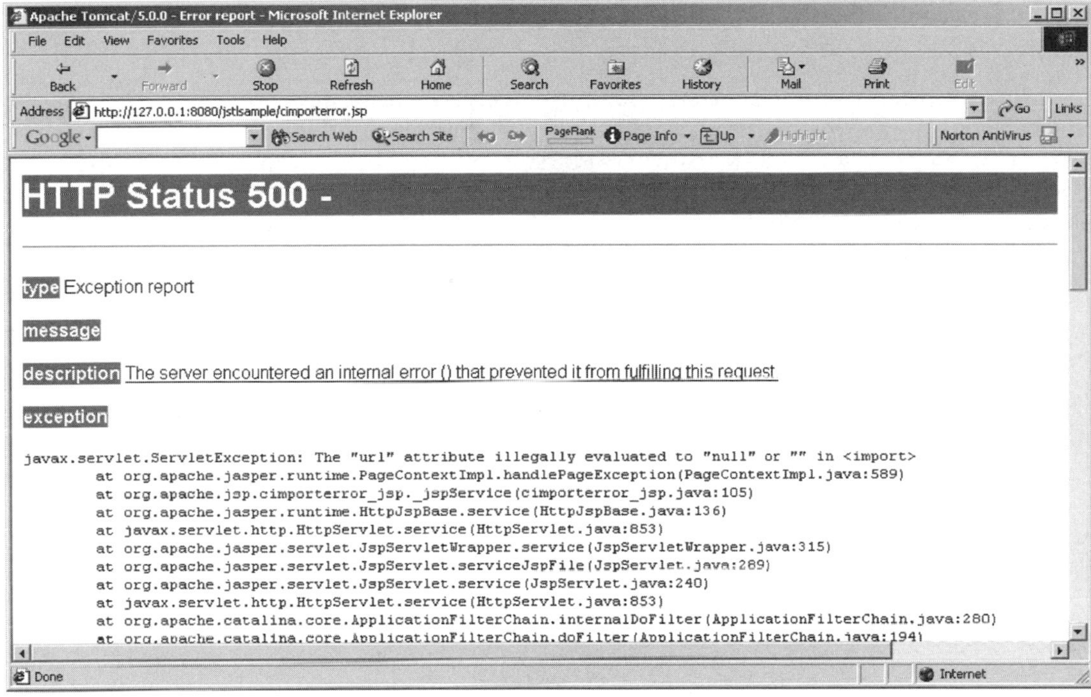

Figure 4.8: Display to the user without a <c:catch>.

Using the test attribute, a boolean expression is evaluated. This expression is constructed using the EL. If the test condition evaluates to true, then the body content of the action is executed. If the test condition is false, then the body content is skipped. It is possible to export the boolean result of the expression evaluation to a scoped variable using the var attribute. The default scope of the var is page, but you can set it to any of the available JSP scopes using the scope attribute. And if you specify a scope, then you also have to specify a var. Otherwise you'll end up getting an error.

4.5.1 Simple Conditional

The <c:if> action provides a simple conditional action. If the test condition specified evaluates to true, then the body content is evaluated and the result is written to the current JspWriter. It is possible to save the results of the test condition into an exported scoped variable by specifying the var and scope attributes. In the following example, a simple conditional is shown by defining an EL expression to evaluate. If it evaluates to true, then the <c:if> action will evaluate the body content.

```
<c:if test="${user.previousOrders == 0}">
```

```
Welcome to the MK bookstore. We hope you find something you like.
</c:if>
```

If we wanted to provide some shopping incentives for a new user, we could use the var attribute and add some additional features. Below we are defining the EL to evaluate, test, store the result of the test in firstTimeBuyer (which is given session scope), and also conditionally evaluate the content of the tag. Then, in the subsequent <c:if>, we are testing the scoped variable firstTimeBuyer again, and we act accordingly.

```
<c:if test="${user.previousOrders == 0}"
      var="firstTimeBuyer"
      scope="session">
Welcome to the MK bookstore. We hope you find something you like.
</c:if>
... other procesing logic in another JSP page
<%-- If a first time buyer, let's give them a 10% discount on the order --%>
<c:if test ="${firstTimeBuyer}">
Congratulations! You get a 10% discount on your first order.
</c:if>
```

4.5.2 Mutually Exclusive Conditionals

When using a mutually exclusive conditional action, only one of the number of possible alternative actions gets its body content evaluated. This is the familiar if/else or if/then/else programming structure. The JSTL actions <c:choose>, <c:when>, and <c:otherwise> are used to construct mutually exclusive conditional statements. Note that the <c:if> and <c:when> actions are different. A <c:if> action always processes its body content if its test condition evaluates to true. Only the first <c:when> action whose test condition evaluates to true will have its body content processed.

The <c:choose> action has no attributes and primarily sets the context for a mutually exclusive conditional. The <c:choose> action can contain the <c:when> and <c:otherwise> nested subtags. When using these actions, at most one of the nested actions will be processed. The test conditional of the <c:when> that evaluates to true will have its body content evaluated and written to the current JspWriter. There can be as many <c:when> actions as desired. The <c:otherwise> action must be the last action nested within the <c:choose>. It isn't required to use a <c:otherwise>, but if it is used, there can only be one.

The body content of the <c:otherwise> is only evaluated if none of the test conditions for the <c:when> actions evaluated to true. For example, the sample code below shows how the text rendered depends on a user's buying habits. Using the EL in the test conditions we can direct our sales strategy to the appropriate purchasing habit of the user:

```
<c:choose>
<c:when test="${user.lastPurchaseAmount > 100}">
Welcome big spender, check out all the new titles you can buy!
```

```
</c:when>
<c:when test="${user.lastPurchaseAmount > 30}">
Welcome, we've got some new titles that you might be interested in!
</c:when>
<c:when test="${user.lastPurchaseAmount > 1}">
Welcome, let us help you find some great books!
</c:when>
<c:otherwise>
Come on, there has to be something that interests you!
</c:otherwise>
</c:choose>
```

In the next set of examples, we are going to change the font color of a table cell depending on the current value of the item. We'll see this example in the context of the <c:forEach> action in just a minute. For now, current is the varStatus attribute, or the current status variable for an iteration, and book is the item attribute in an iteration. Example 4.6 peforms the functionality as switch statement logic, while Example 4.7 shows the logic in if/then/else format.

Example 4.6 Switch Functionality Using <c:choose>

```
<c:choose>
      <c:when test="${current.first}" >
                  <td><font color="#0000FF">
            <c:out value="${book.title}"/>
            </font></td>
      </c:when>
      <c:when test="${current.count % 2 == 1 }" >
                  <td><font color="#FF0000">
            <c:out value="${book.title}"/>
            </font></td>
      </c:when>
      <c:otherwise>
                  <td><c:out value="${book.title}"/></td>
      </c:otherwise>
</c:choose>
```

Example 4.7 If/Then/Else Functionality Using <c:choose>

```
<c:choose>
      <c:when test="${current.first}" >
            <td><font color="#0000FF">
      <c:out value="${book.title}"/>
```

```
        </font></td>
            </c:when>
        <c:otherwise>
            <td><c:out value="${book.title}"/></td>
        </c:otherwise>
</c:choose>
```

4.5.3 Creating Custom Logic Actions

While the simple and mutually exclusive tags provided by the JSTL should provide most of the functionality anyone might require, it is possible to create your own custom logic actions if necessary. These custom logic actions can also be used with the JSTL actions to create a robust and relatively straightforward, simple way to do all kinds of conditional processing. You can expose variables from your custom logic actions the same way that the <c:if> exports its var attribute. The exposed variable can then be used by other actions.

There is an Abstract class, `ConditionalTagSupport`, that extends `javax.servlet.jsp.tagext.TagSupport`. `ConditionalTagSupport` resides in the `javax.servlet.jsp.jstl.core` package and allows a developer to create a custom implementation of conditional actions. Using this class, it's possible for a `boolean` result to be exposed as a JSP scoped variable. The `boolean` result can then be used as the test condition in a <c:when> action in much the same way that we used the var attribute in the earlier sample.

`ConditionalTagSupport` provides support for:

- Conditional processing of the action's body based on the returned value of the abstract method `condition()`.
- Storing the result of `condition()` as a `Boolean` object into a JSP scoped variable identified by attributes var and scope.

While we won't go into the details of how to build a custom logic action, it's important to make the point that the JSTL is extensible and can easily morph to fit an exact need.

4.6 Handling Iterators

There has always been a strong requirement to iterate through collections. In fact, this is probably one of the most common tasks that we need to perform. One can only venture a guess at how many JSP page authors have implemented their own versions of iterating through something. Iterating can certainly be accomplished using scriptlet code in a JSP, but let's face it, there's got to be a better way. Coding iterations and handling different types of collections can get cumbersome. The iterator actions in the JSTL are focused on making iterating as easy as possible over a variety of collection types.

There are two iterations actions <c:forEach> and <c:forTokens>. <c:forEach> repeats over a nested body content so that you can perform various tasks based on a collection, a result set, or a numerical count.

All of the standard J2SE java.util.Collection and java.util.Map types are supported in the <c:forEach> action. These include:

- List
- LinkedList
- ArrayList
- Vector
- Stack
- Set
- HashMap
- Hashtable
- Properties
- Provider
- Attributes

The <c:forTokens> action is useful for parsing through tokens that are separated by some delimiter. Let's look at various samples for using both actions, starting with the <c:forEach>.

4.6.1 <c:forEach>

We have seen throughout some of our previous examples that using the iteration actions makes life a lot simpler for us in JSP-land. If you are like me, you've probably already looked at the various code samples that include iterations actions provided in the JSP files with the sample download before you got up to this point anyway.

The <c:forEach> action uses the items attribute to specify a collection of objects. The action then repeats its nested body content over the items. If items is null, then no iteration is performed since it is treated as an empty collection. The current item in the iteration is exported as a variable. The variable has nested scope visibility. For most Collections, this is an object in the collection. However, if it is an array of primitive types or a Map object, the current item is handled slightly differently. If the collection is of type java.util.Map, then the current item will be of type java.util.Map.Entry. There are two properties exposed:

- key—the key under which this item is stored in the underlying Map
- value—the value that corresponds to this key

There is also an object exported that holds the status information of the iteration. The status is exposed using the public interface LoopTagStatus contained in the javax.servlet.jsp.jstl.core package. There are a number of interfaces exposed with the iteration actions, among them LoopTag and LoopTagSupport. We'll walk through an iteration example in just a moment.

Another nice feature of the iteration actions is their ability to specify ranges for the iteration. This makes it possible to iterate through a specified portion of a collection. The begin and end attributes are the indices used to determine the range. If begin is specified, it must be >=0. If end is specified, it must be >= begin.

The items attribute is not required when using the <c:forEach> action. If the items attribute is not specified, then the value of the current item is set to the integer value of the current index. This makes it very easy to do a "for-loop" if need be. There is a step attribute that allows for the iteration to take place in the specified step amount. If step is specified, it must be >=1. Note, though, that if you are using a Map collection, the Set view of the mappings is obtained from the Map by using the entrySet() method. From the Set, an Iterator object is obtained by using the iterator() method. The items of the collection are processed in the order returned by that Iterator object. Therefore, the begin and end attributes are really dependant on the order of the Map.

Keep in mind that when an object is exported, it is available for other tags also. It becomes possible for tags to collaborate with each other quite easily. It is a common requirement that when iterating over collections, you want to display one item one way and another item differently. Of course, it's usually not possible to determine this until runtime when you can examine the dynamic data being provided by the model in the collections. Using the iteration and conditional actions, it becomes much easier to implement these types of requirements.

For example, let's look at iteration where we are looping through a collection of books.

```
<table>
      <c:forEach var="book" items="${books}" varStatus="status">
            <tr>
                  <td><c:out value="${book.title}"/></td>
            </tr>
      </c:forEach>
</table>
```

Now let's decide that we only want to display the first ten books in our collection. We do this by adding the begin and end attributes:

```
<table>
      <c:forEach var="book" items="${books}" varStatus="status"
                  begin="0" end="9">
            <tr>
                  <td><c:out value="${book.title}"/></td>
            </tr>
      </c:forEach>
</table>
```

Now let's say that when we print the first ten books, we want to highlight the first five. This is done by adding in a collaboration with the conditional <c:choose> action.

```
<table>
      <c:forEach var="book" items="${books}" varStatus="status"
                  begin="0" end="9">
            <tr>
            <c:choose>
                  <c:when test="${status.count < 4}">
                        <td bgcolor="#FFFF00">
                              <c:out value="${book.title}"/>
                        </td>
                  </c:when>
                  <c:otherwise>
                        <td><c:out value="${book.title}"/></td>
                  </c:otherwise>
            </c:choose>
      </c:forEach>
</table>>
```

4.6.2 Paging through a Large Collection

Many tasks require the looping over large collections. Using <c:forEach> these tasks can be accomplished painlessly. As long as there are items remaining in the iteration, the body content of the action will be evaluated. Let's walk through a sample that takes all of the functionality of a <c:forEach> and puts it into a cohesive example.

One of the most common uses for the iteration is to display some set of information. Usually this is some dynamic data where the quantity depends on what the user is doing at the time. When using the <c:forEach>, you probably will be using a collection of some sort. However, it's also possible to just loop through a number sequence. In the examples, I'm using a number sequence so that I can demonstrate all of the features by providing the JSP functionality to page through a sequence.

When using a collection, there is an additional attribute defined called items. Using items allows for the current selection to be the var in the iteration. I'll show a sample using collection data as well so you can see the additional attribute being used.

This sample demonstrates how to solve a common problem: displaying a large result set in a limited amount of space. Usually the way you want to present the results to the users is in smaller chunks, allowing them to page through a selection that they choose. Anyone who has dealt with large database result sets should be familiar with this issue. The way we're going to solve the problem is by using a combination of <c:forEach>, <c:set>, and <c:out> actions.

First we set up some variables on our page as shown in Example 4.8. Note, however, that even though I've assigned values for demonstration purposes, these could just as easily have been set by a request parameter from a form where the user decides how many results they want to view at once.

Example 4.8 Setting the Variables for the Iteration

```
<c:set var="totalSize" scope="session" value="40"/>
<c:set var="chunkSize" scope="session" value="10"/>
<c:set var="start" scope="page" value="1"/>
<c:set var="finish" value="${start + chunkSize - 1}" />
```

The totalSize represents how many total results we have, the chunkSize is how many results to view at a time, the start defines us to start at the beginning, and finish tells us when to end our iteration. We'll see in just a minute how we will pass the start value as a parameter so that users can traverse anywhere in the list they want.

In Example 4.9 we continue by defining our loop. Because we have no items attribute defined, the iteration takes place over a set of numbers. We set the begin and end attributes to the start and finish variables that we previously set in Example 4.8. This allows us to use the same loop with dynamic values. There are a number of statements getting printed so that we can view the values of the item, the current count, and the current index. Item in this case will be just an integer. Using the varStatus attribute, we are able to define a variable that is an exported object of type javax.servlet.jsp.jstl.core.LoopTagStatus. This interface allows us to get various pieces of information about the current iteration.

Example 4.9 <c:forEach> Iteration

```
<c:forEach var="item" varStatus="current"
           begin="${start}" end="${finish}">

Item: <c:out value="${item}"/>
Current count =<c:out value="${current.count}" />
Current index =<c:out value="${current.index}" />
<br>
<c:if test="${current.index == finish}" >
      <c:out value="--------------------------------" />
</c:if>

</c:forEach>
```

It is possible to access the information defined in Table 4.2 from the varStatus variable. These are the properties defined by the LoopTagStatus interface.

In Example 4.9, we print out some status information to see the difference between the count and the index value. In our case, since we are iterating over integers, the index value is equal to the value of the item itself.

Property	Type	Definition
current	Object	The current item in the iteration. No matter how many times current is called, it will return the same value during that iteration.
index	int	0-based indices of the current round of the iteration
count	int	Count is a relative, 1-based sequence number identifying the current round of iteration (in context with all rounds the current iteration will perform).
first	boolean	Determines whether the current round of the iteration is the first one
last	boolean	Determines whether the current round of the iteration is the last one
begin	int	Returns the begin attribute value
end	int	Returns the end attribute value
step	int	Returns the step attribute value

Table 4.2: LoopTagStatus properties.

Last, to add the paging functionality we require the use of another `<c:forEach>` loop as shown in Example 4.10. Here we use our previously defined variables, `totalSize` and `chunkSize`, to create links that the user can select. The link is built by defining a parameter called `start` that will tell us where our display should begin its iteration. Combining the selection, and increasing it by the number defined for the viewable size, allows us to create as many links as required to display the entire result.

Example 4.10 Supply the Paging Functionality Using <c:forEach>

```
<c:forEach var="selection" begin="1"
          end="${totalSize - 1}" step="${chunkSize}">

<a href="?start=<c:out value="${selection}"/>" >
<b>
(<c:out value="${selection}"/>-
 <c:out value="${selection + chunkSize - 1}"/>)
</b>
</a>
</c:forEach>
```

The one additional piece of code that we initially skipped over showed how the start parameter is actually retrieved and used. In Example 4.11 we see how the parameter is referenced and used to determine the start of the iteration.

Example 4.11 Accessing the Start Parameter

```
<c:if test="${param.start > 0}" >
      <c:set var="start" scope="page" value="${param.start}" />
</c:if>
```

Putting this all together is probably easiest by looking at what the browser displays. This is shown in Figure 4.9.

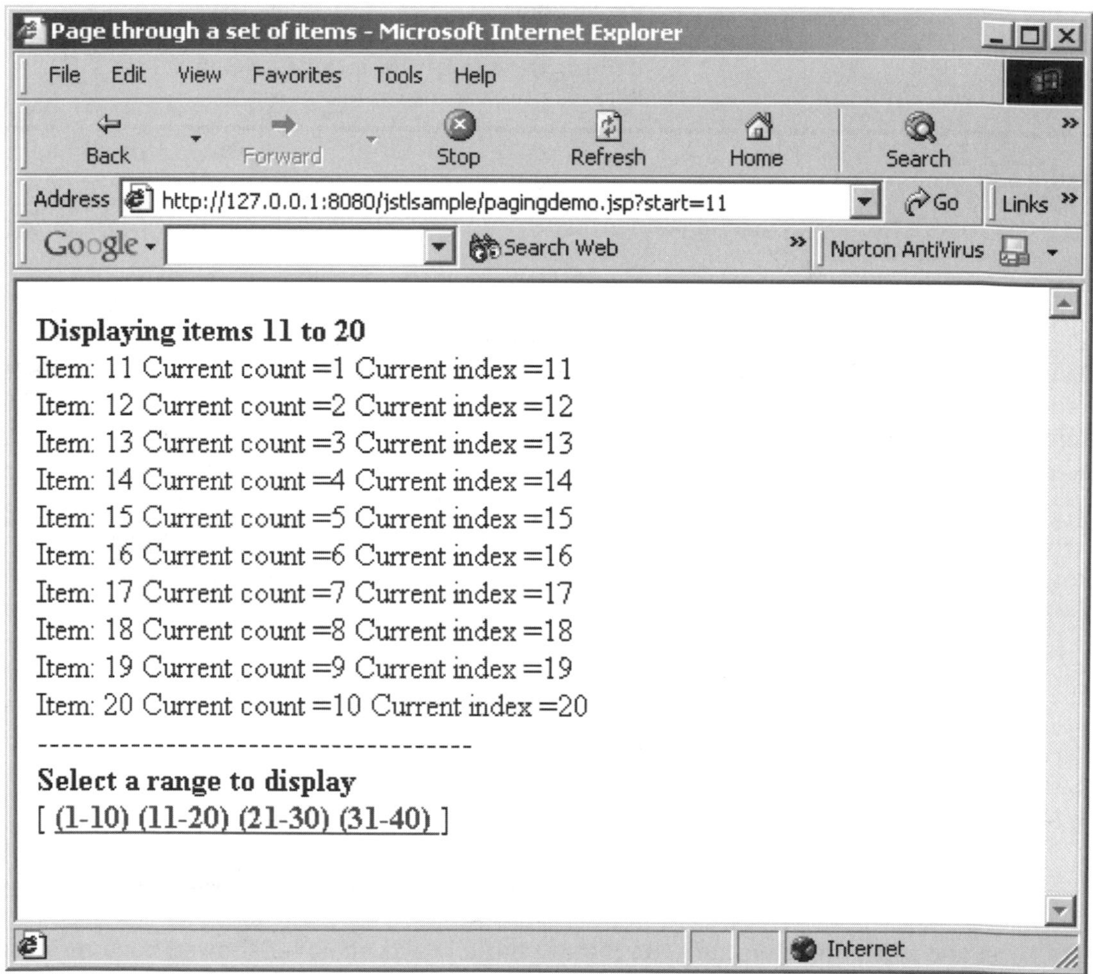

Figure 4.9: Browser display of paging through results.

4.6.3 Looping with a Collection

Now that we have seen how the <c:forEach> action works with a set of integers, let's see how to use it working with a Collection. First, let's look at accessing a java.util.Vector that implements Collection. Then we'll show the difference in how to access a Hashmap, which implements the Map interface.

When using a Collection, the objects are specified in the items attribute. For the sake of simplicity, I'm cheating a bit here. When using a Collection, it will usually be populated from some type of business logic that happens in your Model components. The contents will then be used in the View, which is your JSP file. In Example 4.12 I'm setting up a JavaBean that is a Vector, and manually populating it in a scriptlet so that we have some type of data to work with.

Example 4.12 Setting up the Collection

```
<jsp:useBean id="list" class="java.util.Vector" />
<%-- Add some values to the Vector, so that we can loop over them --%>
      <%
            list.add("apple");
            list.add("orange");
            list.add("plum");
            list.add("peach");
      %>
```

We now have a JavaBean available called list that we can use in our <c:forEach> iteration. By simply setting the items attribute to our newly created Vector, the iteration will set the var to be the current item in the Collection. The code for this is simple and is shown in Example 4.13.

Example 4.13 Looping over the Vector

```
<%-- Print out the Vector collection --%>
<c:forEach var="item" items="${list}" >
<c:out value="${item}" />
<br>
</c:forEach>
```

The items printed out are shown in Figure 4.10.

You'll notice that we didn't have to access anything other than the item to have the correct value of the iteration print to the JspWriter. That's because a java.util.Iterator object is obtained from the Collection (in the action's handler) and the items of the Collection are processed in the order returned by that Iterator object.

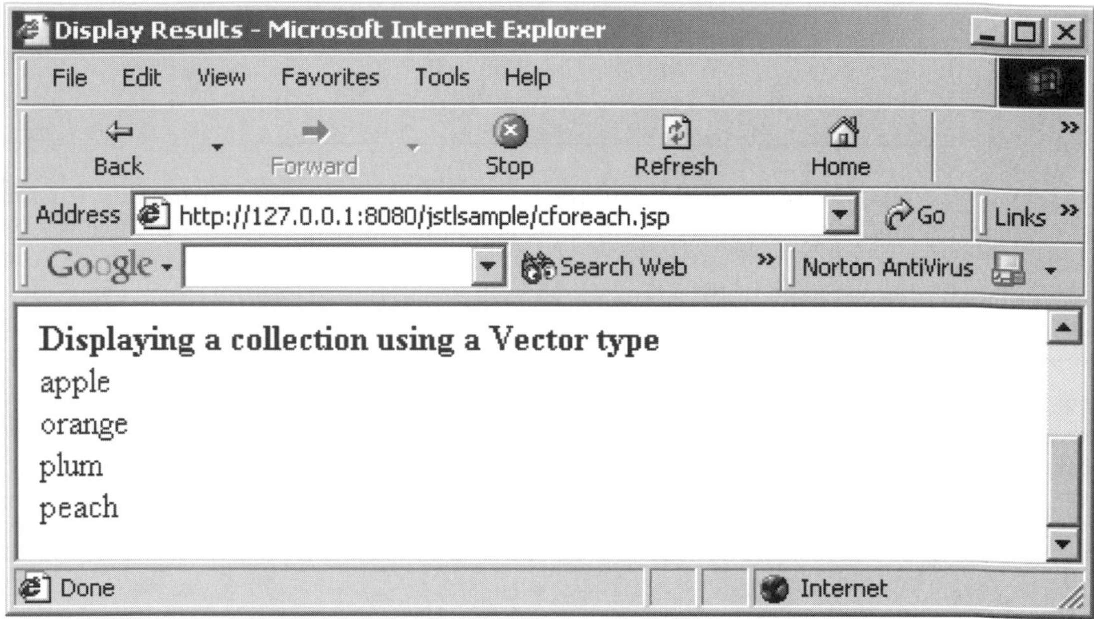

Figure 4.10: Displaying a collection.

We can apply the same begin, end, and step attributes to collections. Remember that the iteration is 0-based, so by setting begin to 1, we actually start on the second item of the collection. Each iteration will display every 2 items, as defined by the step attribute. By setting the end attribute to 5, we see that if the end value is past the size of the collection (in this case the size is 4), it will just be ignored. This is shown in Example 4.14.

Example 4.14 Iterating through the Collection

```
<c:forEach var="item" items="${list}"
           begin="1" step="2" end="5">
<c:out value="${item}" />
<br>
</c:forEach>
```

Using the additional attributes in the <c:forEach>, we can see the difference in the browser output as shown in Figure 4.11.

There is a slight difference to be pointed out when using a java.util.Map. While it's possible to use maps in the same manner as collections, the var attribute is exposed as a Map.Entry Object. A Map Object is one that maps keys to values and cannot contain duplicate keys. Each key can have only one value. The order of a map is defined as the

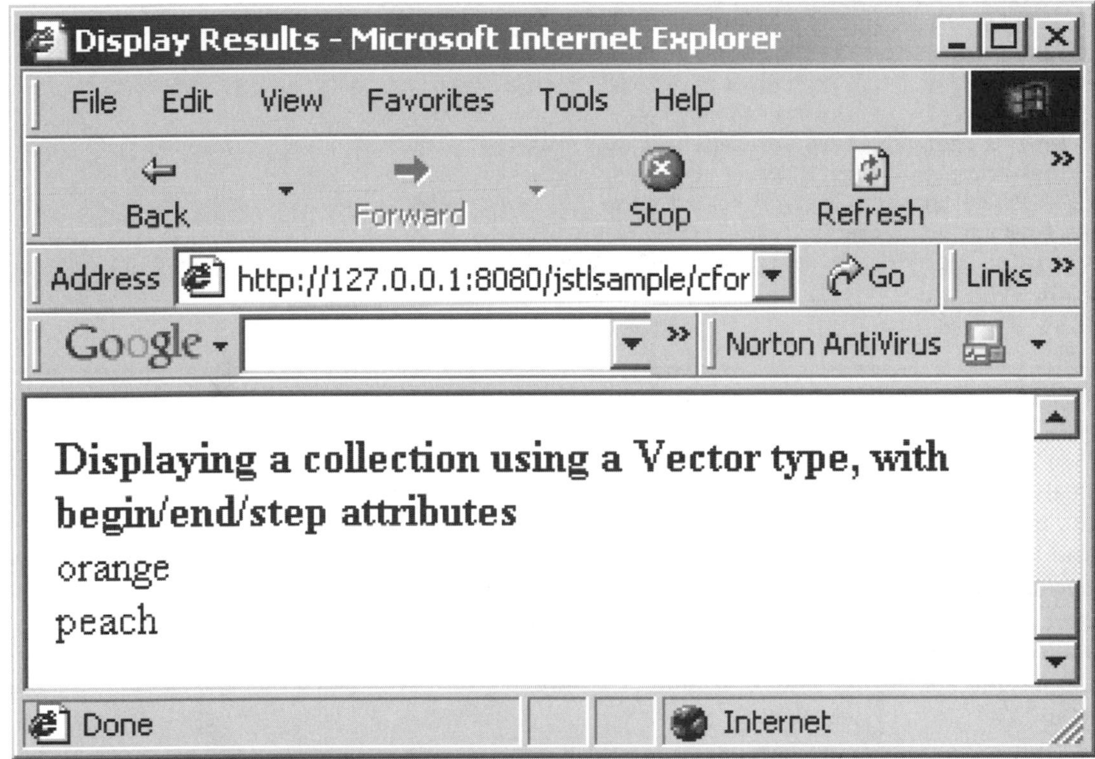

Figure 4.11: Displaying a collection using attributes.

order in which the Iterator object on the map's collection returns the elements. Some map implementations, like the TreeMap class, make specific guarantees as to their order; others, like the HashMap class, do not. The functionality required for your particular application will depend on which class implements the Map interface you are interested in. If you need to read up on the differences in the Map implementations, check out the JDK 1.4.1 JavaDocs.

Let's say that we have a JavaBean setup that is a Map object, the same way we did with our Vector. When iterating over the Map, if we wanted to access the key and value of each item in the Collection, we would do so as shown in Example 4.15. This is the same example that we saw when demonstrating the <c:set> using the target and property attributes. Only now, we are interested in the Map.Entry access of the Map itself.

Example 4.15 Accessing a Map.Entry Object from a Map

```
<jsp:useBean id="list" class="java.util.TreeMap" />
<%-- Add the properties into the TreeMap that we want sorted --%>
```

```
<%-- Note, the order is incorrect when we add the values --%>
<c:set target="${list}" property="${param.name}" value="1" />
<c:set target="${list}" property="Zuni" value="2" />
<c:set target="${list}" property="Amy" value="3" />
<c:set target="${list}" property="Liz" value="4" />
<c:set target="${list}" property="Les" value="5" />
<%-- Print out the list of keys to see the sort --%>
<c:forEach var="item" items="${list}" >
<c:out value="${item.key}" />,<c:out value="${item.value}" />
<br>
</c:forEach>
```

Without beating the <c:forEach> horse to death, let's look at one more sample that deals with a HashMap. We'll use HashMap because this implementation deals with an indexing by a key to obtain a value. While it is possible to use the same mechanism `item.key` and `item.value` to print out the values, there's also an alternative. I'm pointing this out because you can also use this notation if you have a dynamic value in your application that is a key to a Map and you need to access the value of it using the EL. In Example 4.16 we set up a HashMap, add some values to it, and iterate over the collection. Instead of displaying the value that corresponds to the key, we will index the HashMap using the key.

Example 4.16 Indexing a HashMap Value Using a Key

```
<jsp:useBean id="hash" class="java.util.HashMap" />
<%-- Add some values, so that we can loop over them --%>
      <%
            hash.put("apples","pie");
            hash.put("oranges","juice");
            hash.put("plums","pudding");
            hash.put("peaches","jam");
      %>
<br>
<c:forEach var="item" items="${hash}">
 I like to use <c:out value="${item.key}" /> to make
 <c:out value="${hash[item.key]}" />
      <br>
<br>
</c:forEach>
```

Accessing the value in this manner produces the browser output shown in Figure 4.12.

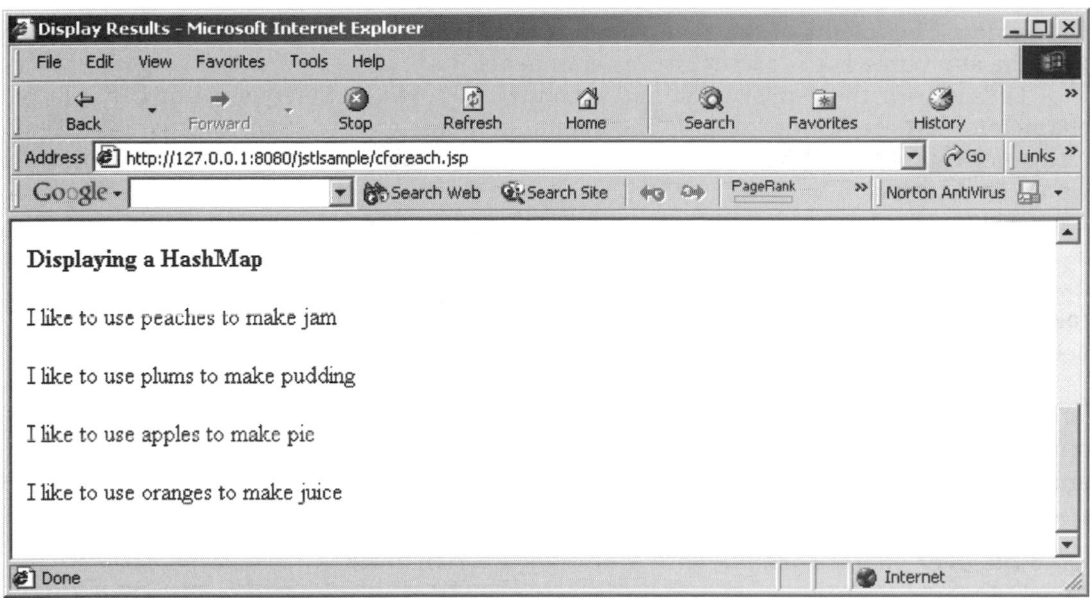

Figure 4.12: Cooking with a HashMap.

At this point, with all the information on <c:forEach> you should be able to iterate over just about anything in any manner required. So let's move along to the other iteration, the <c:forToken>.

4.6.4 Tokenizing Data Using <c:forTokens>

While the <c:forEach> action is powerful for iterating, sometimes data is presented to us in the form of strings. A common reason for getting string data (no matter how much we dislike it) is because we are integrating or interfacing with a legacy system. Many times, the data will come in a form where there is some delimiter (or delimiters) being used, and it's up to our application to get the data into a form in which we can use it. This is just one example of when string data needs to be processed. There might be a specific reason in your application why you are passing string data around on purpose. This is when the <c:forTokens> comes into play.

<c:forTokens> has the same basic attributes as the <c:forEach>, but with two important differences. First, the `items` attribute is a `String` of tokens to iterate over. When iterating over tokenized Strings, it is necessary to define a delimiter to determine the characters that separate the tokens in the `String`. Therefore, the <c:forTokens> also has a `delims` attribute. This is a `String` that contains the set of delimiters to use to iterate through the tokens. If the `delims` is `null`, then the items are treated as one contiguous `String`. If <c:forTokens> reminds you a lot of `java.util.StringTokenizer`, that's a

good thing. The tokens of the string are retrieved using an instance of StringTokenizer with the attributes items and delims as arguments.

Let's clarify the terms token and delimiter. A token is a sequence of consecutive characters that are not delimiters. The delimiter characters are used to separate tokens. As a quick sample, given a string "a-b-c" and a delimiter character of "-" the following tokens would be returned: a b c.

When using the <c:forTokens>, you specify a string in the items attribute. Using the delims attribute, you specify what the delimiter characters are. This can be one character, like a comma, or any number of characters. Each one will be used to determine if a new token is created. If the delims attribute is null, then the items are treated as one token. Let's look at a couple of examples.

Our first sample in Example 4.17 shows a null delims defined. We are using a <c:set> for all of our samples to set a string variable called tokens for our page. The string consists of a number of letters, and various characters. We'll use the tokens variable to see how changing the delims attribute will affect the outcome of the tokenize operation.

Example 4.17 <c:forTokens> with a null delims Attribute

```
<%-- set some tokens to work with --%>
<c:set var="tokens" value="a,b,c:d:e,f#g,h" />
<%-- Tokenize using null delim --%>
<b>Tokenize the string "<c:out value="${tokens}" />" with a null
   delimiter</b>
<br>
<c:forTokens var="token" items="${tokens}" delims="" >
Found token: <c:out value="${token}" /><br>
</c:forTokens>
```

Executing the code above produces the output in Figure 4.13.

By defining a value for delims in Example 4.18, we see in Figure 4.14 how the tokens are now returned. A token is produced only when the character defined in delims is found in the string.

Example 4.18 <c:forTokens> with delims Value

```
<%-- Tokenize using 1 delim --%>
<b>Tokenize the string "<c:out value="${tokens}" />" with delims
   = ","</b>
<br>
<c:forTokens var="token" items="${tokens}" delims="," >
Found token: <c:out value="${token}" /><br>
</c:forTokens>
```

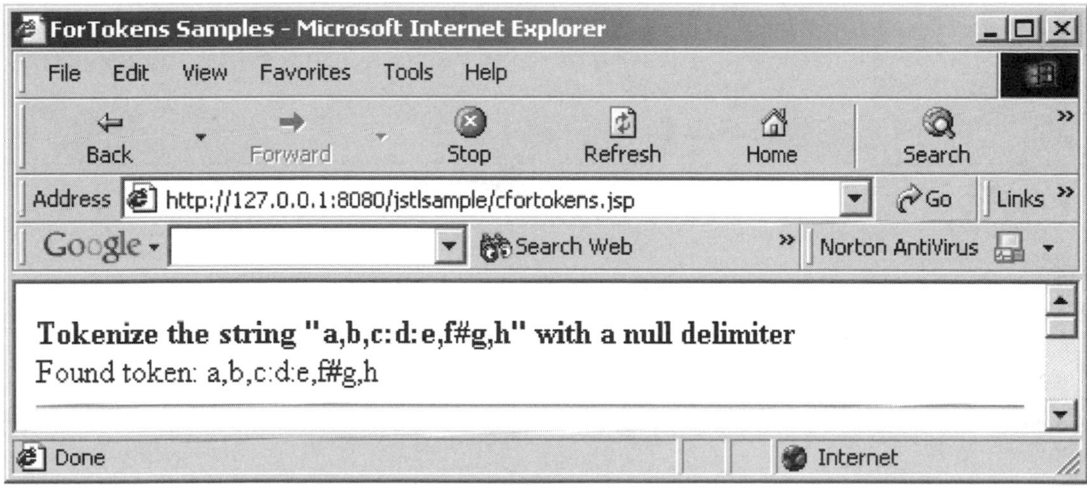

Figure 4.13: Display of *null* delims.

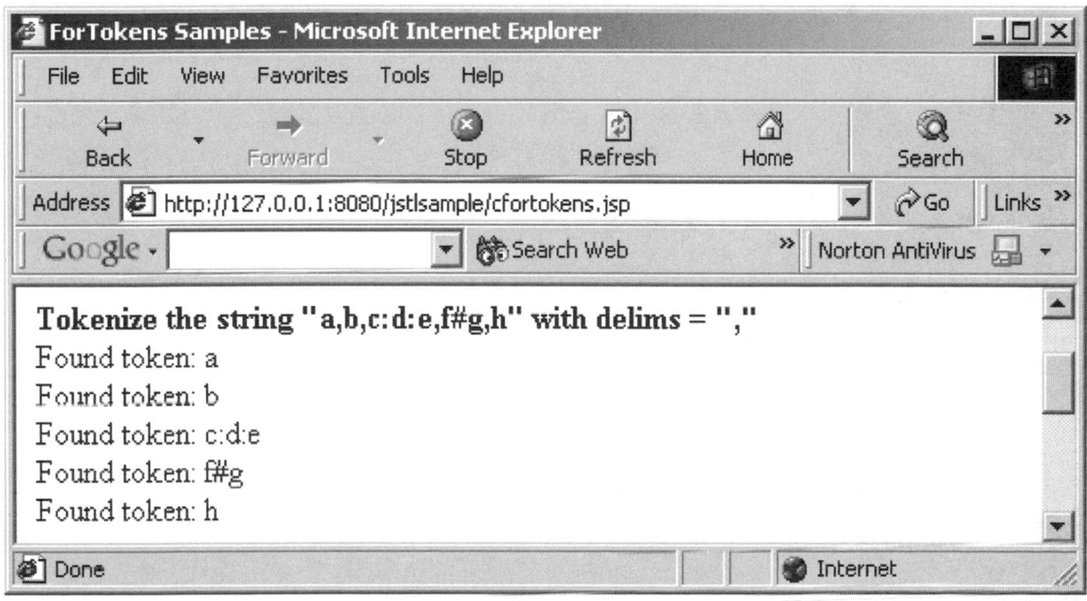

Figure 4.14: Display of tokens using delim value.

Next, we add the whole ball of wax. We define multiple delims so that our string token is completely tokenized. This is shown in the code in Example 4.19 and the display in Figure 4.15.

Example 4.19 <c:forEach> with multiple delims

```
<%-- Tokenize using multiple delims --%>
<b>Tokenize the string "<c:out value="${tokens}" />" with delims
   = ",:#"</b>
<br>
<c:forTokens var="token" items="${tokens}" delims=",:#" >
Found token: <c:out value="${token}" /><br>
</c:forTokens>
```

Obviously, from our samples, it is important to know what the delims are that you are interested in, otherwise your tokens might not be what you are expecting. It's possible to use the EL to access a variable for the delims and then set the data dynamically,

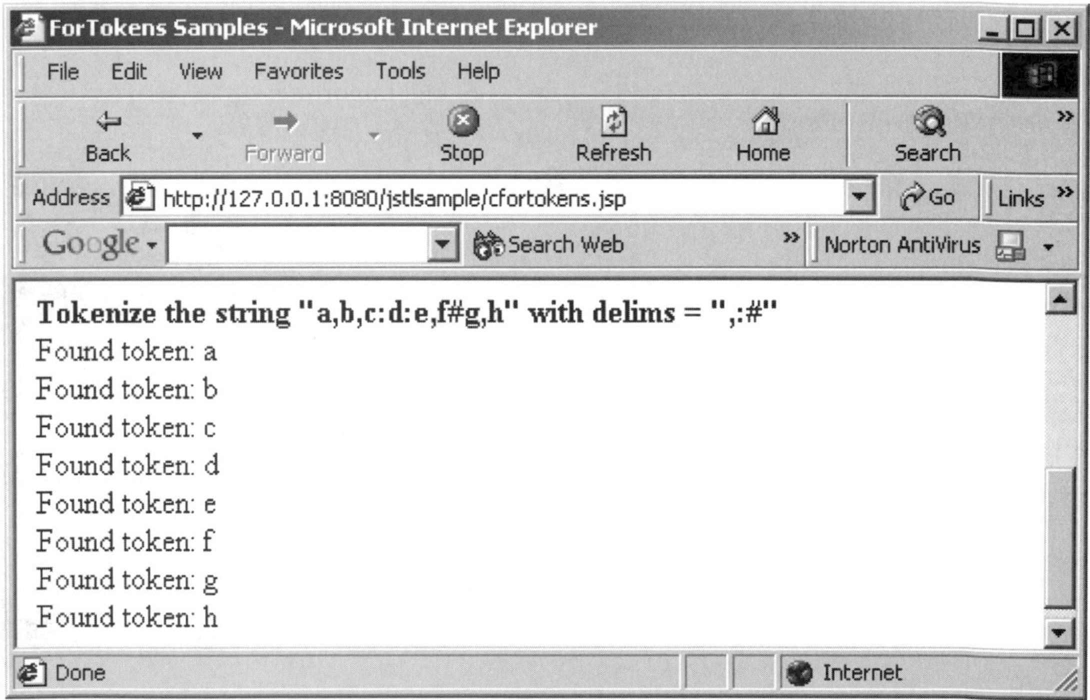

Figure 4.15: Display of tokens using multiple delims.

perhaps with a request parameter that might have been defined on an HTML form. This is shown in Example 4.20.

Example 4.20 Using Dynamic Values for the delims Attribute.

```
<c:forTokens var="token" items="${tokens}"
 delims="${param.delims}" >
Found token: <c:out value="${token}" /><br>
</c:forTokens>
```

The <c:forTokens> action has the same attributes available as the <c:forEach> that we have already gone into in depth. These include the varStatus for accessing status information about the current iteration loop, the begin, end, and step attributes. The step will be used to indicate that the iteration should process only those tokens defined by the step value. All of these attributes work exactly the same in the <c:forTokens> as they do in the <c:forEach>, so I will refrain from going over them again.

4.7 URL-Related Actions

The last group of actions to be covered as part of the Core Tag Library is that of URL-related actions. All of the URL-related tags are related to linking, importing, and redirecting. Dealing with URLs and handling links and redirects are common needs when writing JSPs. Let's take a look at these URL-related actions and then we'll see what they can provide for us in detailed examples.

First we should talk about the types of resources that can be imported. There are a variety of places and types of content that a JSP author might be interested in. Using <jsp:include> has been the way to include both static and dynamic content into JSP pages. <jsp:include> had some limitations as to the types of files that could be included. Then there was the fact that anything included with this standard action had to reside in the same context as the page itself. This is fine for simple web applications, but as web applications grow and cooperate with each other, it is a much better idea to allow for content to come from wherever it needs to. The limitation of <jsp:include> has been overcome with the <c:import> action.

4.7.1 <c:import>

<c:import> is used to import, or include, the content of a URL-based resource. The resource itself can be relative, absolute, within the same context as, or in a foreign context to the requesting JSP. There are a number of ways to use the <c:import> action. The only required attribute is url, which is the URL of the resource to import. We'll look at a simple example using a relative URL in the same context, and then we'll build upon it

by adding some of the other attributes supported in the action. Our first example looks like:

```
<c:import url="/hotoffthepress.html"/>
```

It is possible to specify the scope that the URL resource has by adding the var and scope attributes. The default scope is set to page if it is not specified.

```
<c:import url="/hotoffthepress.html"
     var="hotoffthepress"
     scope="session" />
```

If the latest book releases were being handled by a separate application contained in the context "new releases," but we still wanted to access the hotoffthepress.html file, we'd add a foreign context so the correct file would be imported.

```
<c:import url="/hotoffthepress.html"
     var="hotoffthepress"
     scope="session"
     context="/newreleases" />
```

Let's note here the difference between scope and context. The scope is the JSP scope in which this URL resource will be available. The context is where the resource actually comes from.

The flexibility that is provided for the types of content using the <c:import> action is important. Just as important are the performance gains attained with the <c:import> action. Using <jsp:include> falls short in efficiency in a number of ways. First, when the content of the imported resource is used as the source for another action, unnecessary buffering occurs. The <jsp:include> reads the content of the response and writes it to the body content of the enclosing action. The enclosing action must then re-read the exact same content. This is not the most efficient way to do things but it is typical of the way that custom actions that do transformations where the content is included and then transformed within a different custom action work.

A better approach, and one provided with <c:import>, is to access the input source directly and avoid the buffering involved in the body content of the nested action. By default, any imported content is included inline to the JSP. However, using the var and varReader attributes, it becomes possible to expose the content through either a String or a Reader object. By doing so, the performance issue of the <jsp:include> action is avoided. Using the String or Reader object allows other tags to have direct access to the specified resource content. Let's look at an example:

```
<c:import url="/hotoffthepress.html" var="newReleases"/>
<jstlpg:newbooks in="${ newReleases }"/>
```

Here we are importing a resource and exposing a String object. The custom action <jstlpg:newbooks> can then use this object to perform whatever tasks are necessary. By using the varReader attribute, we could also have exposed the content as a Reader object, like so:

```
<c:import url="/hotoffthepress.html" varReader="newReleases">
     <jstlpg:newbooks in="${ newReleases }"/>
</c:import>
```

Notice that using a varReader has nested visibility. You must enclose the custom action accessing the Reader object because it takes the responsibility away from the consumer tag to prevent resource leaks. If the consumer tag accidentally left the resource open, then memory leaks could occur until garbage collection is performed. The <c:import> tag takes care of closing the appropriate resource. In doing so, after the doEndTag() method of <c:import> is called, you no longer have access to the Reader object.

<c:import> is one of the most valuable and useful actions provided in the JSTL.

4.7.2 <c:url>

When using <c:url>, a URL can be built with the correct encoding and rewriting rules applied. Only a relative URL is rewritten. When using an absolute URL we want to prevent a situation where an external URL could be rewritten that exposes the session ID. With this limitation, if the page author wants to use session tracking, only relative URLs must be used with <c:url> to link to local resources.

<c:url> can be used with or without body content. The body content can be used to specify query string parameters. <c:url> has very similar attributes to <c:import>. For example, the URL can be specified using the value attribute. A context can be specified if necessary. By default, the result of the URL processing is written to the current JspWriter. As with <c:import>, it is possible to export the result as a JSP-scoped variable defined via the attributes var and scope. The var is a String object.

<c:param> subtags can also be specified within the body of <c:url> for adding to the URL query string parameters. If necessary, they will be properly encoded. <c:param> is discussed a bit more in a moment. As for <c:param>, use of this action might look like:

```
<c:url value="/MK/order" var="orderUrl"/>
<a href='<c:out value="${orderUrl}"/>'>Place an order</a>
```

4.7.3 Creating and Using Dynamic Links

The <c:url> action is a powerful action that I'm sure you will see used frequently. <c:url> is used to print out URLs or set a URL into a scoped variable. You might want to set a var that holds a URL because you are going to use that URL in multiple pages or throughout an application. You can then set up the URL once and, when the location changes, you only have to change your <c:url> in one place. It can then be accessed as a variable for other parts of your application. <c:url> is a convenient way to insert URLs into your HTML code that includes dynamic parameters. The same encoding rules apply when using <c:param>, so you don't have to worry about URL encoding issues. If we revisit our earlier Example 4.10 that created paging links from within the <c:forEach> loop, we can now replace our <a> href code with the code shown in Example 4.21.

Example 4.21 Using <c:url> with <c:param> to Build Dynamic Links

```
<c:forEach var="selection" begin="1"
      end="${totalSize - 1}" step="${chunkSize}">

<a href="<c:url value="/pagingdemoURL.jsp">
            <c:param name="start" value="${selection}" />
      </c:url>"
<b>(<c:out value="${selection}"/>-<c:out value
                ="${selection + chunkSize - 1}"/>)</b>
</a>
</c:forEach>
```

Setting a URL as a scoped variable is as simple as the code shown in Example 4.22.

Example 4.22 <c:url> with a Scoped Variable

```
<c:url var="homePage" scope="session"
       value="http://www.switchbacksoftware.com" />

Displaying a URL link by using a scoped variable
<p>
<a href="<c:out value="${homePage}" />">Home page</a>
```

One of the main reasons you want to make use of the <c:url> is that it will handle the session information for you in the link. This is also known as URL rewriting. Therefore, you don't have to depend on browser cookies being enabled to maintain the session ID. Another reason is that when dealing with relative URLs, if the URL starts with a "/", then it will be correctly referenced from the root of your web application context. If you are consistent with your use of <c:url>, there will not be any confusion in a larger application if you are referencing resources from the root of the web server, or from the root of your application. If you want to specify a context, you can use the same context attribute (with the same "/" requirement) that we have already spoken about for other actions.

4.7.4 <c:param>

<c:param> action is used to add request parameters to a URL. It can be a nested action of <c:import>, <c:url>, and <c:redirect>. The name and value are correctly encoded

if necessary. The value of the parameter can be specified as an attribute or in the body content. An example of both utilizations is shown here:

```
<c:url value="/mk/order" var=" orderUrl">
        <c:param name="title" value="${param.title}"/>
        <c:param name="isbn"/>
               ${param.isbn}
        </c:param>
</c:url>
```

If there is no name specified or the name is null, it isn't necessarily an error, although nothing will be processed. A null value is just processed as an empty value. The ordering of the query parameter rules works the same way with <jsp:include>. As defined in the Servlet 2.4 specification, SRV.8.1.1, "The ServletContext and ServletRequest methods that create RequestDispatcher objects using path information allow the optional attachment of query string information to the path. Parameters specified in the query string used to create the RequestDispatcher take precedence over other parameters of the same name passed to the included servlet. The parameters associated with a RequestDispatcher are scoped to apply only for the duration of the include or forward call."

To put this into terms related to the JSTL, this means that new parameters are added to, or replace, the original parameters. The new parameters, with new values, take precedence over existing values. The scope of the new parameters is the parent actions, either the <c:import> or <c:url>. The new parameters (and values) will not apply after the doEndTag() method is called. So in the following example the value of the title parameter would be JSTL, overriding the title Java in the <c:url> action. The value is defined in the <c:param> body content.

```
<c:url value="/mk/order?title=Java">
        <c:param name="title" value="JSTL"/>
</c:url>
```

4.7.5 <c:redirect>

This action sends an HTTP redirect response to the client and aborts the processing of the page. This is done by the action implementation that returns SKIP_PAGE from the doEndTag() method call. The <c:redirect> has two attributes: the url that will be used to redirect to, and an optional context. The URL, relative or absolute, follows the same URL rewriting rules as the <c:url>. The definition of a relative path follows that defined in JSP 2.0 specification, section JSP.1.2.1 and reads:

> "A *context-relative* path is a path that starts with a '/'. It is to be interpreted as relative to the application to which the JSP page belongs, that is to say that its ServletContext object provides the base context URL. A *page relative* path is a path that does not start with a '/'. It is to be interpreted as relative to the current JSP page or the current JSP file depending on where the path is being used."

There are reasons why you would want to use a redirect. If you have finished processing a JSP and then move forward to another page, you might notice that the URL displayed in the web browser is the path to the first JSP. The way to avoid this and have the correct URL displayed is to use a redirect instead of a forward. When doing a redirect, the page informs the browser to make a new request to the target page. The URL shown in the browser therefore changes to the URL of the new page. When doing a redirect, any request scope objects are no longer available to the new page because the browser creates a new request.

Redirecting to a resource in a foreign context is possible by using the context attribute. The URL specified must start with a "/" as context-relative URL, and as defined, the context name must also start with a "/". Using <c:redirect> is simple enough. The following sample would redirect to the booklist.html file in the newrelease context.

```
<c:redirect url="/booklist.html" context="/newreleases" />
```

4.8 Untangling the Web We Weave

Dealing with linking, importing, and redirecting to URL resources is commonplace in web applications. So much so that sometimes it becomes increasingly difficult to follow the flow of pages. Our web becomes a tangled mess. Sometimes it is not all that easy (or interesting for that matter) dealing with the encoding of parameters or the importing of various resources. However, dealing with these issues is a task that requires attention in JSPs. The URL-related actions provide a simplified way for us to deal with these common issues. Let's see how.

4.8.1 The Power of <c:import>

If you look at almost any JSP in a web application, the chances of you finding the standard JSP action <jsp:include> or the JSP directive <%@ include %> on the page are pretty high. Why then do we need another action to import content if there are already two defined in the JSP specification? <c:import> provides more flexibility to the page author by allowing content to be specified from other web applications (also known as contexts) or even other web servers. That functionality is not possible with either of the two existing JSP mechanisms available for doing includes. <c:import> also allows for the content to be available in a scoped variable defined as either a String or a java.io.Reader object. We'll see the difference, and what to take into consideration, between the two in a minute when we go through the example. We'll start with a simple example, and build on it to use some of the more advanced features of <c:import>.

4.8.2 <c:import> and the Composite View Pattern

The Composite View pattern is one that is commonly used in the J2EE presentation tier, and is therefore implemented by many JSPs. The main purpose of the pattern is to create an aggregate View from a number of subcomponents. Think of any website that has a common format, such as a header, content, and a footer. The header, content, and footer are considered included views, while the entire JSP that uses these included views is called the composite view. Using the Composite View pattern is a way to help keep your site more maintainable since, if one of the subcomponents needs to be changed, you only have to do this in one place.

Using `<c:import>`, it's possible to specify the URL of a resource so that you can implement the Composite View pattern easily. The `url` is used to specify what protocol to use to retrieve the resource, as well as its location. The protocol portion, such as `http` or `ftp`, is followed by a : which is then followed by the location of the resource. When using a full URL that specifies the protocol and the resource location, it is called an absolute URL. An example of an absolute URL is `http://www.switchbacksoftware.com`. No matter where you are located throughout the world, if you enter the absolute URL, it will be able to be resolved to the correct resource. If you want to use only a portion of a URL, it is referred to as relative. Relative URLs are commonly used when dealing with a specific web application directory structure. Table 4.3 shows some common ways a relative URL can be specified and the location it would refer to. `<c:import>` allows both absolute and relative URLs to be specified.

For our initial sample we'll use a relative URL. Using relative URLs is usually best when you are dealing with locations inside your application. This is because if you relocate your application to a different server, none of your links will break. When referencing external sites from your application, it's best to use an absolute URL.

We'll start with defining a `header.jsp` and `footer.jsp` file. The `header.jsp` is slightly more interesting because it makes use of a parameter for displaying the title in the browser. This is done using:

```
<title><c:out value="${param.title}"/></title>
```

The footer just has some information to display a logo image along with a contact address for yours truly. These are straightforward files that are used so that we consistently display what we want to appear in our header and footer.

URL	**Location Reference**
test.jsp	Another page in the same directory as the current page
subdir/test.jsp	The directory called subdir beneath the current pages directory
../test.jsp	The parent directory from the current page
/dir1/dir2/test.jsp	The path starting from the domain root of the web server
#something	This refers to an anchor called something on the current page

Table 4.3: Common ways to define relative URLs.

The JSP file of more interest is the one that implements the composite view. The url attribute of the <c:import> action is used to define what resource we want to import. We also show that there is a parameter defined for the first import that passes the title information to be used by the header we just mentioned. Using the param allows the header file to be customized by each composite view using it. This is shown in Example 4.23.

Example 4.23 Importing a Resource

```
<c:import url="/header.jsp" >
 <c:param name="title" value="Import Action Samples" />
</c:import>
```

This is a sample of using the import action to implement the Composite View pattern

```
<c:import url="/footer.jsp" />
```

This is the first use that we've seen of the <c:param> action. The name attribute describes the name of the parameter while the value attribute defines its value. Both the name and the value are encoded correctly. For example, if you have a parameter whose value has a space, like ours does, it will be passed to the imported resource as Import%20Action%20Samples. Therefore, there is no need to worry about encoding your parameters; it's taken care of for you. The browser display rendered from the code in Example 4.23 is shown in Figure 4.16.

Now we'll get a little fancier. In our sample so far, we have accessed a relative URL without using any of the additional available attributes. Let's see how absolute URLs can be used along with some of the more advanced features of <c:import>.

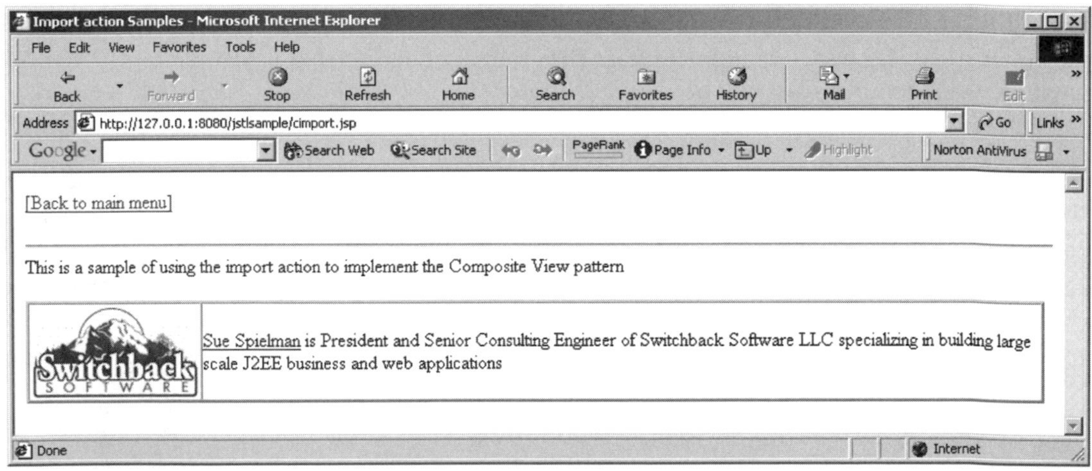

Figure 4.16: Browser display from our <c:import> actions.

It is possible to import a resource from another web site using the http protocol. We simply include the web address in the url attribute like so:

```
<c:import url="http://www.switchbacksoftware.com" />
```

We could also import an ftp resource by using the ftp protocol:

```
<c:import url="ftp://ftp.switchbacksoftware.com/jstl/samples.zip" />
```

One of the more powerful features introduced to the <c:import> action is the ability to specify a context attribute. This lets us import a resource from another web application that resides on the same web server as our application. When using the <jsp:include>, this was not possible. Therefore, if there were resources common to a suite of web applications (like images or header/footer files), they would have to be duplicated for each web application. Using <c:import>, you can share the resources and only have to have them reside in one place. Let's hear it for maintainability.[13] The value of the context attribute is the name of the web application. When specifying the context, both the context and the url must start with a "/". In Example 4.24 we are accessing an html file from a web application called shared. This web application is the context for all shared resources between our web applications.

If you are using Tomcat and you try to import a resource from another context and get an error that looks similar to

```
javax.servlet.ServletException: Unable to get RequestDispatcher for Context:
"/shared" and URL: "/resource.html"
```

you need to verify the value and/or enable crossContext access. This is done in your server.xml file. If application WAR files are being auto-deployed, then the default context values are used. The crossContext attribute defaults to false for security reasons. This is the attribute that allows for a RequestDispatcher to be created for contexts outside of your application. The way to avoid this problem is either to set <DefaultContext crossContext="true"/> within your <host> element, or to define a specific context for your application using the <context> element. Refer to Tomcat (or your vendor) documentation for more details if you need them.

Example 4.24 Importing a Resource from Another Context

```
<c:import url="/header.jsp" >
      <c:param name="title" value="Import action using a context" />
</c:import>
This resource is imported from another web context called "shared"
<hr>
```

[13]However, you might consider that if you have to move your application to another server, you also have to move any shared contexts along with it.

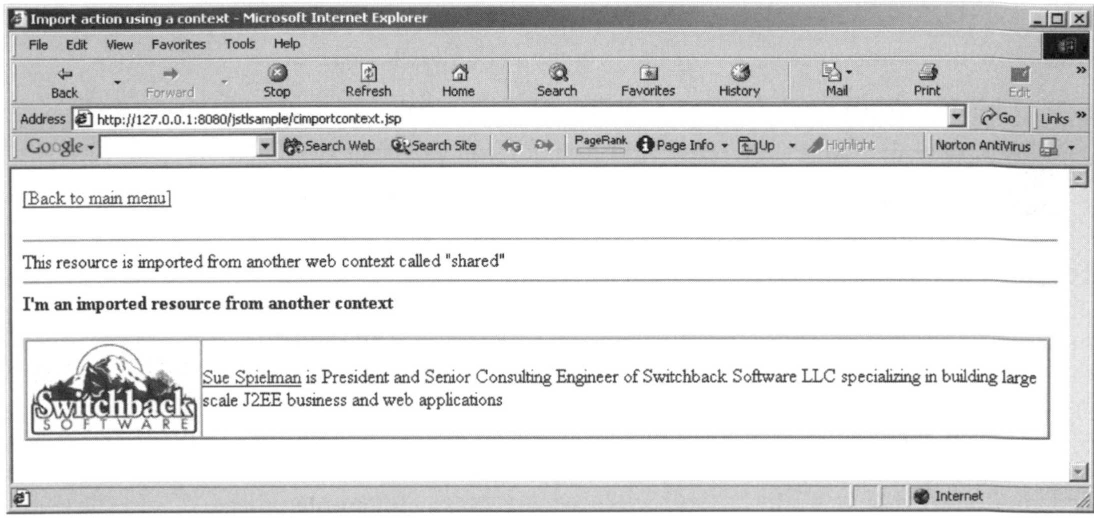

Figure 4.17: Browser display of imported context resource.

```
<c:import context="/shared" url="/resource.html" />

<c:import url="/footer.jsp" />
```

The resource.html will be resolved to the location /shared/resource.html. The browser output is shown in Figure 4.17.

Most of the time when using <c:import>, you will be interested in including the resources directly into your page. However, there are times when you might want to store the content into a scoped variable for later use. There are two ways to do this with the <c:import> action, using the var or varReader attribute.

4.8.3 Storing Imported Content

It is helpful to store content into a variable when you have repeatable content that is used multiple times on a page. Using a scoped variable is also a way to help your application performance. If there is a resource that will be accessed from many pages, you can import it once into a variable and then set the scope appropriately so that other pages can also access it. Additionally, when you import a resource there's a good chance that you might want to use it with other actions. Having the content in a variable allows the other action to make use of the content without having to access the URL again. The var attribute specifies the variable that is used to read the content into a java.lang.String object. The scope attribute only applies to var, not varReader.

Using var is fine until you have a large document being read in. If this is the case, you are probably more interested in using the varReader attribute. Using the var Reader exposes the content as a java.io.Reader object. This can be helpful because it allows for nested tags to access the content as necessary without reading in large quantities of information. However, when using a varReader, it is only valid for the scope of the <c:import>. This is because the action needs to be responsible for the closing of the Reader object so that there isn't an unintentional resource leak. Maybe this restriction will be changed in future versions of the JSTL, but for 1.0 that's the fact.

Basically the <c:import> action opens a connection to the specified URL, and then it can be accessed by another action or script within the <c:import> body content. This is slightly different than when dealing with just a URL or a var. In both of those situations, there can be no body content specified, unless it's the <c:param> action that we've already seen. One thing to note is that if you need to pass a parameter to a url that uses a varReader, you must first build the URL using the <c:url> action. We'll talk about how to use <c:url> next section. First, let's look at a sample using both a var and a varReader.

In Example 4.25 we create a var called commonHeader that will hold the contents of header.jsp. We're setting the scope to be session, so that other pages that might want to use the same header can reference the variable while the user has a valid session. Note that when we write the contents of the var to the JspWriter, we need to set the escapeXml attribute of <c:out> to false. That's because in this particular case, our header has HTML elements included and we want them to be rendered correctly on the page.

Example 4.25 shows how we can import an XML file into a reader object, and then let a subtag access the reader and process it. We're using the <x:parse> and the <x:out> tag here to show that some type of processing actually went on against the varReader object. Don't worry about the details of the various XML actions, XML file, or XPath statements we're using here. We'll be going into the XML tags in the next chapter. For now, I just want to give you a full sample using the <c:import>. Figure 4.18 shows the completed output in the browser.

Example 4.25 Using var and varReader in <c:import>

```
<c:import var="commonHeader" url="/header.jsp" scope="session" >
      <c:param name="title" value="Import action using var and
       varReader" />
</c:import>
<c:out value="${commonHeader}" escapeXml="false" />
<c:import url="/authors.xml" varReader="reader">
      <x:parse xml="${reader}" var="doc"/>
</c:import>
The author's name is: <x:out select="$doc/authors/author/name"/>
<br>
```

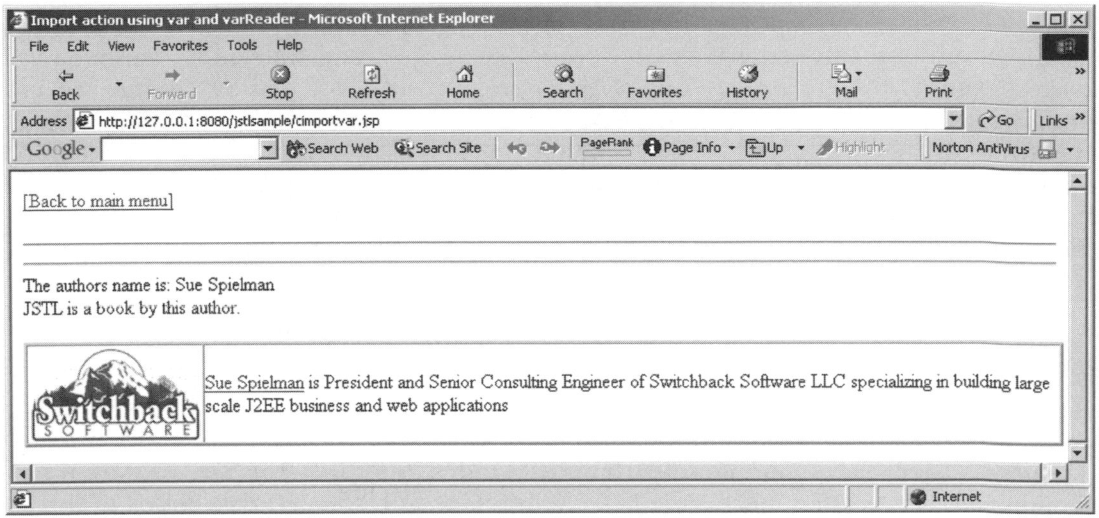

Figure 4.18: <c:import> results.

```
<x:out select="$doc/authors/author/books/book"/> is a book by
this author.

<c:import url="/footer.jsp" />
```

4.8.4 Using Character Encoding

The last thing to talk about regarding <c:import> is the charEncoding attribute. This is used so that you can explicitly tell the import how you would like the incoming information to be encoded. Character encoding is also sometimes referred to as character sets. These are various ISO numbers. The default that <c:import> uses is ISO 8859-1, which is frequently called Latin-1. ISO 8859-1 is the default value of the charset for the contentType attribute of the JSP page directive. It is also the primary encoding in the USA and Western Europe. However, since this is an 8-bit encoding scheme, it doesn't work for languages that require 16-bit character representations like Japanese or Chinese. This is where Unicode comes into play.

In Unicode, every character from all of the world's writing systems is assigned a unique 2-byte code. The first 128 codes of Unicode are identical to 7-bit ASCII, and the first 256 codes, to ISO 8859-1, so that it remains backward compatible to those encodings. It really is only necessary to use charEncoding attribute when accessing an absolute URL resource with a protocol other than HTTP, and the encoding is different from ISO-8859-1.

For example, to explicitly set the character encoding to UTF-8, which is an 8-bit, higher performance Unicode-compatible standard called Universal Transformation Format,[14] you would simply do:

```
<c:import url="http://www.switchbacksoftware.com"
 charEncoding="UTF-8" />
```

4.9 Redirecting

We've spent a fair amount of time on when you want to bring something into a JSP using <c:import>, but what if you want to go somewhere else. This is where the <c:redirect> action comes into play. The standard <jsp:forward> action is used to send the current request to a static resource. You might ask, "How do I decide when to forward and when to redirect?" The answer depends on the needs of your application, but there are a couple of important differences to consider that can help you decide.

When you forward, the target page is invoked by the JSP container through an internal method call on the server. Therefore, the same request is used for the processing on the new page and the browser still shows the original URL on the address line. When doing a redirect, the page doing the redirect informs the browser with an HTTP redirect to make a new request to the target page. The processing of the current page stops. When doing a redirect, any request scope objects are no longer available to the new page because the browser creates a new request. It's possible to use the <c:param> nested in the <c:redirect> to pass along any parameters you might want. Another option is to save the data in a session or application scope object using <c:set>.

<c:redirect> also allows for specifying a context so you can actually redirect to a page outside of the current web application. This is functionality that is not possible with <jsp:forward>. If you are redirecting to a page within the current application or using an absolute URL, then you can just specify the url attribute. Example 4.26 shows a redirect to an absolute URL. Notice that nothing past the <c:redirect> action is going to be executed.[15]

Example 4.26 Performing a <c:redirect>

```
<c:redirect url="http://www.switchbacksoftware.com" />
<c:out value="Herein lies the meaning of life." />
```

[14]You can find more details here: *http://www.ietf.org/rfc/rfc2279.txt?number=2279*

[15]For those servlet programmers among us, the <c:redirect> is the same as if you had done HttpServletResponse.sendRedirect().

4.10 Summary

The Core tag library is a critical piece of the JSTL. This chapter introduced the various functional areas provided in the Core Library. These include actions in the general-purpose, conditional, iterations and URL-related areas.

You should now have a firm grasp of how all of the actions provided in the Core tag library can be used in your JSP development.

We've also looked at all of the actions, along with all of the available attributes for each one, used in a practical way. From the basics of the `<c:out>` action to the more complicated uses of generating dynamic links based on loop variables, I'm sure you will find many other uses for the actions in the Core tag library as you continue your application development.

chapter 5

Working with the XML Actions

The XML tag library brings us to actions that deal with XML manipulations. I am hard pressed to think of any application that I've developed in the last few years that didn't use XML to represent the data in the web tier. XML is the data format of choice for exchanging information. Keeping this in mind, it's relevant to discuss the number of actions that JSTL provides to help a page author deal with XML.

You will find a strong similarity between the XML core actions and the actions provided in the Core tag library. But there is a difference; that being that the XML core actions use XPath for their expression language.

XML is omnipresent in today's web applications. Most applications work XML documents into their being, if for no other reason than to keep the résumés of developers beefed up with the latest acronyms. XML has its benefits, but it also requires a whole slew of X's to make any sense out of it. This chapter contains a brief overview of many (if not all) of the supporting technologies that can be used in some way, shape, or form within the JSTL. Consider it a whirlwind tour. There are plenty of books, actually bookshelves, of resources available on these topics, so plan to spend some quality time with any one of them. I feel it's necessary to have some understanding of semantics for each of the technologies so that we can discuss the JSTL actions in detail. Once we have our vocabulary and concepts under our belt, we'll put the XML tag library actions to good use.

5.1 Overview of Supporting Technologies

Let it be said that no man is an island, or in this case, no technology is. When you are dealing with the space we know as the web, it is common for technologies to work in tandem. Each serves its own purpose and has its own set of issues to be learned and dealt with. Granted, at times all this can be overwhelming even to the most seasoned engineer. But if you become familiar with the purpose of a technology and then have an understanding of what it does for the applications it's applied to, you will find that the technologies themselves become easier to learn and deal with. If you are already familiar with all of these related technologies, feel free to skip right along. Otherwise, pay attention because each of these X's marks a lot of spots.

5.2 eXtensible Markup Language (XML)

I am fairly certain that if you are reading this book, you have at least heard the acronym XML. But just because it seems to be a popular buzzword doesn't mean it's understood by all who use it. XML first made its appearance in its 1.0 form in 1998, but it is an evolution of SGML (Standard Generalized Markup Language) that was the international standard for descriptive markup approved in 1986 by ISO.

If you are one of those people who keep hearing the term but don't really know what XML does, don't feel bad because you're not alone. Many people still don't know exactly what it's for and how to apply it. So here's the secret: XML doesn't actually *do* anything. Understanding this secret lies at the root of all evil for some. In other words, this one small—but vital—point is a source of great confusion for many people.

XML is a markup language much like HTML (which by the way also evolved from SGML), but *it's not a replacement* for HTML. The two were designed with different goals in mind. HTML was designed to display data and to focus on how data looks. For example, using HTML, the code sample:

```
<b>Sue Spielman</b>
```

says *display* the text as Sue Spielman in bold. XML, on the other hand, was designed to *describe* data and to focus on what data is. Therefore, using the same code sample, I would describe the data as an element as shown in Example 5.1.

Example 5.1 Simple XML Document

```
<person>
      <firstname>Sue</firstname>
      <lastname>Spielman</lastname>
</person>
```

To recap, HTML is about *displaying* information while XML is about *describing* information.

There are no predefined tags in XML, unlike in HTML, so you must define your own. Even though I used <person> to describe myself, I could have also used <engineer> or <author> or whatever tag I thought was appropriate to describe the data. <procyclist>

would be good, but that's for another lifetime. I could have also added a <profession> tag and described the data as:

```
<person>
      <firstname>Sue</firstname>
      <lastname>Spielman</lastname>
      <profession>Geek</profession>
</person>
```

XML is a way to structure, store, and send information in whatever way is appropriate for describing that data. Using XML, a related set of information is described in a treelike hierarchical fashion. It is up to the author to describe the data however he or she sees fit. Now you see how the "extensible" fits in. This is why it can be said that XML doesn't actually do anything. It is up to the consumer of the data to decide what to do with the data and how to parse it. XML is just a structured way to get it there.

You can see why XML isn't a replacement for HTML. They actually complement each other in the following ways. As web development progresses, XML will be the data mechanism while HTML will be a description mechanism. XML allows for a separation of data from display. When HTML is used to display data, the data is stored inside the HTML. With XML, data can be stored in separate XML files. Doing it this way, changes in underlying data will not require any changes to your HTML or layout.

5.2.1 Using XML Files for Data Storage

While XML is used to describe data, it can also be used to store data. A store can take the form of files or can be stored as text in a database. Applications can be written to store and retrieve information from the store and generic applications can be used to display the data. Since XML operates independently of the hardware, the software, and even the application, you can make the data available to more than only standard HTML browsers. Other clients and applications can access XML files as data sources just as they access databases.

5.2.2 XML APIs

There are a number of API sets available for dealing with XML. This book isn't really concerned with learning the ins and outs of how to correctly parse through an XML document and what issues you should worry about when deciding which API to use. However, since the terms DOM and SAX are frequently thrown around (and we do make use of them in the XML actions), I want to briefly touch base on them.

DOM stands for Document Object Model. The definition from the W3C site (*http://www.w3.org/DOM/*) states: "The Document Object Model is a platform and language-neutral interface that will allow programs and scripts to dynamically access and update the content, structure and style of documents." Basically this means that you can use the DOM API to get an XML document into a data structure so that you can access the various elements. DOM gives you access to the information stored in your XML document as a hierarchical object model. DOM creates a tree of nodes (based on the structure and information in your XML document) and then you can access your information by interacting with various nodes in the tree. DOM tends to be easier to use, but slower and more expensive in terms of memory. The DOM is parsed once; therefore, the entire document must be stored in memory.

Simple API for XML, or SAX,[16] lets you access the information in the XML document as a sequence of events. This is very different from using the DOM approach of creating a Java object model from the document. Using event processing makes SAX faster in terms of performance but means that you have to create your own custom object model as well as the SAX event handler class that listens to SAX events and processes the events correctly. SAX gives you the flexibility to create your application design as you see fit in terms of trade-offs and goals, but at the expense of time in terms of engineering effort to build the handler classes.

5.3 eXtenstible Stylesheet Language (XSL)

XSL is the stylesheet language of XML. It is much more sophisticated than the Cascading Style Sheets (CSS) used by HTML. Unlike in HTML, element names in XML are only concerned with data, and not with presentation semantics. Without a stylesheet, there is no way for a processor to know how to render the content of an XML document other than as an undifferentiated string of characters. XSL provides a comprehensive model and a vocabulary for writing such stylesheets using XML syntax.

Using CSS is a simple process. You basically tell the browser to display each element using a special font or color that is specified in the CSS. This works for a simple reason: HTML uses predefined tags and these tags are well understood. HTML tags contain presentation semantics. A <p> indicates a paragraph. We all know that. The browser knows what each element means and how to display it. XML, on the other hand, doesn't have predefined tags. So how does the browser know how to display it? It doesn't. That is what XSL provides. Although it is possible to use CSS in XML documents, XSL really is the preferred way.

5.3.1 Allowing for Transformation

XSL is a language that can transform XML into HTML. The transformation of documents is just one of the things that make up XSL's functionality. XSL is also a method for defining XML parts and patterns that can then be used for sorting and filtering XML data. And last but not least, XSL can be used for formatting XML documents.

---

[16]SAX is de facto standard API that is public domain and not controlled by any consortium or corporation. You can find the official SAX site at *http://www.saxproject.org/*.

By formatting documents I mean such things as bolding or coloring data based on some attribute or value, or being able to display XML data on various devices differently. The same XML document can be used to display data to a browser or a handheld. However, the way the data is displayed will be quite different on those two devices. XSL handles determining how to format documents given differing attributes.

5.3.2 XSL Languages

XSL actually consists of three languages: XSLT, XPath, and XSL Formatting Objects (sometimes called XSLFO). We will not be talking at all about XSLFO because there is no support in the JSTL for it. Hold onto your hat. Here is the relationship between XSL, XSLT, and XPath.

XPath is a language to define XML parts or patterns. XSLT is a language for transforming XML documents into other types of documents or into other XML documents. XSL uses XSLT to take an XML source tree (or source document) and transform it into a results tree (or results document). This is shown in Figure 5.1. We will go into a further overview in the next section on XSLT, but it bears mentioning here so that the relationship between XSL, XSLT, and XPath is clear.

5.3.2.1 *Stylesheet Processor*

An XSL stylesheet processor is what does most of the work. The processor takes two parameters, a document or data in XML and an XSL stylesheet. It then produces the presentation of that XML source content that was intended by the designer of that stylesheet.

The first thing the processor does is to construct a result tree from the XML source. The result tree is then used to produce formatted results. A formatter may simply be the rendered output of a browser.

The structure of the result tree can be significantly different from the structure of the source tree. For example, source data can be rearranged to appear in a sorted fashion. When the result tree is constructed, the tree transformation process also adds the appropriate information so that the result tree can be formatted correctly.

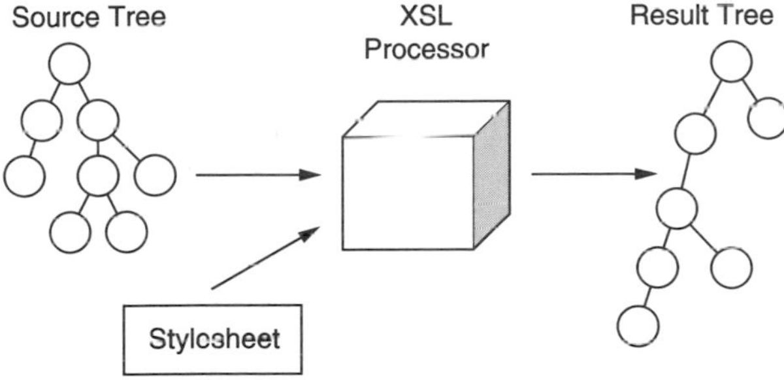

Figure 5.1: Performing an XSL transformation.

5.4 XML Path Language (XPath)

XPath, one of the major elements of XSLT and a W3C recommendation,[17] is a set of syntax rules for defining parts of an XML document. While not written in XML, XPath uses path expressions to make it possible to locate specific nodes within an XML document. These expressions look a lot like how we access traditional file paths. For example, if we had a simple XML document as shown in Example 5.2, we could access the title by using the XPath expression

```
/catalog/book/title
```

Example 5.2 XML Document

```
<?xml version="1.0" encoding="ISO-8859-1"?>
<catalog>
      <book edition="1" >
            <title>JSTL</title>
            <author>Sue Spielman</author>
      </book>
<catalog>
```

XPath is a language for addressing parts of an XML document. XPath is designed to be used primarily by XSLT. Formatting is the process of turning the result of an XSL transformation into a suitable output form for some type of display. During the transformation process, XSLT uses XPath to define parts of the source document that match one or more predefined templates.

XPath is very file system-like in the way that its structure is maintained. Using XPath you can specify nodes in the XML tree and how they relate to other nodes. When a match is found, XSLT will transform the matching part of the source document into the result document. If there is a part of the source document that doesn't match any of the templates, usually that part of the source will be unmodified in the result.

XML documents hold content in a structured tree hierarchy. There must be a way to address nodes in the document to make the tree useful in processing. When transforming documents, it's necessary to allow for addressing and locating of nodes within the document. When using stylesheets, this is accomplished for the processor by using XPath.

XPath uses a string-based syntax for building addresses to the information found in an XML document. It looks very directory-like. For example, `$doc/person/firstname` would represent an XPath address to the `firstname` element in our XML Example 5.1. XPath is used to specify the locations of document structures or data found in an XML document when processing that information using XSLT. XSLT and XPath work closely together. In addition

[17] *http://www.w3.org/TR/xpath.*

to its use for addressing, XPath is also designed so that it has a natural subset that can be used for matching (testing whether or not a node matches a pattern) and is commonly used this way in XSLT.

XPath allows for any location to address any other location or content within the tree structure. In order to address components, you have to know the addressing scheme with which the components are arranged.

5.4.1 Library Functions

There is a library of standard functions available in XPath for working with strings, numbers, and booleans. XPath supports numerical, equality, relational, and Boolean expressions. Expressions can be used to access nodes, sets of nodes, and attributes. A default function library comes with the XPath engine provided with the JSTL. Some engines provide extension functions or allow customization to add new functions. The XPath function library in JSTL is limited to the core function library of the XPath specification. The supported XPath functions are defined in Tables 5.1–5.4.

5.5 Variable Mappings

In order to make it as easy as possible to access data from within a JSP in specific scopes, the XPath engine provides variable mappings. The scopes are defined in exactly the same way as those implicit objects we are familiar with in the EL. Table 5.5 shows the available mappings.

Through these mappings, JSP scoped variables, request parameters, headers, and cookies, as well as context init parameters, can all be used inside XPath expressions.

Method name	Description
`count`	Returns the number of selected elements
`id`	Selects elements by their unique ID
`last`	Returns a number equal to the context size from the expression evaluation context
`local-name`	Returns the local part of the expanded-name of the node in the argument node-set that is first in document order
`name`	Returns the name of an element
`namespace-uri`	Returns the namespace URI of the expanded-name of the node in the argument node-set that is first in document order
`position`	Returns a number equal to the context position from the expression evaluation context

Table 5.1: XPath node set functions.

Method name	Description
concat	Returns the concatenation of its arguments
contains	Returns true if the first string contains the second string, otherwise it returns false
normalize-space	Removes leading and trailing spaces from a string
starts-with	Returns true if the first string starts with the second string, otherwise it returns false
string	Converts an object to a string
string-length	Returns the number of characters in a string
substring	Returns a substring
substring-after	Returns a substring after a substring
substring-before	Returns a substring before a substring
translate	Translates letters in a string

Table 5.2: XPath string functions.

Method name	Description
ceiling	Returns the smallest integer that is not less than the argument
floor	Returns the largest integer that is not greater than the argument
number	Converts its argument to a number
round	Returns the integer that is closest to the argument
sum	Returns the sum, for each node in the argument node-set, of the result of converting the string-values of the node to a number

Table 5.3: XPath number functions.

Method name	Description
boolean	Converts its argument to Boolean
false	Returns false
lang	Returns true or false depending on whether the language of the context node as specified by `xml:lang` attributes is the same as or is a sublanguage of the language specified by the argument string
not	Returns true if its argument is false, and false otherwise
true	Returns true

Table 5.4: XPath Boolean functions.

For example, using some more XPath syntax, we show that it is possible to access an XML element attribute by using the @ symbol. The code snippet

```
/catalog/book[@edition=$param:current]
```

Expression	Variable mapping
`$foo`	pageContext.findAttribute("foo")
`$param:foo`	request.getParameter("foo")
`$header:foo`	request.getHeader("foo")
`$cookie:foo`	the cookie's value for name foo
`$initParam:foo`	application.getInitParameter("foo")
`$pageScope:foo`	$pageScope:foo pageContext.getAttribute("foo", PageContext.PAGE_SCOPE)
`$requestScope:foo`	pageContext.getAttribute("foo", PageContext.REQUEST_SCOPE)
`$sessionScope:foo`	pageContext.getAttribute("foo", PageContext.SESSION_SCOPE)
`$applicationScope:foo`	pageContext.getAttribute("foo", PageContext.APPLICATION_SCOPE)

Table 5.5: XPath variable mappings.

would find the book element with an attribute `edition` equal to the value of the HTTP request parameter `current`.

5.6 Using the Select Attribute

All of the XML actions of JSTL allow a way to specify XPath expressions. This is accomplished by using the `select` attribute. The `select` attribute is always specified as a string literal that is evaluated by the XPath engine. It was decided to have a dedicated attribute for XPath expressions so as to avoid confusion. Since some of the XML actions have similar functions to the Core actions, it was important not to get the XPath expression confused with the JSTL expression language. The `select` attribute is shown in this simple sample where the XPath expression specifies the title to be selected from the XML document and output to the `JspWriter`.

```
<x:out select="$catalog/book/title"/>
```

5.7 Accessing Resources

When using XML actions, obviously one of the first things we want to do is access some type of resource like an existing XML document. This is done by importing resources using the Core URL action `<c:import>` that we already talked about in Chapter 4 on "Working with the Core Actions." The resource can then be used by such XML actions as `<x:parse>` and `<x:transform>`. For example, we can import a URL resource and then export it into a variable named `xml`. This variable is then used as the XML document to the parse action as shown in the sample below.

```
<c:import url="http://www.mkp.com/book?id=12345" var="xml"/>
<x:parse xml="${xml}" var="doc"/>
```

We'll see how it's possible to resolve references to external entities using various attributes when we get to the <x:parse> and <x:transform> actions.

5.7.1 Node Types

XML trees contain nodes. A node is one of seven types: root, element, text, attribute, namespace, processing instruction, or comment. The root node is the root of the tree. There is only one per tree. The root node can have element, processing instruction, and comment nodes.

A LocationPath is used to describe the type of node and where it can be found. For example:

`child::*` selects all element children of the context node.
`child::node()` selects all the children of the context node, whatever their node type.

There are two kinds of location paths: relative location paths and absolute location paths. A relative location path consists of a sequence of one or more location steps separated by "/". The steps in a relative location path are composed together from left to right. Each step in turn selects a set of nodes relative to a context node. An absolute location path consists of "/" optionally followed by a relative location path. A "/" by itself selects the root node of the document containing the context node.

5.7.2 Node Functions

XPath includes a set of node set functions, string functions, boolean functions, and number functions. A sample of each type of function in each category is shown in Table 5.6. While I'm not going to go into specifics for the functions, you'll at least have an idea of what's available. This is when your favorite XPath book should come in handy.

Node functions	**Function names**
Node set functions	`last, position, count, name, local-name, id, namespace-uri`
String functions	`string, concat, starts-with, contains, substring-before, substring-after, substring, string-length, normalize-space, translate`
Boolean functions	`not, true, false, lang`
Number functions	`number, sum, floor, ceiling, round`

Table 5.6: Some of the available XPath functions.

5.8 eXtensible Stylesheet Language Transformation (XSLT)

When using XSL, an XML page may go through n number of transformations. XSLT allows the user to define a set of transformation rules that will be applied to one XML document, resulting in a new document with an entirely new format. The format of the resulting document may or may not be XML. In fact, it is frequently *not* XML.

Typically, an XML document will get transformed into an HTML document so that it can be easily rendered in a browser. How is this accomplished? XSL defines a stylesheet that conforms to the XSL Transformations specification. In general, templates are used to accomplish this. The stylesheet defines a set of selection criteria (or templates) that will match one or more elements in the source XML file. Then the processor will apply all templates that match existing elements and output the final result. The XSLT processor takes a stylesheet and a source document and does the dirty work of the transformation.

A sample transformation fragment for our previous Example 5.1 might look like:

```
<xsl:template match="person">
            <p><xsl:text>Firstname: </xsl:text>
            <b><xsl:value-of select="firstname"/></b>
      <xsl:text> Lastname: </xsl:text>
            <b><xsl:value-of select="lastname"/></b>
</p>
</xsl:template>
```

In this case, the XPath addressing in the select is trivial because the firstname and lastname are children of the tag we are currently processing, which is person. Using our previous simple XML example, and using this stylesheet, the HTML output would look like:

```
Firstname: Sue Lastname: Spielman
```

5.8.1 XSLT Namespace

The XSLT namespace URI is http://www.w3.org/1999/XSLT/Transform. At the top of every XSLT stylesheet, this namespace must be declared in the stylesheet element tag to bind it to a local prefix. Out of common sense, you probably want to use xsl as the XSLT namespace prefix:

```
<xsl:stylesheet xmlns:xsl
   ="http://www.w3.org/1999/XSL/Transform">
```

However, any prefix you like can be used to bind the namespace. I could have just as easily used

```
<xsl:stylesheet xmlns:myxsl
   ="http://www.w3.org/1999/XSL/Transform">
```

to access the XSLT elements through the XML document and referred to them with a myxsl prefix.

So what do you know? Well, in less than a handful of pages, you know everything there is to know about XML, XSL, XSLT, and XPath. Well, maybe not, but at least you have a good understanding of where all the pieces fit together. We can now start using the JSTL actions related to dealing with XML.

5.9 Parsing XML Documents

The first step required before being able to access any of the information contained in an XML document is that it must be parsed. Usually there is an existing document that you want to be working with. This document might be the result of some business logic that was performed in the business tier of your application. We want now to deal with it in the presentation tier so that we can display the results appropriately. Using the `<x:parse>` action is how we get the information from XML format into some format that can be used by XPath, and XSLT. `<x:parse>` takes a source XML document, parses it, and produces a scoped variable that holds the results. The variable can be defined by either using the `var` or `varDom` attribute. There are two different types of attributes because there are a number of ways to represent XML documents. JSTL provides the flexibility for the implementer of the specification to return an object of its choosing in the var attribute.

5.9.1 <x:parse> Action

The `<x:parse>` action is used to parse an XML document. The resulting object is then saved into a scoped variable as defined by either the `var` or the `varDom` attribute. The `varDom` attribute is a `String` that holds the name of the scoped variable. The type of the scoped variable is an `org.w3c.dom.Document`. The type of the var attribute depends on the implementation of the `<x:parse>` action, so you will need to consult the documentation for it. In the reference implementation of the JSTL, the type of the scoped variable as defined by var is also of type `org.w3c.dom.Document`. The `<x:parse>` action performs the parse on the document; it does not perform any validation against Document Type Definition files (DTDs) or Schemas. The XML document to be used for the parse can either be specified with the `xml` attribute, or it can be specified inline by including it the action's body content.

The `varDom` attribute exposes a DOM document, making it possible to use the variable for collaboration with other custom actions you might have created. Objects exposed by `var` and `varDom` can be used to set the context of an XPath expression. This is exactly what we'll see in our `<x:set>` and `<x:out>` example when we reference the `$doc` in the select attribute. In the sample below, we import a document using the `<c:import>` action. Then we use that XML document for the parse. The results are stored in the var attribute of the parse action. We then use doc as the context for our other XML actions.

```
<c:import url="http://www.mkp.com/catalog.xml" var="xml"/>
```

```
<x:parse source="${xml}" var="doc"/>
<x:out select="$doc/catalog/book/title"/>
```

If your source XML document is null or empty, a JspException will be thrown.

A systemId attribute can also be used as the system identifier (URI) for parsing the XML document. We'll look at how to use the systemId attribute later in this chapter.

5.9.2 Filtering

The filter attribute can be used to apply an object that implements the org.xml.sax.XMLFilter interface to the source document. This can be used if the implementation of the XML tagset being used is based on DOM-like structure. If you have dealt with large DOM objects before, you are well aware of the performance issues associated with them. Using a filter can help reduce the performance impact, but frankly, to go into how to set up and build a filter is beyond the scope of this book.

The filter attribute can be used to allow filtering of the input data prior to having it parsed by the implementation. This filtering will produce a smaller (and, hopefully, more manageable), DOM-like structure. If your filter is null, then no filtering is performed. Using filtering is a good example of when you might want to create your own custom tag that implements setting up and creating a filter. This allows you to expose the configuration of a filter through a custom tag so that a page author can perform whatever filtering is appropriate in a given situation. The filter object is then used in the <x:parse> action. The XMLFilter Object, which is part of SAX2, isn't the focus of this book so I'll leave it up to you to locate your favorite book on SAX2.

In Example 5.3 we have the same XML sample that we looked at in the previous section included in the body content of the <x:parse>. You'll also notice the use of <x:out> in this example. It performs the same functionality as <c:out> except that we use <x:out> specifically for dealing with XML documents. Instead of the value attribute that we've seen in <c:out>, <x:out> uses the select attribute. The select attribute works with XPath expressions. What is happening in this example is that <x:parse> is parsing the body content and making it available as the var called doc. We then select the value of an element from that variable by prefixing the variable name with a $. The XPath syntax $doc refers to the object, which is slightly different from the ${doc} syntax that would be used by the EL. We then continue by specifying the location we are interested in using the XPath expression $doc/person/firstname. The content of that element is Sue, and then it is printed out. Figure 5.2 shows the resulting browser output.

Example 5.3 You Always Remember Your First Parse

```
<x:parse var="doc">
<person>
      <firstname>Sue</firstname>
      <lastname>Spielman</lastname>
</person>
```

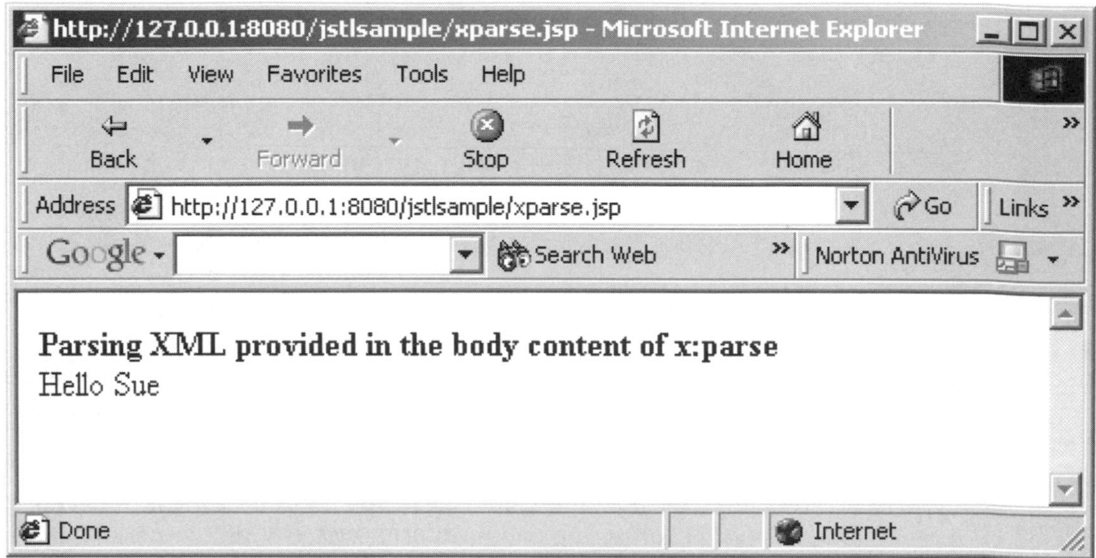

Figure 5.2: <x:parse> output.

```
</x:parse>

Hello <x:out select="$doc/person/firstname" />
```

A more common way to identify the XML file is to use the parse to expose it as an imported resource. By using the <c:import> action, we access the XML file and then use the EL to pass it to the <x:parse>. This is shown in Example 5.4. There is no functional difference in providing the XML file this way, so the output to the browser remains the same as Figure 5.2.

Example 5.4 <x:parse> Using an Imported XML Document

```
<c:import var="xmlfile" url="/people.xml" />
<x:parse var="doc" xml="${xmlfile}" />
Hello <x:out select="$doc/person/firstname" />
```

In fact you can combine the two types of ways to specify the document by doing something like:

```
<x:parse var="doc" >
      <c:import url="/people.xml" />
</x:parse>
```

In this case the XML file is specified in the body content of the <x:parse>, but it is being imported using the <c:import>. Both ways of importing a document work equally well and it is totally up to the way you prefer to write the code. My personal preference is to import first and then use a scoped variable as the content for the xml attribute in the <x:parse>.

It is important to note that whether or not your XML is specified in the body content or is provided as a document, the <x:parse> action does not perform any type of validation against a DTD or schema. If you want to validate your documents first, then you might want to consider writing your own custom tag to do the validation before the document is passed to <x:parse>.

5.9.3 Using the Advanced <x:parse> Attributes

There are a couple of attributes of <x:parse> that might be of interest to advanced page authors. They are filter and systemId. Let's look at the filter attribute first. If you have dealt with large XML documents, you are already aware of the performance issues surrounding them. These issues include their large memory requirements, since a DOM document must be completely read at once, as well as slower performance if you are making many references within the document. Using the filter attribute is a way to help mitigate the performance ramifications. The filter is an object that implements the org.xml.sax.XMLFilter interface. This interface allows for a Java programmer to provide a SAX-based filter to use on the XML document. Let's look at a scenario to see where using a filter would be beneficial.

Say you have a large company and you want to write an application that displays contact information. It is possible that some business logic queries the appropriate databases to gather all of the information and then stores the data into an XML document. This could be a very large document. However, you're only interested in people whose last names begin with an "S". You can substantially reduce the size of your XML document by applying a filter to it that eliminates all of the data except those whose last name begins with an "S".

As I have already mentioned, I'm not going into the technical details regarding how to program your own XMLFilter since it would be beyond the scope of this book. However, if you want to look at an implemented sample, one is provided in the JSTL reference implementation. All of the related files are located in the org.apache.taglibs.standard.extra.spath package, so if you download the source code, you can peruse the files at your leisure.

The second attribute to talk about is the systemId. The systemId is used to help identify where an XML file comes from. Under normal circumstances, the <x:parse> doesn't really care where your XML document comes from as long as it can access it. However, it's possible that there are other files that might be required to complete the parse that are referenced relative to the location of the XML file. In those cases, the systemId helps identify where the parser should look to resolve them. The systemId can contain either an absolute or a relative URL.

5.10 Using <x:out> and <x:set>

The <x:out> and <x:set> actions should already be familiar to you. They look exactly like the ones we have already detailed in the previous chapter on the Core Tag Library. The only difference is that instead of using the EL as we have been doing for the various Core actions, we use XPath to specify variables and content in the select attribute. To clarify, the actions that use XPath can also use the EL for dynamic attributes, the only exception being the select attribute because it only takes an XPath expression. So that there is no confusion over the actual variables, instead of using the value attribute like we did in the Core actions, we use the select attribute. value always takes an EL expression; select always takes an XPath expression. That should be easy enough to remember. All of the other attributes that we have already discussed in the <c:out> and <c:set> actions are available in <x:out> and <x:set>. This includes escapeXML in <c:out>, and var and scope in <c:set>.

5.10.1 <x:out> Action

The <x:out> action provides the same functionality as the Core <c:out> action. It allows for an XPath expression to be evaluated and then outputs the result of the evaluation to the current JspWriter object.

As previously mentioned, the select attribute is used to hold the XPath expression to be evaluated. Once the expression is evaluated, the result is converted to a String and written to the current JspWriter. Using <x:out> is the same as if you had used either the standard JSP syntax <% =...%> to display the result of an expression or <c:out> to display the result of an expression in the EL syntax.

<x:out> also has an optional Boolean attribute called escapeXML. This attribute determines whether the characters <, >, &, ', and " should be converted to their corresponding character entity codes as shown in Table 5.7. This attribute defaults to true.

As an example, using the XML document in Example 5.2, the following statement would output the book title:

```
<x:out select="$doc/catalog/book/title"/>
```

Character	Entity code
<	<
>	>
&	&
'	'
"	&# 034;

Table 5.7: XML character entity code.

You might wonder, since we are referencing the XML document using the $doc in the XPath expression, how we actually got the XML document into scope to start with? This is done using the <x:parse> action and using the var attribute that we just talked about.

5.10.2 <x:set> Action

We also have a corresponding <x:set> action to the <c:set> action. This action evaluates an XPath expression and then saves the result into a scoped variable as defined by the var attribute. In addition to the var and scope attributes that we have seen in other actions, the <x:set> also has the select attribute for defining the XPath expression. This action uses the mapping of XPath types to Java types when storing the result. In the sample below, using the XML document shown in Figure 5.2 as the source, we see how we would use <x:set> to access an element in an XML document and then save the value into a request scoped variable named title. The contents of the variable bookTitle would be JSTL.

```
<x:set var="bookTitle" scope="request" select
  ="$doc/catalog/book/title"/>
```

5.11 <x:set> and <x:out> in Action

When using <x:set> it is important to point out that you are setting a variable that contains a subset of an XML document. This is useful if you have a large document and you are only interested in a portion of the elements but you need all of the nested elements included. Using <x:set> allows a way to optimize the XML document so that it works best for what you are interested in.

We'll use both of these actions in one example so you can see how the XML actions work together nicely. In Example 5.5, we import and parse the people.xml document that we saw in Example 5.1. This allows us to have a document that we can work with and reference using XPath. We print out a value from the element called firstname by using <x:out> and the XPath expression $doc/person/firstname. Then we use <x:set> to set a variable to the subset of content from our people.xml document. Again, using <x:out> shows how we are accessing the same data value but are using a different XPath expression. This is because our lastname element is now at the level of our document root, instead of being nested in the <person> element.

Example 5.5 Using XPath with <x:set> and <x:out>

```
<c:import var="xmlfile" url="/people.xml" />
<x:parse var="doc" xml="${xmlfile}" />
Hello <x:out select="$doc/person/firstname" />
<x:set var="name" select="$doc/person" scope="request" />
```

```
Print out lastname from a subset of the person.xml document : <x:out
   select="$name/lastname" />
```

I am intentionally keeping the XML samples simple. I want to make sure that you get a good understanding of how the JSTL actions work. However, it should be apparent that using XML and XPath requires a fairly good understanding of those technologies to take full advantage of them.

5.12 Using XML Documents to Determine Flow Control

While the XML core actions provide the basic functionality to parse and access XML data, the XML flow control actions are used to do conditional processing and iterations. The same way that we used various Core actions for flow control in our JSPs can be applied to the conditional actions available in the XML tag library. In fact, the XML actions mimic the Core actions. The actions available are:

```
<x:if>
<x:choose>
<x:when>
<x:otherwise>
<x:forEach>
```

The only difference between the two libraries, which you might have guessed by now, is the fact that the select attribute uses XPath instead of the EL when working with the <x> actions. Using XPath expressions, the XML control flow actions determine whether to process JSP code. These actions act in much the same way as the Core tag library flow control actions we already talked about, except for the utilization of XPath instead of the expression language. Therefore, to avoid redundant information, I am going to point out the differences between the XML and the Core actions (<c:if>, <c:choose>, and <c:forEach>), where appropriate. If you want the full action information, refer to Chapter 4 "Working with the Core Actions."

The biggest difference is that the select attribute is evaluated to a boolean expression according to the semantics of the XPath boolean() function. Otherwise, everything that you've already learned in that chapter that applies to the control flow actions can be applied here as well.

You'll notice that before you do any type of control flow, you always have to have a document available. This means that you always have to do an <x:parse> on the document so that it can be accessed through a variable.

Before we start going through the actions, let's add a little bit more of the XML flavor. Let's go back to our previous book samples and use an XML file that contains a book catalog. To make the file a little more interesting, I've added an XML attribute to one of the elements. The catalog.xml file that we'll use for the rest of these samples is shown in Example 5.6.

Example 5.6 catalog.xml File

```
<catalog publisher="MK">
      <book>
           <title>JSTL</title>
           <author>Sue Spielman</author>
           <edition>1</edition>
      </book>
      <book>
           <title>Struts</title>
           <author>Sue Spielman</author>
           <edition>2</edition>
      </book>
      <book>
           <title>Java</title>
           <author>Sikora</author>
           <edition>1</edition>
      </book>
</catalog>
```

5.12.1 <x:if> Action

The <x:if> action uses the select attribute to specify the XPath expression. The expression is evaluated and the resulting object is converted to a boolean. The result is determined according to the semantics of the XPath boolean() function. These semantics are as follows.

- A number is true if, and only if, it is neither positive or negative, zero nor NaN.[18]
- A node-set is true if, and only if, it is non-empty.
- A string is true if, and only if, its length is non-zero.

If the result is true, then the <x:if> will render its body. So, for example, if we want to see whether we have the XML data for a selected book, we could do so by evaluating the XPath expression shown in the select attribute:

```
<x:if select="$doc/catalog/book/[title='JSTL']">
      You've made a fine choice!
</x:if>
```

You can make use of the familiar var and scope attribute when using the <x:if> action to save the Boolean result.

---

[18]Going back to your mathematics courses, if you need a refresher, NaN stands for Not a Number.

5.12.2 Using <x:if>

For a more interesting example, we will do a conditional based on the publisher attribute of the <catalog> element. We might be generating catalogs for many different publishers, so we'd like to print the name of the publisher for the user. The code is shown in Example 5.7.

Example 5.7 Using <x:if> for Control Flow

```
<c:set var="publisher" value="MK" />
<c:import var="xmlfile" url="/catalog.xml" />
<x:parse var="doc" xml="${xmlfile}" />

<x:if select="$doc/catalog[@publisher=$pageScope:publisher]">
   Welcome to the <c:out value="${publisher}" /> book catalog.
</x:if>
```

We're starting to combine various JSTL actions now so you can see how they interact with each other. First, we set a variable that holds the name of the publisher we are interested in so that we can print the appropriate message. Then we import and parse our XML file. Next, we do a conditional test to see if there is a match in the attribute publisher of the catalog element with that of our defined variable.

You'll notice a couple of new features in this one line of code. First, we're using the `[@]` XPath syntax to refer to an attribute of an element. Next, we are doing a comparison using XPath notation. And last, we're using a new variable called `$pageScope`. The XML actions have the same available implicit variables as the EL. However, since we don't use the EL `${var}` notation to access variables, these implicit variables use the `$var:` syntax specific for XPath. For the list of available implicit variables, see Section 8.1.11 in Chapter 8. With that slight detour, we are therefore doing a comparison between the attribute value in the element contained in the XML file and the variable value that we set ourselves. The outcome of this appears in Figure 5.3.

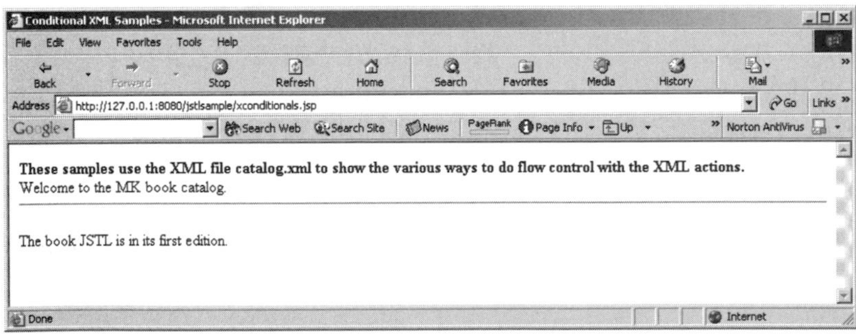

Figure 5.3: Browser output of <x:if> conditional.

Keep in mind that, if we wanted to, we could save the boolean result into a variable for later use just like we did with the <c:if> action.

5.12.3 <x:choose>, <x:when>, and <x:otherwise> Actions

I'll cover all of these actions in one lump since they are related to each other. For all intents and purposes, these tags are analogous to a Java switch statement. The <x:choose> action selects one of any number of possible alternatives. The alternatives consist of a sequence of <x:when> elements followed by an optional <x:otherwise>.

Each <x:when> element has the single select attribute. When an <x:choose> element is processed, each of the <x:when> elements has its expression evaluated in turn. The result is converted to a boolean following the same rules as for <x:if>. Only the body of the first <x:when> whose result is true is rendered. If none of the test conditions of nested <x:when> tags evaluates to true, then, if an <x:otherwise> tag is present, its body is evaluated.

The following are constraints on the <x:choose>. The body of the <x:choose> action can only contain the following:

- White spaces, which may appear anywhere around the <x:when> and <x:otherwise> subtags
- 1 or more <x:when> actions, which must all appear before <x:otherwise>
- 0 or 1 <x:otherwise> action, which must be the last action nested within the <x:choose>

The following are constraints on the <x:when> and <x:otherwise>:

- Both must have <x:choose> as an immediate parent.
- <x:when> must appear before an <x:otherwise> action that has the same immediate parent.
- <x:otherwise> must be the last action in the nested <x:choose>.

To put all of these tags together, let's go through an example. Using multiple <x:when> is like implementing a switch statement, while using one <x:when> and an <x:otherwise> is like if/then/else functionality. Using the only available attribute, select, we've created a switchlike statement in Example 5.8. Here we're checking the value of the edition element. We use that comparison to know whether or not to print out the message. Actually we'll build upon Example 5.8 in the next section on <x:forEach> so that we can see how everything fits together in a practical situation by iterating over an entire XML document.

Example 5.8 <x:choose>, <x:when>, <x:otherwise> in Action

```
<x:choose>
     <x:when select="$doc/catalog/book/edition=1">
```

```
            The book <x:out select="$doc/catalog/book/title" /> is
            in its first edition.
      </x:when>
      <x:when select="$doc/catalog/book/edition=2">
            The book <x:out select="$doc/catalog/book/title" /> is
            in its second edition.
      </x:when>
      <x:otherwise>
            The book <x:out select="$doc/catalog/book/title" /> is
            a best seller in its third edition!
      </x:otherwise>
</x:choose>
```

5.13 Going Loopy with <x:forEach>

In reality, or whatever altered reality we each live in, it seems logical that we'd want to process a number of nodes within an XML document. Usually there is lots and lots of data being returned in an XML document. This is exactly the case in our simple XML sample. We'd like to loop through each of the nodes in the XML document so that we can display information from each node. We do this using <x:forEach>. The <x:forEach> action evaluates the given XPath expression in the select attribute and iterates over the result, thereby setting the context node to each element in the iteration. When using the <x:forEach>, if the select attribute is null, then a JspException is thrown. As long as there are items to iterate over, the body content is processed by the JSP container and written to the current JspWriter. To demonstrate, the following sample will evaluate all of the nodes that have a book element and then print out the edition attribute.

```
<x:forEach select="$doc//book">
      This book is in its <x:out select="@edition"/> edition.
</x:forEach>
```

In Example 5.9 we import an XML document and then parse it. We then have the document available to iterate over. We loop over the entire XML document and print out a table containing information about each book in the catalog. Using the XPath statement //book, we are basically saying "select each book node in the XML document." Each node that we come across that starts with a <book> element becomes the current node. It is then possible to reference any elements within that node. In our example we are using title, author, and edition of the current node. Note that it's also possible to refer to these elements using the ./ notation, like ./title.

Example 5.9 <x:forEach> Processing

```
<c:import var="xmlfile" url="/catalog.xml" />
<x:parse var="doc" xml="${xmlfile}" />
```

```
<table><tr><th>Title</th><th>Author</th><th>Edition</th></tr>
<x:forEach select="$doc//book">
      <tr>
      <td><x:out select="title" /></td>
      <td><x:out select="author" /></td>
      <td><x:out select="edition" /></td>
      </tr>
</x:forEach>
</table>
```

Executing the code in Example 5.9 renders the result shown in Figure 5.4 in the browser.

5.13.1 Nested forEach Loops

A common task is also to have nested <forEach> loops. We make a slight adjustment in our XML file so that we can have multiple catalogs. This is easily done by adding a new root element called <catalogs> as shown in Example 5.10. In Example 5.11 we see how to perform a nested <x:forEach> loop over an XML document. There are a couple of slight

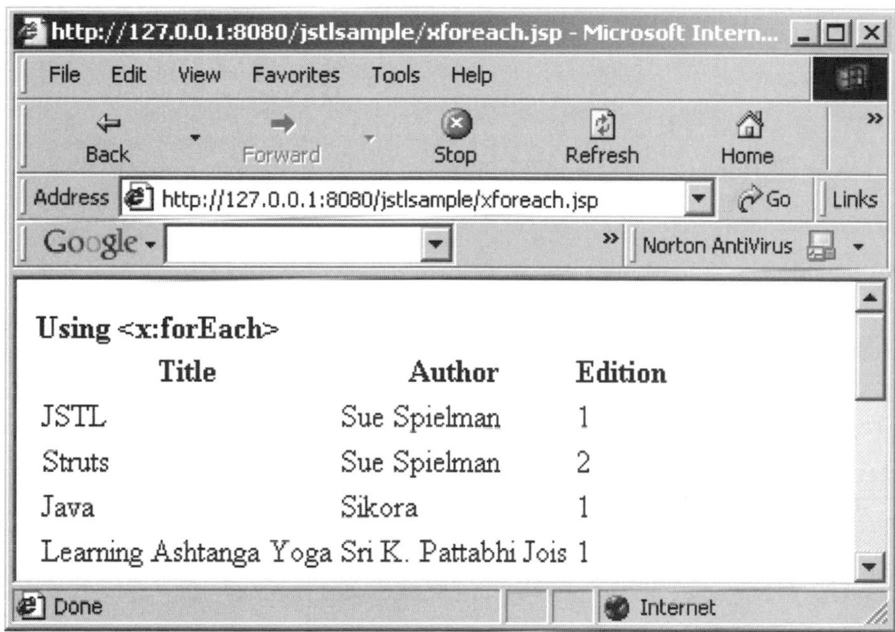

Figure 5.4: <x:forEach> display.

XPath changes that should be noted. When doing nested <x:forEach> loops, the current node of the outer loop is inherited by the inner loop (or loops). Because of this, we want the books only to be listed relative to the current catalog. To do this, we change the XPath from //book, indicating to find all books in the XML document, to just book. This will cause only the book elements of the current catalog node to be iterated over. The result as shown in the browser is displayed in Figure 5.5.

Example 5.10 catalog.xml File for Nested Iterations

```
<catalogs>
<catalog publisher="MK">
      <book>
                  <title>JSTL</title>
                  <author>Sue Spielman</author>
                  <edition>1</edition>
      </book>
      <book>
                  <title>Struts</title>
                  <author>Sue Spielman</author>
                  <edition>2</edition>
      </book>
            <book>
                  <title>Java</title>
                  <author>Sikora</author>
                  <edition>1</edition>
      </book>
</catalog>
<catalog publisher="New Age Books">
      <book>
                  <title>Learning Ashtanga Yoga</title>
                  <author>Sri K. Pattabhi Jois</author>
                  <edition>1</edition>
      </book>

</catalog>
</catalogs>
```

Example 5.11 Using Nested <x:forEach>

```
<x:forEach select="$doc//catalog">
      <h2>Catalog listing for <x:out select="@publisher" />
      <table><tr><th>Title</th><th>Author</th><th>Edition</th></tr>
      <x:forEach select="book">
            <tr>
            <td><x:out select="title" /></td>
            <td><x:out select="author" /></td>
```

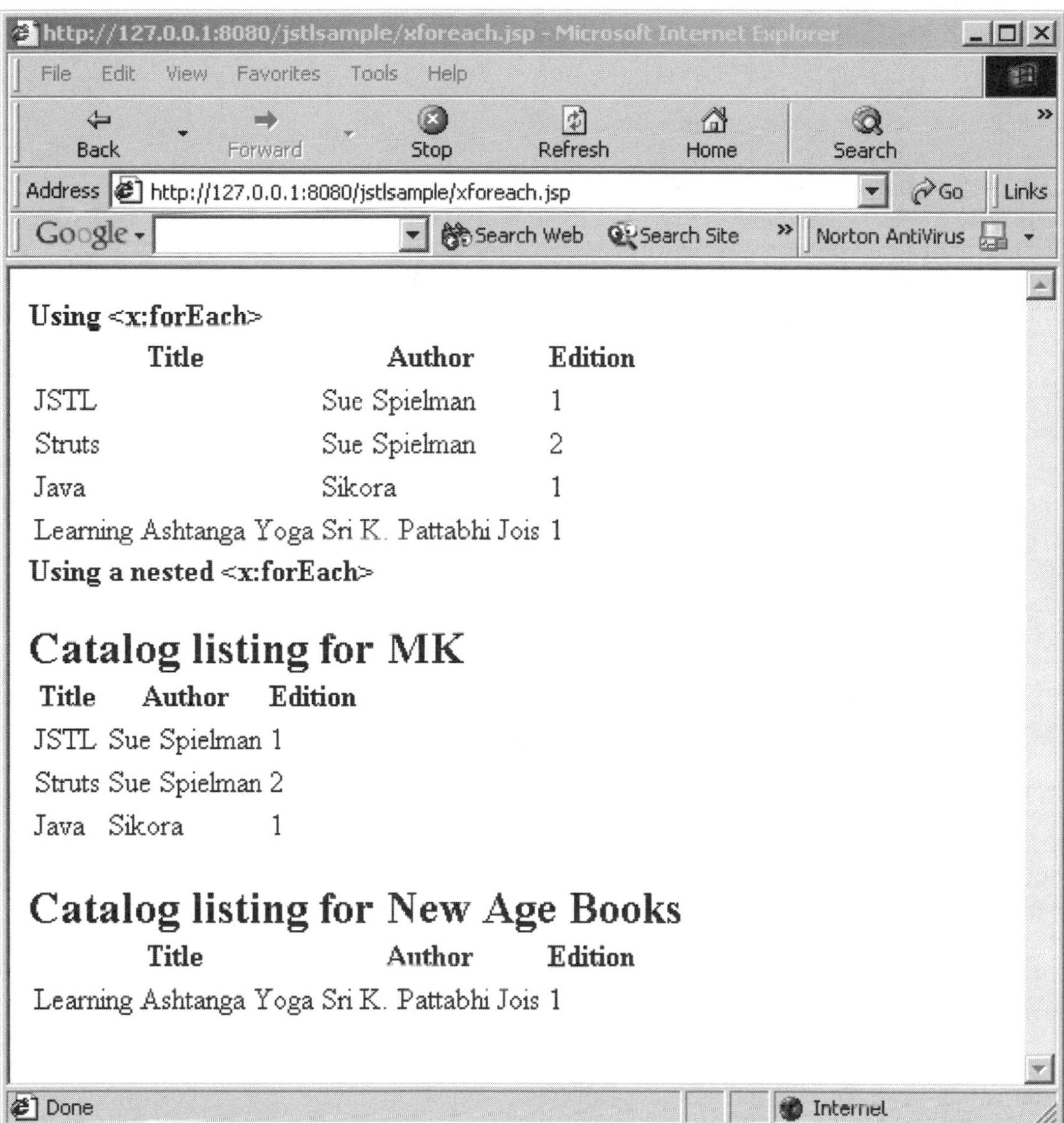

Figure 5.5: Nested forEach browser display.

```
            <td><x:out select="edition" /></td>
            </tr>
      </x:forEach>
      </table>
</x:forEach>
```

5.14 XML Transformation Actions

The XML transformation actions provide a mechanism for page authors to use XSLT stylesheets. XSL is the eXtensible Stylesheet Language and is used for expressing style sheets. To quickly review what we covered earlier, XSL is of three parts: XSLT, XPath, and XSL Formatting Objects. XSLT is the part of XSL that is used to do transformations. Typically, transformations take an XML document and turn it into another XML document, or into another type of document that is recognized by a browser or device. This is the mechanism used to turn XML into, say, XHTML or WML. Using XSLT stylesheets is a common way to support multiple client devices from a web application. Each device (PC, mobile device, PDA) might have its own XSLT stylesheet associated with the client type. The data can then be formatted correctly and specifically for that targeted device.

XSLT is quite powerful and can add new elements into an output file, remove elements, and rearrange and sort elements. It can also perform evaluations to determine which elements to display from a given XML document. XSLT is a whole beast unto itself and to teach it in this book is way beyond the scope of JSTL. If you are planning on using XSLT and haven't yet, it probably makes sense to spend some time coming up to speed on it.

It is frequently a requirement that the same stylesheet is used to transform different source XML documents. The overhead of constantly loading the stylesheet can become a burden on the application. JSTL allows for the stylesheet to be processed once and then saved into what is called a transformer object. This transformer object can then be cached and used for future transformations so that a performance gain is realized. Let's take a look at how the transformations are handled.

5.14.1 <x:transform> Action

The `<x:transform>` action applies an XSLT stylesheet to an XML document. If either the XML document or the source XSLT document supplied to the action is `null`, then a `JspException` will be thrown. Either the XML document can be provided in the `xml` attribute, or it can be included as the body content of the action. The XSLT stylesheet is provided in the `xslt` attribute. Like the other XML actions, the `<x:transform>` does not provide any DTD or Schema validation.

The result of the transformation is written to the current `JspWriter` by default; however, it's possible to capture the result of the transformation in two other ways. First a `javax.xml.transform.Result` object can be specified by using `result` attribute. Second, an `org.w3c.dom.Document` object can be saved in the scoped variable specified by (you guessed it!) the var and scope attributes.

It is also possible to specify the `xmlSystemId` and the `xsltSystemId` attributes that identify a system identifier URI for an XML document or an XSLT stylesheet, respectively. The following code completes a transformation given XML and XSLT documents.

```
<c:import url="http://www.mkp.com/catalog" var="xml"/>
<c:import url="/WEB-INF/xslt/catalogList.xsl" var="xslt"/>
<x:transform xml="${xml}" xslt="${xslt}"/>
```

5.15 Transforming Content

XML documents communicate the data. When we want to specify how to display the data, we must use one of the many X technologies. XSL is used to define style sheets that are used for doing transformations of XML data for display. It is fairly easy to do this using the <x:transform> action. However, it requires you to have the XSL style sheets already defined. Doing transformations can be quite useful if your application supports multiple devices. For example, if you render to a browser but also want to render on a mobile device, a different markup language needs to be generated. It would be quite cumbersome (and not really practical) to have separate JSP files for each of the different devices you want to render to. Instead, you can use the XML data and transform it using the appropriate XSL file. This is much more maintainable in the long run for your application, as well as for your sanity.[19] Keep in mind that this is not an XSLT book, so I'm assuming that if you are interested in using the <x:transform> action, you have an understanding of how to create and use XSL style sheets. Let's walk through a sample to put it all together.

When using <x:transform> you must provide both an XML document and an XSL style sheet. We'll continue using our catalog.xml document as shown in Example 5.10. It is common to have browser-specific items in an XSL file so that content can be rendered for a particular user's environment. In this sample, we will just create a more aesthetically pleasing table, without getting too complicated in the XSL file. The XSL is shown in Example 5.12. We are simply going to create a table similar to the one that we saw in Figure 5.5; however, we'll add a nicer border and some color. Keep in mind that this is a very simplistic sample, and there are many more things you can do in your XSL files.

Example 5.12 XSL File to Use for Transformation

```
<xsl:stylesheet version="1.0" xmlns:xsl="http://www.w3.org/1999/
XSL/Transform">
<xsl:template match="/">
      <html>
      <body>
            <h2>Using an XSL stylesheet to transform an XML file</h2>
            <table border="1">
            <tr bgcolor="#FF00FF">
                  <th align="left">Title</th>
                  <th align="left">Author</th>
                  <th align="left">Edition</th>
            </tr>
            <xsl:for-each select="catalogs/catalog/book">
            <tr>
                  <td><xsl:value-of select="title"/></td>
```

[19]Your JSTL implementation can cache the transformer objects if it so chooses. You might want to check the documentation from the vendor to see what caching mechanism they are using.

```
                <td><xsl:value-of select="author"/></td>
                <td><xsl:value-of select="edition"/></td>
            </tr>
            </xsl:for-each>
            </table>
    </body>
    </html>
</xsl:template>
</xsl:stylesheet>
```

Our JSP file in Example 5.13 now becomes much simpler than the file we saw in Example 5.11. We import the two documents consisting of the XML file and the XSL file and then apply the transformation. The browser output is shown in Figure 5.6.

Example 5.13 Using <x:transform>

```
<c:import var="xmlfile" url="/catalog.xml" />
<c:import var="xslfile" url="/catalog.xsl" />
```

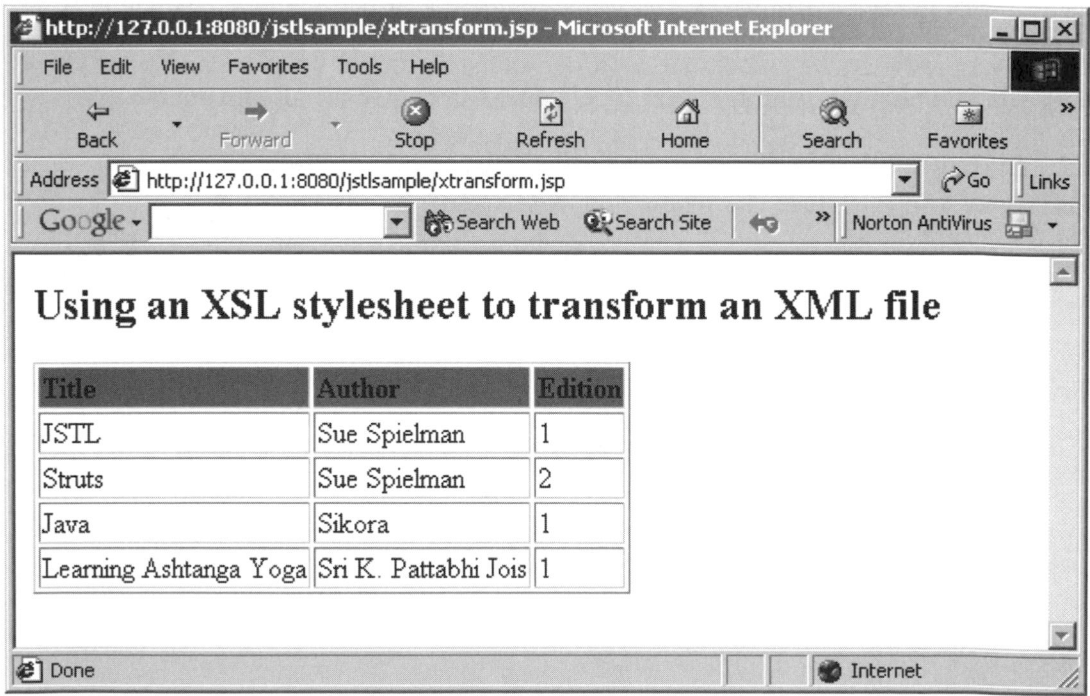

Figure 5.6: Browser output using <x:transform>.

```
<x:parse var="doc" xml="${xmlfile}" />
<x:transform xml="${xmlfile}" xslt="${xslfile}" />
```

5.16 Providing Parameters to Transformations

It is possible to provide local or global parameters by using the xsl:param element when working with XSL files. The <x:param> action in JSTL allows for specifying parameters to the XSL file used in a transformation <x:param>, but it must be nested within a parent <x:transform> action. Example 5.14 shows a very simple sample of how to define a global parameter in an XSL file and then access it.

5.16.1 <x:param> Action

Using the <x:param> action, it is possible to set transformation parameters to the <x:transform> action. The <x:param> action can only be nested within an <x:transform> action. A parameter name and value can be provided by using the name and value attributes. It is also possible to specify the value within the body content of the <x:param>.

If we look at our previous example using the <x:transform> action, we can add a parameter to it by simply doing:

```
<x:transform xml="${xml}" xslt="${xslt}">
      <x:param name="displayAll" value="true"/>
</x:transform>
```

When using the <x:param> action, the name attribute that defines the parameter must match that which is defined in your XSL file. The value is then specified using the value attribute or the body content to the <x:param> action. This is shown in Example 5.15 and the browser output is shown in Figure 5.7.

Example 5.14 XSL File with Parameters

```
<xsl:stylesheet version="1.0" xmlns:xsl="http://www.w3.org/1999/
XSL/Transform">
<xsl:param name="publisher" />
<xsl:template match="/">
      <html>
      <body>
            <h2>Using an XSL stylesheet to transform an XML file</h2>
            <table border="1">
            <tr bgcolor="#FF00FF">
                  <th align="left">Title</th>
                  <th align="left">Author</th>
                  <th align="left">Edition</th>
```

```
                <th align="left">Publisher</th>
            </tr>
            <xsl:for-each select="catalogs/catalog/book">
            <tr>
                <td><xsl:value-of select="title"/></td>
                <td><xsl:value-of select="author"/></td>
                <td><xsl:value-of select="edition"/></td>
                <td><xsl:value-of select="$publisher"/></td>
            </tr>
            </xsl:for-each>
            </table>
        </body>
        </html>
</xsl:template>
</xsl:stylesheet>
```

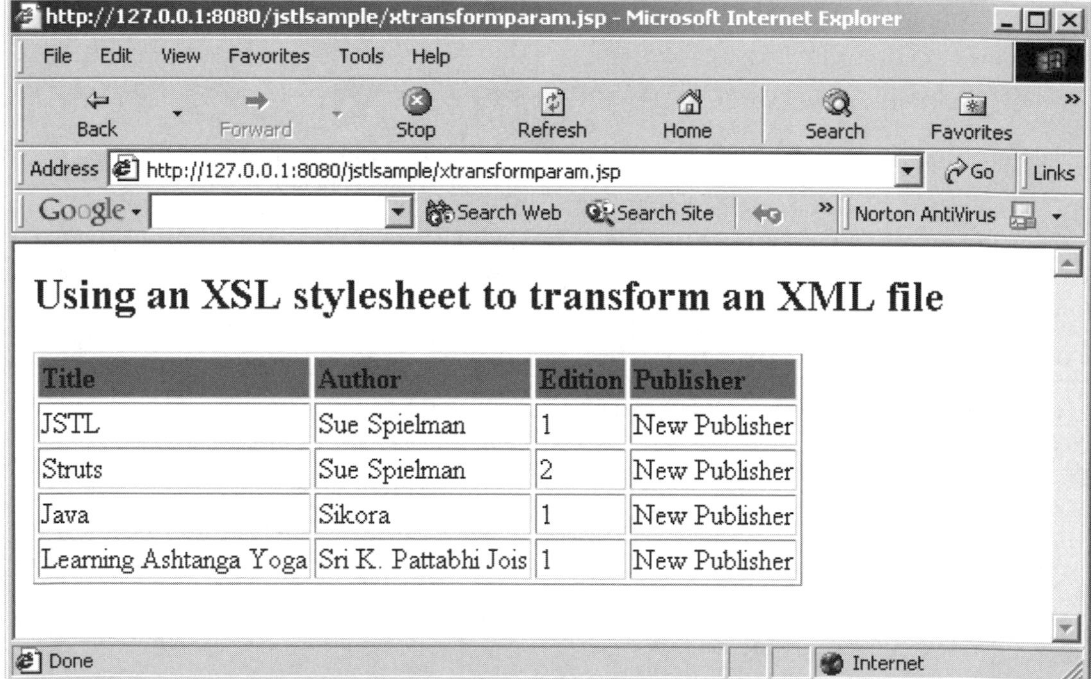

Figure 5.7: Browser output using XSL param.

Example 5.15 Using the <x:param> Action

```
<x:transform xml="${xmlfile}" xslt="${xslfile}" >
 <x:param name="publisher" value="New Publisher" />
</x:transform>
```

5.16.2 Performing Multiple Transformations

It is not uncommon to have the output of one transformation become the input of another. This is referred to as chaining. Typically there are a number of XSL files that are specific to various tasks so that you don't end up having extremely large, complicated XSL files.

It's possible to perform chaining easily using the var attribute of <x:transform>. Instead of <x:transform> writing to the JspWriter, it will write the output to the variable, which can then be used as input to the next transformation. You can use as many transformations as required to complete your tasks. Another approach is to nest <x:transform> actions, so that the output of one transformation becomes the body content of the next. Personally, I prefer to use variables instead of nesting transformation actions because it seems easier to understand and maintain when you are working with variables. Example 5.16 shows both ways to chain a transformation. This sample shows a simple chain consisting of two transformations, but you can nest as many as you like.

Example 5.16 Chaining Transformations

```
Using a var
<x:transform var="transform1" xml="${xmlfile}" xslt="${xslfile}"/>
<x:transform var="final" xml="${ transform1}" xslt="${xslfile2}"/>

Nested transformation with var

<x:transform var="final" xslt="${xslfile2}">
      <x:transform xml="${xmlfile}" xslt="${xslfile}" />
</x:transform>
Nested transformation written to current JspWriter
<x:transform xslt="${xslfile2}">
      <x:transform xml="${xmlfile}" xslt="${xslfile}" />
</x:transform>
```

5.17 Summary

In this chapter we've taken a look at the actions available in the XML tag library. Many of these actions are similar to those provided in the Core tag library, but with one major difference. The XML actions allow for the use of XPath as the expression language. XPath is a common way to define access to an XML document structure.

Also in these pages, we took a brief introductory tour of the various technologies it is required to understand when working with XML documents, including XPath, and then covered the available XML actions. We saw that, in addition to the core and conditional XML actions, there are also transformation actions. These allow for XML documents to be transformed using XSLT.

The XML actions play an important role in today's web applications. Since XML is omnipresent, dealing with XML documents becomes much easier with the actions provided in the XML tag library. Using the XML actions, it's possible to do all sorts of data comparison, iteration, and transformations using XSLT. All of these actions should make your page authoring that much easier. In order to make the best use of the XML actions, it is important to have a firm understanding of XPath and XSL at the very least.

chapter 6

Working with the Internationalization and Formatting Actions

More than likely, the application you are developing today will have to be internationalized tomorrow. Wouldn't it be great if the effort required to internationalize your application could be reduced to zero? Well okay, that might be too optimistic to hope for since anyone who has developed applications for international use knows there is always something that needs to be tweaked. Luckily, the internationalization and formatting actions provided in the JSTL are a comprehensive set of actions that can be used to minimize the headaches of having to internationalize your application.

These actions come under the functionality of the I18N umbrella. I18N, which refers to the 18 letters between the *I* and the *N* in *internationalization*, is a common acronym used when talking about internationalization features. It is also common to use the term L10N, for localization. In this chapter, we'll explore these internationalization actions. All of the actions related to I18N are contained in the custom tag library with the URI `http://java.sun.com/jstl/fmt` and are frequently accessed by using the `fmt` prefix.

The I18N functional area can be broken down into two main areas:

1. Locale and resource bundles that include such actions as:
   - `<fmt:setlocale>`
   - `<fmt:bundle>`
   - `<fmt:setBundle>`
   - `<fmt:message>`
   - `<fmt:param>`
   - `<fmt:requestEncoding>`

2. Formatting for numbers, dates, and currency, which includes such actions as:
   - `<fmt:timeZone>`
   - `<fmt:setTimezone>`
   - `<fmt:formatNumber>`
   - `<fmt:parseNumber>`
   - `<fmt:formatDate>`
   - `<fmt:parseDate>`

To address both of these functional areas, let's first take a cursory look at what pieces are involved in creating international applications. Then we'll look at how these pieces can be put to work using the various actions available in the JSTL.

6.1 Locales

Understanding locales is the first order of business we need to discuss. A locale is commonly referred to as the language support used for a particular region. In general, the locale is a geographic, political, or social region. There are basically two ways to specify a locale. The first is by using a standard lowercase two-letter language code as defined in ISO-639. A complete listing of these codes can be found on the Unicode site at *http://www.unicode.org/unicode/onlinedat/languages.html.* It is typical (but not required) also to specify a country code along with the language code. The uppercase country codes are defined by ISO-3166 and can be found at *http://www.iso.ch/iso/en/prods-services/iso3166ma/02iso-3166-code-lists/index.html.* The reason for using a country code is to be able to distinguish between various dialects. For example, English (en) spoken in the United States (en_US) is different from English spoken in Great Britain (en_GB). Anyone who has been to both countries can attest to that.

If your application is internationalized, it means that your program can support multiple locales. Localizing an application is the support for the specifics of a particular locale. Any operation an application performs that requires specifics from a locale is called locale-sensitive. What this means is that you want to make sure that if you display a formatted number or percentage, a currency amount, or a time or date, the information will appear to the users in the way that they are used to seeing it according to the customs and conventions of the users' native country or region. This information is accessible by using the `Locale` class located in `java.util` package.

6.1.1 Internationalization vs. Localization

The terms internationalization and localization are frequently used interchangeably. However, they really are two separate things. Internationalization is the process of enabling a program to run correctly regardless of what country it is being used in. Once a program is internationalized, the next step is to localize it.

Localization is when you translate any user-visible text into the native language as defined by that particular locale. A locale defines the customary format used for things like displaying numbers, dates, currency values, decimals, and sorting orders. Dealing with different locales also involves the basic issue of character encoding. Any input and output of text requires that the program understands how to deal correctly with the character encoding. If you have ever visited a website that shows garbled characters, you've gotten a taste of when the browser and website are not speaking the same character encoding. Basically, once your site is internationalized, you can deal with the issues related to localization relatively easily.

6.2 Why be Language Independent?

There are many reasons for making sure your site is I18N ready from the beginning. For one, it keeps the text, labels, messages, and other locale-sensitive information from being embedded into the source code. Having these items separate helps to maintain a single source code base for all language versions of your product. It also allows for fast translations, because all localizable resources are in one place and can easily be identified. Second, even if there is not an immediate requirement to have your product available in multiple languages, I can confidently assure you that eventually it will be a requirement. The third reason for ensuring I18N readiness is that it's easy. Java has always been geared toward making internationalization easy by using Unicode as its internal character set. With the actions now available in the JSTL, there is no good reason to forgo being I18N compatible.

6.3 Localizing an Application Using Resource Bundles

The Locale is used to specify which of the localized language files to use. Each user can have their own locale set so that multiple users can all access the application concurrently while viewing it in different languages. This is done by using resource files, also called resource bundles. Resource bundles are used to hold the text and messages that are used by your application. The `java.util.ResourceBundle` is an abstract class that allows for subclasses to define localized resources. A common way to do this is to use `java.util.PropertyResourceBundle`, which is a concrete subclass of `ResourceBundle`. A `PropertyResourceBundle` manages resources for a locale using a set of static strings from a property file. Using resource bundles, you can write your application code largely independently of the user's locale, isolating most, if not all, of the locale-specific information in resource bundles.

`PropertyResourceBundle` allows for name/value pairs to be defined in a properties file in the format key=value. This can include button labels, text strings, ... basically anything that can be displayed to the user. These resources are stored in a properties file that is specific to the locale. For example, we might have MyResources.properties to hold the default key/message pairs. The contents of this file could contain:

```
welcome=Welcome
testString= This is a test string
buttonLogon=Logon
buttonLogout=Logout
```

Whenever the key name is referenced by a resource, it will be replaced with the value of that key. This property file might be translated into whatever language support is required. Therefore, whenever the required resource file is needed, and according to the locale specified, the correct translated text will appear to the user. We will see as we continue through the JSTL I18N actions how locales and resource bundles interact with the actions so that applications can be easily internationalized.

6.4 Types of I18N Architectures

Typically there are two basic approaches used when designing web applications that require I18N support. The first approach is shown in Figure 6.1.

In this approach, the web application uses a controller Servlet to manage incoming requests. Each request is then sent to the appropriate locale-specific JSP page. This amounts to having one JSP per locale that your application will support. You should be getting a headache just thinking about what the maintenance requirements will be. In this case, you will have to make sure that all changes made to any JSP are propagated to all of the JSPs. Not a very desirable solution, but it might be sufficient for doing prototyping or for very small applications.

In the second approach, as shown in Figure 6.2, we have a more practical approach to most web application development.

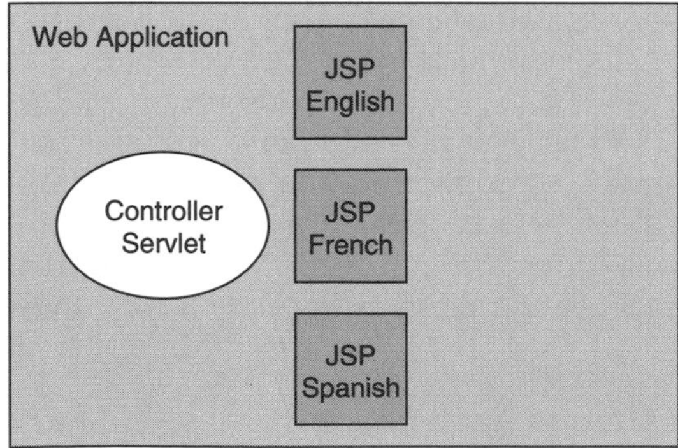

Figure 6.1: International design using separate JSP pages.

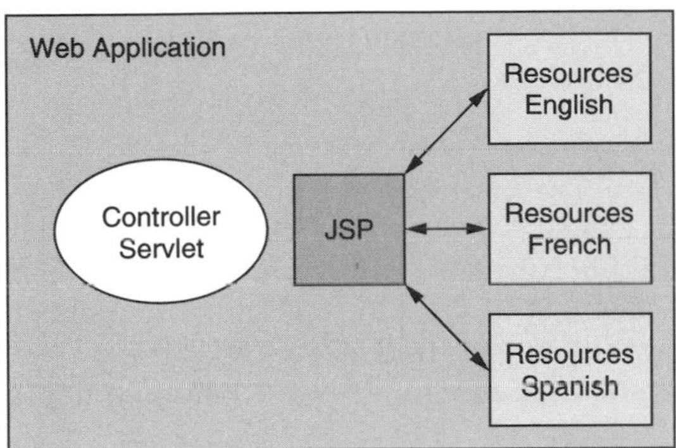

Figure 6.2: International design using one JSP with resource bundles.

Doing it this way, we have one JSP file that can use the appropriate resource bundle depending on the `Locale` specified in the request. This approach is more maintainable for the application in general. However, don't overlook the small fact that the resource bundles still need to be maintained in each of the supported languages. There are rules that are used to determine the order of resource bundles, which we discuss in Section 6.10, "How Resource Bundles are Decided." I mention these two approaches because it is important to note that, whichever one you choose, JSTL actions can support your choice. The architecture of your application should not be dictated by whether or not the actions will work correctly. Being able to use JSTL regardless of your architecture is actually one of the advantages of using the JSTL.

6.5 First, the <fmt:message> Action

Before we start talking about the various actions available in the I18N, let's introduce the `<fmt:message>` action. If you really wanted to do the bare-bones amount of work necessary to build an internationalized application, `<fmt:message>` is the only action that you'd need to consider. The `<fmt:message>` action takes advantage of the `LocalizationContext` (which we talk about in the next section). By using the `<fmt:message>`, you can output values from your resource bundles as simply as:

```
<fmt:message key="welcome"/>
```

The appropriate resource bundle will be used to look up the key "welcome" and the translated string will be provided. This is about as easy as it gets to incorporate international support into your application.

The `<fmt:message>` action also supports parameterized content, also called parametric replacement. For example, you can provide variables that will be used within the string used by the key attribute. Say we want to personalize our welcome page and pass the name of a user so that we can welcome them. To do this, we use the `<fmt:param>` subtag.

We will talk about this in more detail later in this chapter, but as a quick example, so that you are familiar with the format, the action might look like:

```
<fmt:message key="welcome" >
      <fmt:param value="${userNameString}"/>
</fmt:message>
```

In this example, we would be accessing a variable already set, called userNameString, that would then be used as a parameter to the message. If we were accessing the English version of the resource bundle, "Welcome Sue" would appear in the JspWriter.

Now, with the basics of the <fmt:message> under your belt, let's take a more in-depth look at how the I18N actions work.

6.6 Localization Context

All of the I18N actions work with a localization context. This context is used when determining how to localize the data provided to the action. The class LocalizationContext is found in the javax.servlet.jsp.jstl.fmt package. This class is used by quite a few of the JSTL I18N actions, including <fmt:message>, <fmt:formatNumber>, <fmt:parseNumber>, <fmt:formatDate>, and <fmt:parseDate>.

There are two main pieces of data the context uses: the resource bundle and the locale for which the resource bundle was found. There is an order of precedence used by the context to determine what is the correct resource bundle to be using. This precedence is determined as follows.

First, the bundle attribute of the <fmt:message> actions is used if it is specified. The I18N localization context associated with it is used for localization specific to that message action. If no bundle attribute was specified, then the next place to check is the <fmt:bundle> action.

<fmt:message> actions can be nested inside of a <fmt:bundle> action. If this is the case, then the I18N localization context of the enclosing <fmt:bundle> action is used for localization. When we go into the details of the <fmt:bundle> action, we'll talk about how the resource bundle is actually determined and what the algorithm looks like when using the basename attribute. The basename is the bundle's fully qualified resource name. The basename is represented similarly to a fully qualified class name, using the dot notation. However there is no defined suffix for a basename. An example of a basename is:

```
jstlpg.Resources
```

This basename is then used as the base for creating the appropriate named resource bundle. Thus, if an English resource bundle was being used, the locale and country codes could be set to en_US. The complete name of the resource bundle would be created using the basename and the appropriate locale information:

```
jstlpg.Resources_en_US
```

If neither the bundle attribute nor the <fmt:bundle> action is specified, then the default localization context is used. This is done by using the configuration setting variable javax.servlet.jsp.jstl.fmt.localizationContext. If the configuration setting is of type Config.FMT_LOCALIZATION_CONTEXT, its resource bundle component javax.servlet.jsp.jstl.fmt.LocalizationContext is used for localization. Otherwise, the configuration setting is of type String. When the type is String, the value is interpreted as a resource bundle basename.

6.7 Localization Context Sample

Let's walk through a couple of samples to see how the various ways of setting the localization context work when used on a JSP page. These samples are probably extreme cases of when you want to change the resource bundles. Usually you have a locale that is used throughout the page, but these samples will give you an idea of how the various precedence levels work if the following actions appeared on the same page.

```
<%-- This action would use the configuration setting --%>
<fmt:message key="welcome" />

<%-- Use the bundle with the specified base name --%>
<fmt:bundle basename="jstlpg.Resource">

<%-- Localization context established by parent <fmt:bundle>
tag --%>
<fmt:message key="welcome" />

<%-- Localization context established by attribute bundle --%>
<fmt:message key="welcome" bundle="jstlpg.NewResource " />

</fmt:bundle>
```

6.8 Preferred Locales

We've been talking about the localization context and locales so far, but haven't really gone into the details of how to set and change the preferred locale. Doing so is useful since you might have different locales being used by different users of the same application at the same time. There are a couple of ways that the resource bundle of the localization context can be retrieved and we'll address those processes in the next section. The algorithm used to retrieve the resource bundle requires two pieces of information:

1. The basename of the resource bundle
2. The preferred locales

6.8.1 Setting the Preferred Locales

There are two ways to set the preferred locales. You can either do it in the application itself or you can use the browser to determine the correct locale. If both ways are used, the application-based locale setting will take precedence.

6.8.1.1 *Application-based Method*

When using the application-based method, the locale is set using the configuration setting variable `javax.servlet.jsp.jstl.fmt.locale`. Using this variable will effectively disable the browser-based locales. This variable can be set to `String` constant `Config.FMT_LOCALE` if you want to set it programmatically. If a `String` value is used, it is interpreted as the printable representation of a locale. This must contain a two-letter (lowercase) language code (as defined by ISO-639), and optionally a two-letter (uppercase) country code (as defined by ISO-3166). Language and country codes must be separated by hyphen (-) or underscore (_).

It is useful to set the locale using the application-based method in situations where you want your users to be able to pick their preferred locale. After the appropriate locale is selected, a scoped variable can be set accordingly. Another case where this may be useful is where a client's preferred locale is retrieved from a database and installed for the page using the `<fmt:setLocale>` action. The `<fmt:setLocale>` action may be used to set the `javax.servlet.jsp.jstl.fmt.locale` configuration variable as follows:

```
<fmt:setLocale value="en_US" />
```

6.8.1.2 *Browser-based Method*

In the browser-based locale setting, the client determines which locale(s) should be used by the web application by using its browser. The action retrieves the client's locale preferences by calling `ServletRequest.getLocales()` (or `pageContext.getRequest().getLocales()`) on the incoming request. This returns an enumeration of the locales (in order of preference) that the client wants to use. If the client's request doesn't provide an `Accept-Language` header—which is what specifies the supported languages for the response of this request—the returned locale enumeration contains the runtime's default locale, so there will always be at least one element in the enumeration.

It doesn't really matter which method you use to determine the locale setting. In both cases, the algorithm defined to determine which resource bundle to use for the localization context uses an enumeration of the preferred locales.

6.9 Formatting Locales

The formatting actions also need to use information from the localization context. If for some reason a formatting action cannot leverage the locale from the localization context (maybe because the context doesn't have a locale set or the formatting action can't establish a reference to the existing localization context) it must establish the formatting locale on its own. To do so, an algorithm similar to that we have just discussed is used.

The algorithm compares preferred locales against the set of locales that are available for a specific formatting action. The available locales are found in two different ways depending on whether we are talking about number or date actions. The locales available for actions <fmt:formatNumber> and <fmt:parseNumber> are determined by using the available Java class method calls. For numbers, this is java.text.NumberFormat.getAvailableLocales(). The locales available for <fmt:formatDate> and <fmt:parseDate> are determined by a call to java.text.DateFormat.getAvailableLocales().

Once we have the available locales, a lookup can be done. The locale lookup is similar to the resource bundle lookup as described in the next section, except that instead of trying to match a resource bundle, the locale lookup tries to find a match in a list of available locales. A match of the specified locale against an available locale is attempted in the following order:

- Language, country, and variant are the same.
- Language and country are the same.
- Language is the same and the available locale does not have a country.

So basically there is a two-step process to find the formatting locale. First, when there are multiple preferred locales, they are processed in the order in which they were returned by a call to ServletRequest.getLocales(). If a match wasn't found, a locale lookup is done for the fallback locale as specified in the javax.servlet.jsp.jstl.fmt.fallbackLocale configuration setting. If this match is found, then that is used as the formatting locale. Otherwise, it is up to the action to take some type of corrective steps to remedy the problem.

6.10 How Resource Bundles are Decided

Once we have the basename and the ordered set of preferred locales, the resource bundle for the localization context is determined according to a mechanism very similar to that already found in the J2SE platform. By using similar semantics, the JSTL takes advantage of the getBundle() method in the java.util.ResourceBundle. Use of this method is shown below.

```
ResourceBundle myResources =
ResourceBundle.getBundle(baseName, locale, this.getClass().
getClassLoader());
```

This is how the bundle lookup is usually done in the J2SE; we'll see later what the differences are in the JSTL. When searching for candidate bundles to use, the J2SE getBundle works as follows:

1. The basename, specified locale, and default locale generate the list of candidate bundle names.
2. If the specified locale's language, country, and variant are all empty strings, then the basename provided is used as the only candidate bundle name.
3. If any of the other strings mentioned are indicated, then the sequence used to generate the candidate bundles is a combination of the specified locale and the default locale.

As a sample, candidate bundles are evaluated in the following order:

1. basename + "_" + languageSpecified + "_" + countrySpecified + "_" + variantSpecified
2. basename + "_" + languageSpecified + "_" + countrySpecified
3. basename + "_" + languageSpecified
4. basename + "_" + languageDefault + "_" + countryDefault + "_" + variantDefault
5. basename + "_" + languageDefault + "_" + countryDefault
6. basename + "_" + languageDefault
7. basename

Candidate bundle names, where the final component is an empty string, are omitted. For example, if countrySpecified is an empty string, the second candidate bundle name is omitted.

`getBundle` then iterates over the candidate bundle names to find the first one for which it can instantiate an actual resource bundle. For each candidate bundle name, it attempts to create a resource bundle.

First, it attempts to load a class using the candidate bundle name. If such a class can be found and loaded using the specified class loader, and if it is assignment compatible with `ResourceBundle`, and if it is accessible from `ResourceBundle`, and if it can be instantiated, then `getBundle` creates a new instance of this class and uses it as the result resource bundle.

Otherwise, `getBundle` attempts to locate a property resource file. It generates a path name from the candidate bundle name by replacing all "." characters with "/" and appending the string `.properties`. It attempts to find a resource with this name using `ClassLoader.getResource`. If it finds a resource, it attempts to create a new `PropertyResourceBundle` instance from its contents. If successful, this instance becomes the result resource bundle. If no result resource bundle is found, a `MissingResourceException` is thrown. This can be summarized in the activity diagram shown in Figure 6.3.

Once a result resource bundle is found, its parent chain is instantiated. `getBundle` iterates over the candidate bundle names that can be obtained by successively removing variant, country, and language (each time with the preceding "_") from the bundle name of

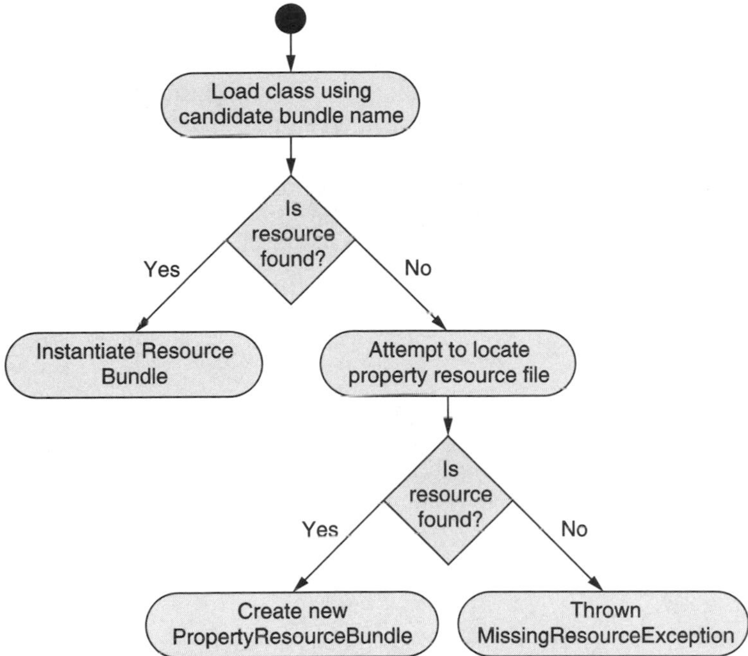

Figure 6.3: Locating a resouce bundle activity diagram.

the result resource bundle. As above, candidate bundle names—where the final component is an empty string—are omitted. With each of the candidate bundle names it attempts to instantiate a resource bundle as described above by the algorithm above. Whenever it succeeds, it calls the previously instantiated resource bundle's `setParent()` method with the new resource bundle, unless the previously instantiated resource bundle already has a non-null parent.

Implementations of `getBundle` may cache instantiated resource bundles and return the same resource bundle instance multiple times. They may also vary the sequence in which resource bundles are instantiated as long as the selection of the result resource bundle and its parent chain are compatible with the description above.

The returned resource bundle contains locale-specific objects. When an I18N action requires a locale-specific resource, it simply loads it from the appropriate resource bundle.

We see how the J2SE implementation handles resource bundle lookups. Let's see what the differences are in the JSTL implementation.

6.10.1 Resource Bundle Lookup Differences

JSTL omits doing lookups on the current default locale as returned by `Locale.getDefault()` as well as omitting doing lookups on the root resource bundle, which is the basename. The reason for these omissions is so that other locales may be considered before applying the JSTL fallback mechanism. The lookup on the fallback locale is performed by using the `javax.servlet.jsp.jstl.fmt.fallbackLocale` configuration setting. If a match is found, the fallback locale and the matched resource bundle are stored in the I18N localization context.

The root resource bundle is only considered if there is no fallback mechanism, or if the fallback mechanism fails to determine a resource bundle. If such a resource bundle exists, it is used as the resource bundle of the localization context but doesn't have any locale. If the resource bundle doesn't exist, then the localization content will not contain a resource bundle (obviously) or a locale. In this case the I18N action is required to take the appropriate steps to make sure that the action can still function correctly.

Once a resource bundle has been found and selected for the localization context, the searching stops. The order for the lookup is determined by the enumeration from the `getLocales()` call. This is an important point to be clear about because, if you have browser-based locale settings that contain both English and Spanish, in that order, and English is defined by just the language code for English (en) but the language and country code for Spanish (es_ES) is used, the resource bundle for en will be used if it is found and the search will be stopped.

When using resource bundles for a specific language and country, it is preferable that there be a language resource available. If you are expecting the language/country resource to be used for the lookup, you need to specify both the language and the country code so that the exact match will be found. For example, `Resources_fr_FR` should be backed by a resource bundle covering just the language in a resource bundle called `Resources_fr`. You typically create a country-specific bundle if the differences are too great for just the single language reference, for example, `Resources_en_US` and `Resources_en_GB`.[20]

Now that you have made it through the entire explanation for how the resource bundle lookups are accomplished, the simplified version of the search order is:

1. basename + "_" + language + "_" + country + "_" + variant
2. basename + "_" + language + "_" + country
3. basename + "_" + language
4. fallback Locale
5. basename

[20] A resource bundle can be referenced not only by a language and country code, but also by an optional variant. Variants can be useful in web applications that have different messages for different users based on some profile information of that user.

Settings	Available resource(s)	Resulting localization context settings
Basename: MyResources Ordered preferred locales: en_US, fr_CA Fallback locale: fr_CA	MyResources_en MyResources_fr_CA	Resource bundle: MyResources_en Locale: en
Basename: MyResources Ordered preferred locales: de, fr Fallback locale: en	MyResources_en	Resource bundle: MyResources_en Locale: en
Basename: MyResources Ordered preferred locales: ja, en_GB, en_US, en_CA, fr Fallback locale: en	MyResources_en MyResources_fr MyResources_en_US	Resource bundle: MyResources_en Locale: en
Basename: MyResources Ordered preferred locales: fr, ja Fallback locale: en	MyResources_fr_CA MyResources_ja MyResources_en	Resource bundle: MyResources_ja Locale: ja

Table 6.1: Resource bundle lookup samples.

6.11 Resource Bundle Lookup Samples

Let's take a look at a few sample situations. We will define the basename, the order of the preferred locales that would be returned in the enumeration, the fallback locale, and the available resource bundles. By following the logic of the resource bundle lookup algorithm, we'll see which resource is selected and then set in the resulting localization context. This is shown in Table 6.1.

6.12 Using the LocaleSupport Class

The logic we just discussed for doing resource bundle lookups is exposed as the general convenience method getLocalizedMessage() in the javax.servlet.jsp.jstl.fmt.LocaleSupport class. Using this class is very helpful if you have a tag handler implementation that needs to do message lookups. A tag handler may take advantage of the getLocalizedMessage() method so that the tag handler can produce localized messages easily. If you are producing exception messages or application-specific errors that will be used on error pages, using the getLocalizedMessage() with a provided message key will make it simple to find the resource. Either a basename can be specified or the default resource bundle in the localization context will be used for doing the lookups. The default resource bundle from the localization context is located by retrieving it from the javax.servlet.jsp.jstl.fmt.localizationContext configuration setting. It is also

```
public static String getLocalizedMessage(PageContext pc,
                     String key)
public static String getLocalizedMessage(PageContext pc,
                     String key, String basename)
public static String getLocalizedMessage(PageContext pc,
                     String key, Object[] args)
public static String getLocalizedMessage(PageContext pc,
                     String key, Object[] args, String basename)
```

Table 6.2: Method signatures of LocaleSupport class.

possible to take advantage of using parametric replacement in the messages. This is accomplished by using the args parameter, as shown in the available method signatures in Table 6.2.

6.13 Setting and Using Locales

Let's assume that you have already created your ResourceBundle files with your text strings from your application. The first step you need to take is to make sure that your application knows what Locale it is working with.

It is possible to just let the locale be specified based on what the user's web browser sends as its default. This is what the Accept-Language header value signifies. However, it's good practice to set a default for your application. This can be especially useful if you get a locale request from a browser that is not supported by your application. The page author can set the default application locale by using the <fmt:setLocale> action. The default locale can also be specified using the javax.servlet.jsp.jstl.fmt.locale configuration setting as shown in Example 6.1.

Example 6.1 Using the Locale Configuration Setting

```
<context-param>
      <param-name>javax.servlet.jsp.jstl.fmt.locale</param-name>
      <param-value>en_US</param-value>
</context-param>
```

6.13.1 <fmt:setLocale> Action

The <fmt:setLocale> action stores the locale specified by the value attribute in the javax.servlet.jsp.jstl.fmt.locale configuration variable. This action has three attributes defined: The value, which is either a String or a java.util.Locale; a variant, which is vendor- or browser-specific (for example, WIN for Windows or MAC for Macintosh);

and a scope that specifies the scope of the locale configuration variable. The scope can be any of the standard JSP scopes: page, request, session, or application. If value is of type java.util.Locale, the variant attribute is ignored. If this action is used, it has the effect of disabling browser-based locale capabilities. Therefore, if you are going to use this action, make sure that you do so at the beginning of the JSP prior to using other I18N actions. While the value attribute is required, if it is null or empty the runtime default locale is used.

To demonstrate how locales effect the formatting of dates, times, and numbers, let's look at Example 6.2. This sample first lets the user select from a form an option for the language they would like to use. Using an incoming parameter called currentLocale, we can see the difference in how dates and numbers are formatted according to the current locale. For this sample, I've selected French as my preferred language. By first displaying the browser output using the default Locale configuration setting (which is English), we can see how using the <fmt:setLocale> and setting the value to be that of fr changes our display. The browser output is shown in Figure 6.4.

Example 6.2 Changing Locales Using <fmt:setLocale>

```
<fmt:setLocale value="${param.currentLocale}" />
Today's date is: </b><fmt:formatDate type="date" value="${now}" />
The current time is: </b><fmt:formatDate type="time" value="${now}" />
Formatting a number: </b><fmt:formatNumber value=
"${param.myNumber}" />
```

6.13.2 Having a Fallback Locale

There are many different locales, and it is not expected that your application support all of them. Unless you are writing software for the UN, chances are that you will have just a handful of locales that you need to support. However, it's still possible that you'll get a request for a locale type that isn't supported and you certainly want to make sure that your application can gracefully decline the request. Setting the javax.servlet.jsp.jstl.fmt.fallbackLocale configuration setting allows a way to have your application use a best guess at what will suffice for the client. The fallbackLocale is different from the locale setting we already talked about. The default locale is used to make sure that the application has a default set so that the page author doesn't have to be bothered with setting a locale each time. The fallbackLocale is used if we get a request for a locale that we don't know how to handle.

Setting the variable is shown in Example 6.3. In this case, if we get any locale that we don't know how to handle, we will use the English locale as the default value. The browser output shown in Figure 6.5 is a result of getting a locale for HootyTooty, which is not a known locale. Therefore the fallbackLocale is used from the configuration setting and we get formatting from the English locale.

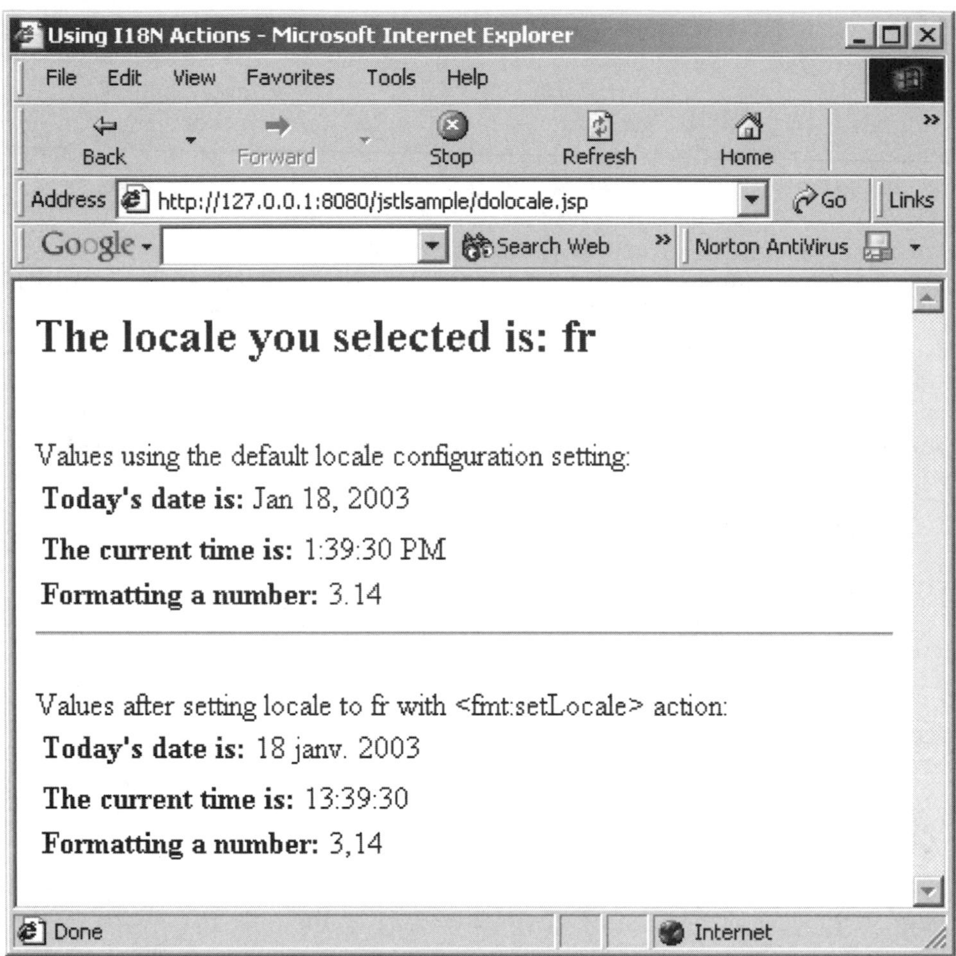

Figure 6.4: Showing the difference in locale settings.

Example 6.3 Setting the fallbackLocale

```
<context-param>
      <param-name>javax.servlet.jsp.jstl.fmt.fallbacklocale
      </param-name>
      <param-value>en_US</param-value>
</context-param>
```

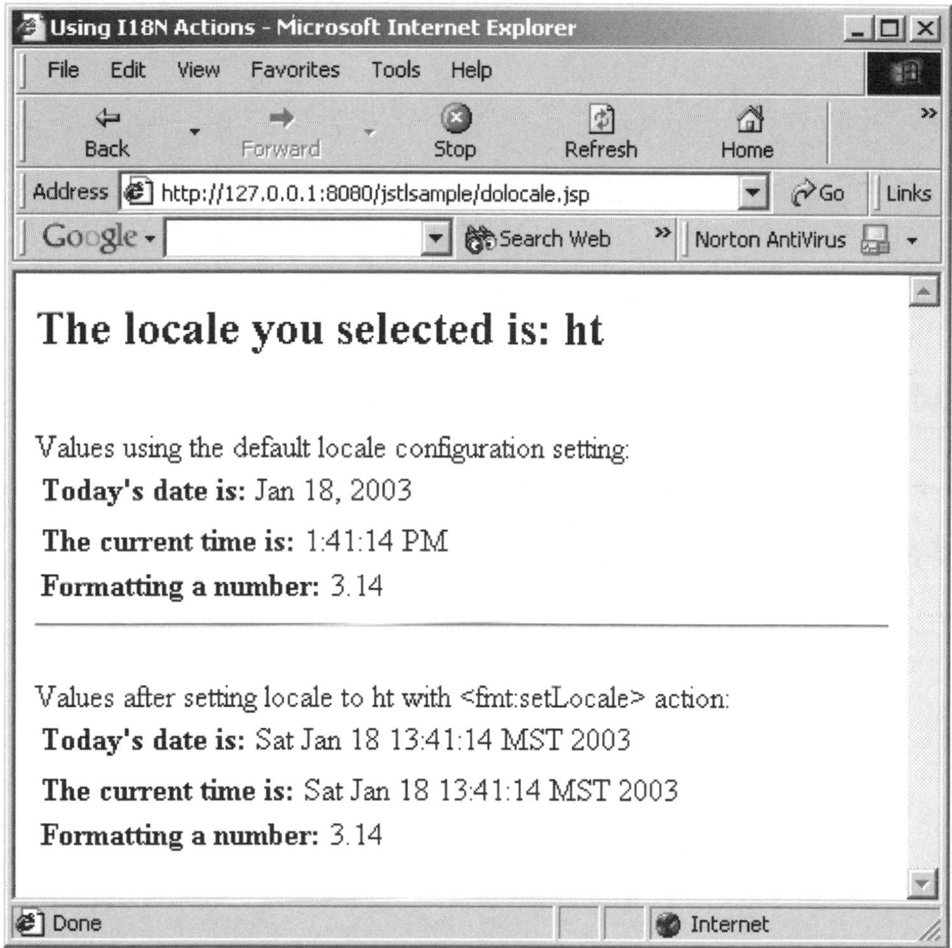

Figure 6.5: What happens when using a fallback locale.

6.14 Using Messages and Resource Bundles

Since we are on the subject of locales, let's talk about how you deal with your localized messages for specific locales. We mentioned earlier that even though a program is internationalized, you still need to localize the message strings for the languages that you are going to support. The messages are contained in a resource bundle. Usually there is a separate resource bundle for each language you are supporting. For all intents and purposes, the resource bundles are really nothing more than a file that contains a name/value pair and that includes a key and a message string. The message string is what gets translated into the appropriate language. Let's first take a detailed look at each of the actions we'll be using and then we can go through the sample.

6.14.1 <fmt:bundle> Action

The <fmt:bundle> action is used to create the localization content and load a resource bundle into that context. This action is used when you want a bundle to be specific to the body content of this action. The basename attribute is used to specify the fully qualified resource name to use for the resource bundle. This looks a lot like a class name reference using the "." notation we are used to. However, keep in mind that there is no file type suffix. If the basename is null or empty, or a resource bundle cannot be found, the null resource bundle is stored in the I18N localization context. The resource bundle algorithm that we discussed to determine which bundle is actually loaded then uses this name to do the resource bundle lookup. The scope of the I18N localization context is limited to the action's body content. The prefix attribute is provided as a convenience for very long message key names. If the prefix is specified, it is used by any nested <fmt:message> actions. The prefix is prepended to the key attribute of the nested action. For example:

```
<fmt:bundle basename="Resources">
      <fmt:message key="mk.samples.jstl.title"/>
</fmt:bundle>
```

and

```
<fmt:bundle basename="Resources" prefix="mk.samples.jstl.">
      <fmt:message key="title"/
</fmt:bundle>
```

are equivalent references to the key attribute used in the <fmt:message> action.

6.14.2 <fmt:setBundle> Action

<fmt:setBundle> might appear similar to <fmt:bundle>, but there are significant differences. <fmt:setBundle> provides a way to create an I18N localization context and then provides a way to store it in a defined scoped variable. If the var attribute is not defined, then the javax.servlet.jsp.jstl.fmt.localizationContext configuration variable is used to store the context. When this configuration variable is used, it becomes the new default localization context in the defined scope attribute. If the var attribute is used, then the class type is javax.servlet.jsp.jstl.fmt.Localization Context.

As in the <fmt:bundle> action, if the basename is null or empty, or a resource bundle cannot be found, the null resource bundle is stored in the localization context.

A quick sample of using the <fmt:setBundle> actions looks like:

```
<fmt:setBundle basename="mk.samples.jstl.Resources"
```

```
             var="enBundle"
             scope="page"/>
```

This sample is defining a page-scoped variable called enBundle (for English bundle), which can be found using the basename defined. As we'll see in a moment, we can then use this variable in other actions.

6.14.3 <fmt:message> Action

If you are a true minimalist, the only I18N action you really need to know is the <fmt:message> action that we briefly talked about at the beginning of this chapter. Everything else related to resource bundles and locales can be taken care of by defaults. The <fmt:message> action is the actual mechanism for looking up a message from the localized string messages provided in a resource bundle. These are the string messages that appear on your JSPs through using the current JspWriter. <fmt:message> can be used without any body content, or it can contain the <fmt:param> action that allows for parametric replacements.

The <fmt:message> must have a key attribute that defines the message key to use in the resource bundle as well as a number of optional attributes. These include a bundle attribute that contains a specific localization context to use for the message key lookup; a var that is the name of an exported scoped variable that holds the localized message; and a scope attribute that defines the scope of the var if one was defined. There is no default on the scope of the var, so if you specify the var attribute you must also define the scope for it. When using the var attribute, the result is stored in the named var attribute and is not written to the current JspWriter object.

In the case when a specified key cannot be found, or it's null or empty, the message is processed as if undefined. In this case a message is returned that contains "??????". If the localization context that this action is using does not have any resource bundles associated with it, an error message of the form "???<key>???" is produced. The "<key>" portion would be replaced with the name of the given key.

Keep in mind that when the key specifies the message by using the key attribute, if the action is nested inside a <fmt:bundle> action, and the parent <fmt:bundle> action contains a prefix attribute, the specified prefix is prepended to the message key.

6.14.4 <fmt:param> Action

It is possible to do parametric replacement in messages by using the <fmt:param> subtag. One <fmt:param> subtag can be used for each parameter value required. The parametric replacement is done in the order of the <fmt:param> subtags. Using parameters within messages takes advantage of the functionality already provided in the JDK by using the java.text.MessageFormat . If there is more than one <fmt:param> subtag, the message is supplied to the method MessageFormat.applyPattern(); the values of the <fmt:param>

tags are collected in an array of Objects, and are supplied to the method Message Format.format(). The locale of the MessageFormat is set to the appropriate localization context locale before MessageFormat.applyPattern() is called. If the message is compound (i.e., has more than one parameter) and no <fmt:param> subtags are specified, then MessageFormat is not used.

When using <fmt:param> you are able to specify the parameter value by using the value attribute or by including the value in the body content of the tag. <fmt:param> tags must always be nested inside a <fmt:message> action.

6.15 Setting the Resource Bundle for <fmt:message>

Using <fmt:message> you can access the key in a resource bundle and a corresponding message string will be printed to the current JspWriter. By default, the browser locale or the result of a <fmt:setLocale> will determine the resource bundle to use according to the algorithm that's explained earlier in this chapter . You can explicitly set the resource bundle by using a base name. The base name can be used to override an existing resource bundle. If you use <fmt:setBundle>, you can specify the scope so that the bundle is used for a longer duration than just the page, if that's what you require. Specifically, a new basename is shown in the sample below. In this case, we are using a resource bundle in our resources directory of our web application called jstlpgtz. This would be the resource bundle for the country code tz, which happens to be Tanzania, just in case you're interested in learning how to speak Swahili. A resource bundle base name has the same form as a fully-qualified resource name, that is, it uses "." as the package component separator and does not have any file type such as .class or .properties suffix.

```
<fmt:setBundle basename="resources.jstlpgtz" />
<fmt:message key="hello" />
```

It is also possible to have a bundle used just for the scope of the element. For example, the code below would accomplish the same thing as the code above.

```
<fmt:bundle basename="resources.jstlpgtz" >
     <fmt:message key="hello" />
</fmt:bundle>
```

Both sets of code produce Figure 6.6.

Alternatively, keep in mind that you may specify the resource bundle base name as the value of the javax.servlet.jsp.jstl.fmt.localizationContext context initialization parameter in your web.xml. In this case, we're setting our default to use the English version of the resource bundle as our base name.

```
<web-app>
     <context-param>
          <param-name>
               javax.servlet.jsp.jstl.fmt.localizationContext
```

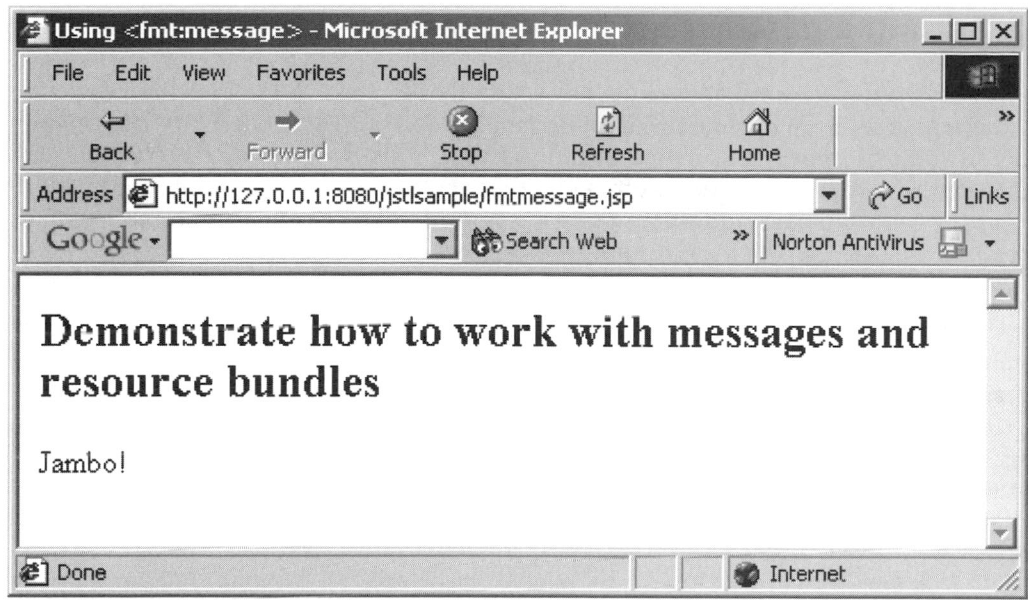

Figure 6.6: Hello in Swahili.

```
                </param-name>
                <param-value>
                    resource.Jstlpg
                </param-value>
            </context-param>
        </web-app>
```

According to Section 8.3.2 of the JSTL specification, if there is no resource bundle for any of the requested locales, the root resource bundle with the given base name is used if present. The root resource bundle for a given base name is the bundle returned by a call to `java.util.ResourceBundle.getBundle()` with a locale argument whose language, country, and variant components are all empty strings.

I'd like to point something out when you are using the resource bundles. An application can choose how to store its localized strings. It can be in a `.property` file or a `ResourceBundle` class, or in a database. If you decided to use a database (which many applications do) and a new localized key/value pair is inserted, you will have to restart Tomcat before you can use that key/value pair in the JSTL. A modified resource bundle is not considered changed until a Tomcat restarts because of the call made to `java.util.ResourceBundle.getBundle()` in the reference implementation (RI). Any resource bundle that is instantiated is then cached. This might be different in other implementations for web containers as they become available, but if you see similar behavior this is probably the reason.

6.16 Adding a parameter to <fmt:message>

Using <fmt:message> we were able to specify a key that is used to look up the key/value pair in the resource file. This is all well and good, but it seems like there are times when we'd like to add a bit more information to the message. This is when we use <fmt:param>. The <fmt:param> action allows us to do parametric replacement. Using <fmt:param> with <fmt:message> you can pass things like EL expression values and request parameters. This is shown in Example 6.4. The browser output is shown in Figure 6.7.

Example 6.4 Say a Personalized Hello in Swahili

```
<fmt:bundle basename="resources.Jstlpgtz" >
<fmt:message key="hellopersonal" >
      <fmt:param value="${param.username}"/>
</fmt:message >
</fmt:bundle>
```

When you are using parameters to resource messages, you need to make sure that you are passing your parameters in the correct order. Sometimes the translation of different languages puts the necessary parameters in a different order. You'll need to check with whoever is responsible for doing the translation exactly what order is required for the language you are working with.

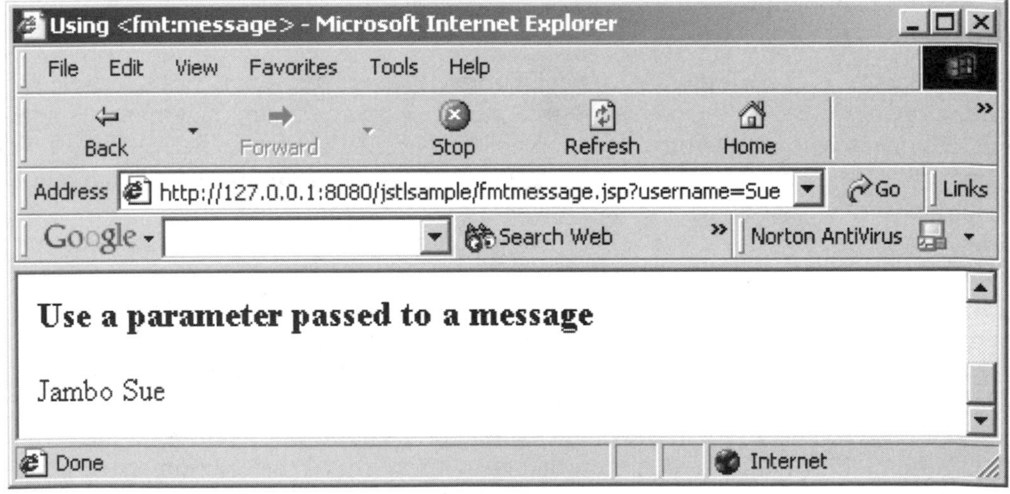

Figure 6.7: Browser personalized hello in Swahili.

6.17 Formatting Actions

Formatting actions are the second major group of actions that fall under the I18N umbrella. These actions are for data that contains numbers, dates, and times to be formatted and parsed correctly according to the current locale settings. The formatting actions handle such pieces of data as percentages, currency, or numbers. All of the available formatting actions are listed below.

```
<fmt:timeZone>
<fmt:setTimeZone>
<fmt:formatNumber>
<fmt:parseNumber>
<fmt:formatDate>
<fmt:parseDate>
```

It is possible to define specific patterns to use so that you can customize how the formatting appears for certain actions. We'll look at a few samples of this when we talk about the <fmt:formatNumber> action. The same pattern options, as well as style options, are available in terms of doing date and time formatting. Time information on a page may be tailored to the preferred time zone of a client by using the <fmt:timeZone>. This is useful if the server hosting the page and its clients reside in different time zones.

While the formatting actions can be defined as a group of actions, a subset of these actions actually works in concert with the I18N resource bundle and locale actions by using the locale settings found in the localization context. This subset is listed in Table 6.3.

These actions follow similar rules as the resource bundle and locale actions in terms of determining which localization context to use. If a formatting action is nested inside a <fmt:bundle> action, the locale of the localization context used in the enclosing <fmt:bundle> is used. If there is no locale defined in that localization context, then the default localization context as specified in the javax.servlet.jsp.jstl.fmt.localizationContext configuration setting is used if it exists and if the value is of type LocalizationContext. Remember, it's possible for the value of that configuration setting to be either a type or a String. If the value is a String, then the formatting action will establish its own localization context and use its locale as the formatting locale.

<fmt:formatNumber>
<fmt:parseNumber>
<fmt:formatDate>
<fmt:parseDate>

Table 6.3: Formatting actions using locale settings.

The resource bundle of this newly established localization context is determined in the same manner that we already talked about in "How Resource Bundles are Decided" (Section 6.10). If we still don't have a locale defined in the localization context, then a formatting locale lookup is done to establish the preferred locale to use. Refer to Section 6.9 "Formatting Locales" to see again how that is accomplished.

6.17.1 Determining the Time Zone

The date formatting actions also take advantage of the time zone setting. The appropriate time zone setting to use is determined in the following order:

1. Use the time zone from the action's `timeZone` attribute.
2. If the `timeZone` attribute is not specified and the action is nested inside of a `<fmt:timeZone>` action, use the time zone from the enclosing `<fmt:timeZone>` action.
3. Use the time zone given by the `javax.servlet.jsp.jstl.fmt.timeZone` configuration setting.
4. Use the JSP container's time zone.

Let's go through the available formatting actions and see what they provide.

6.17.2 <fmt:timeZone> Action

The `<fmt:timeZone>` action is used to specify the time zone in which time information is to be formatted or parsed for any nested actions it contains. It takes a value attribute that can be either a `String` or a `java.util.TimeZone`. If value is a `String`, then it is interpreted as one of the time zone IDs that are supported by the Java platform or a custom time zone ID. This is done by using the `java.util.TimeZone.getTimeZone()` method call. (If you need more information on the types of supported time zone formats, reference the JavaDocs for the `java.util.TimeZone` class.) If no value is specified, then the default is the GMT time zone.

6.17.3 <fmt:setTimeZone> Action

The `<fmt:setTimeZone>` action is used to store a specified time zone into a variable that is scope defined or into the time zone configuration variable. The value attribute follows the same rules as those applied in the `<fmt:timeZone>` action. The var attribute is a `String` that is used to export a variable that stores an instance of a time zone of type `java.util.TimeZone`. If no var is specified, then the time zone configuration variable `javax.servlet.jsp.jstl.fmt.timeZone` is used. The scope of this var, or time zone configuration variable, is determined by the setting of the scope attribute that can be any of the standard JSP scopes.

6.18 Setting and Using Time Zones

Whenever applications (or people) deal with time, time zones need to be taken into consideration. For example, I know when my phone rings at 6:00 a.m. Mountain Standard Time (MST) that it is someone calling me from the East coast in Eastern Standard Time (EST). Having grown up on the East coast, I know that the people there assume that EST is the center of the universe and everyone adheres to that time zone. Unfortunately, this is not the case. Time zone abbreviations are just an easier way to reference the location's time offset from Greenwich Mean Time. It's possible to do this with time zone abbreviations like EST, CST, MST, etc. However, make sure you check the latest Javadocs for the `java.util.TimeZone` class to make sure how time zones are specified. In Java 1.4, the three-letter abbreviations have been deprecated because of overlapping abbreviations, although they are still valid for backward compatibility. JSTL will support whatever `TimeZone` supports.

While it is relatively easy for people to deal with time zones—for example, I just don't answer the phone at 6:00 a.m.—applications need a more structured way to do so. This is an important issue, to ensure that the parsing and formatting of dates and times is correct. JSTL allows the setting of the time zone for specific actions, the setting of the time zone for a group of actions, and the setting of the time zone for a specific scope in the application. Each way is demonstrated in Example 6.5. The browser display is shown in Figure 6.8. Keep in mind that we are using the same time zone because it is being passed in as a parameter.

There are different ways to set the time zone because it might be that you have different areas of your application that require different formatting. It is left up to the page author to decide which is the most efficient way to set the time zone. When using the `<fmt:setTimeZone>` action, it will set the configuration variable `javax.servlet.jsp.jstl.fmt.timeZone` for the specified scope as the new default time zone. This will only happen if no var attribute is specified. If using a var, then that variable will have the scope as defined.

Example 6.5 Various Ways to Set the Time Zone

```
The current time is:
<fmt:formatDate timeZone="${param.currentTimeZone}"
                type="time"
                value="${now}" />
The current date is:
<fmt:formatDate timeZone="${param.currentTimeZone}"
                type="date"
                value="${now}" />
<fmt:timeZone value="${param.currentTimeZone}" >
The current time is:
</b><fmt:formatDate type="time"
                    value="${now}" />
The current date is:
</b><fmt:formatDate type="date"
                    value="${now}" />
```

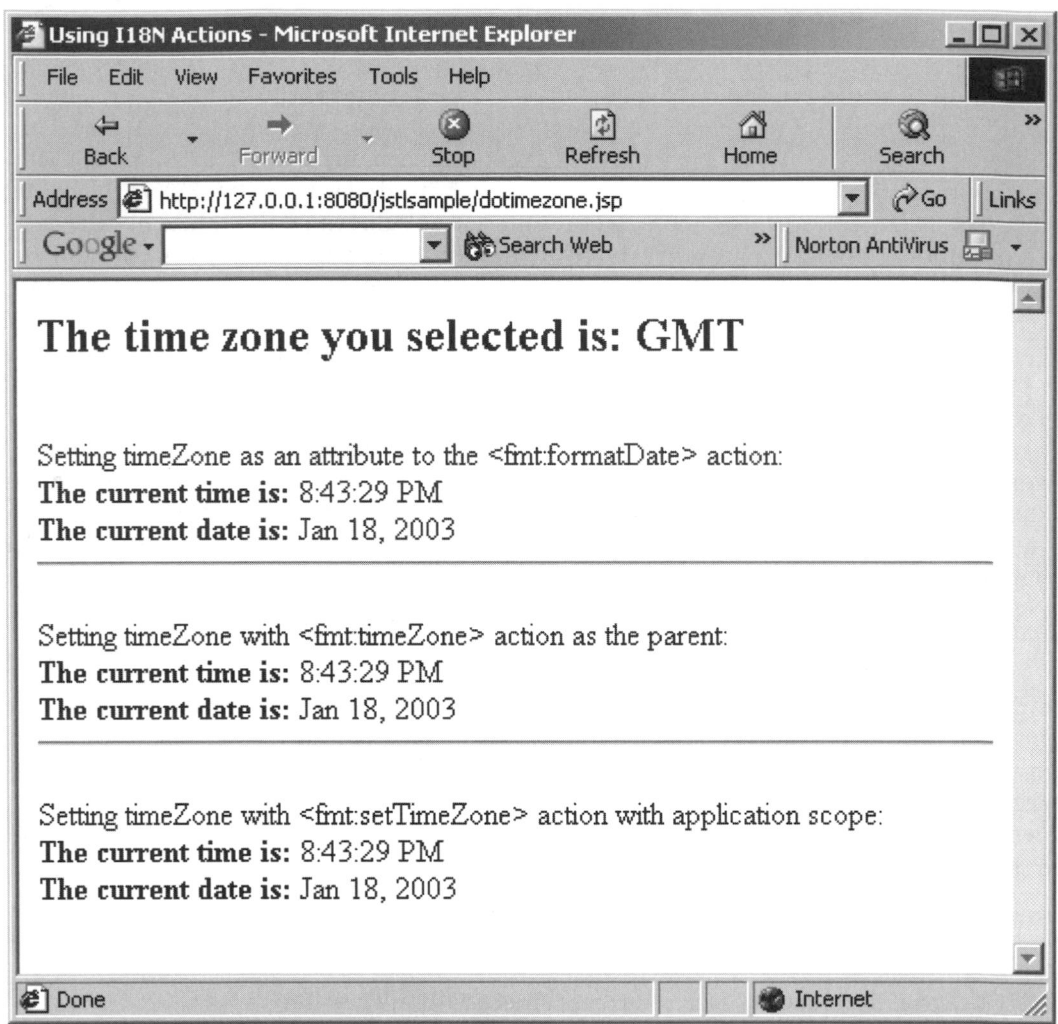

Figure 6.8: Displaying time zone information.

```
</fmt:timeZone>
<fmt:setTimeZone value="${param.currentTimeZone}"
                 scope="application"/>
The current time is:
<fmt:formatDate type="time"
                value="${now}" />
The current date is:
<fmt:formatDate type="date"
                value="${now}" />
```

6.19 Working with Timestamps

Throughout our samples so far we've been using the <fmt:formatDate> action to demonstrate how locale and time zones affect an application. <fmt:formatDate> is quite useful when dealing with timestamps. A timestamp can be a date, a time, or both. <fmt:formatDate> and <fmt:parseDate> work with both dates and times. As we've seen, <fmt:formatDate> (or <fmt:parseDate> for that matter) doesn't work in a vacuum. The output of either of these actions depends on the locale and the current time zone that is being used. The java.util.Date class represents dates in Java. The Date represents a specific instant in time with millisecond precision, represented in coordinated universal time (UTC). Therefore, when dealing with dates, we are dealing with a complete date and time. We'll see how to customize <fmt:formatDate> so that your output reflects the style necessary for your application. For a complete description of java.util.Date refer to the javadocs at http://java.sun.com/j2se/1.4/docs/api/index.html.

6.20 Formatting and Parsing Timestamps

First, let's get familiar with the basics of <fmt:formatDate> before going into how to customize it with patterns. When using <fmt:formatDate>, the value attribute must contain a valid date. This can done by either using an instance of java.util.Date, or using the output of <fmt:parseDate>. Let's take a look at all of the available attributes for formatting and parsing dates, then we'll dive into some more examples.

6.20.1 <fmt:formatDate> Action

<fmt:formatDate> is used to format dates and times in such a way that they are locale-sensitive or formatted according to a custom pattern. This action handles both date and time styles so that it's possible to format just a date, just a time, or both date and time from a given value. The attributes available in this action reflect this and are shown in Table 6.4.

The date/time value to be parsed may be specified by using the value attribute. If value is not specified, it is read from the action's body content. Depending on the value of the type attribute, only the time, the date, or both the time and date components of the date specified are formatted. The format used will depend on what formatting style was specified in the dateStyle attribute and/or timeStyle attribute.

It is also possible to apply a customized formatting style to the times and dates by specifying the pattern attribute. If a pattern is specified, the type, dateStyle, and timeStyle attributes are all ignored. The specified formatting pattern must use the pattern syntax specified by java.text.SimpleDateFormat.

If the string representation of a date or time needs to be formatted, the string must first be parsed into a java.util.Date using the <fmt:parseDate> action. This parsed result can then be supplied to the <fmt:formatDate> action using a variable. For example:

```
<fmt:parseDate value="9/7/02" var="parsed" />
<fmt:formatDate value="${parsed}" />
```

Attribute	Description
value	A date and/or time to be formatted.
type	Specifies whether the date, time, or both should be formatted. Defined using time|date|both. Defaults to date.
dateStyle	Predefined formatting style for dates. Used if type is missing, or set to date or both. Otherwise it is ignored. Can be default|short|medium| long|full. Defaults to default.
timeStyle	Predefined formatting style for times. Used if type set to time or both. Otherwise it is ignored. Can be default | short | medium|long|full. Defaults to default.
pattern	Custom formatting for dates and times.
timeZone	Either a String or java.util.TimeZone to determine which time zone to use when representing time.
var	Exported scoped variable containing a String of the formatted result.
scope	Scope of var.

Table 6.4: Attributes of <fmt:formatDate> action.

As with the other actions that have a var attribute, the result is output to the current JspWriter object. However, if the var attribute is specified, it is stored in the named scoped variable and will be available for the scope specified in the scope attribute.

6.20.2 <fmt:parseDate>

As with the <fmt:parseNumber>, the <fmt:parseDate> action produces the string representation of dates and times that have been formatted in a locale-specific or custom manner; it is then parsed correctly. The date string to be parsed may be specified either by using the value attribute or by including the string in the tag's body content. The string specified must conform to the parsing format that is going to be used. Otherwise, the parse will fail. The type attribute indicates whether the string specified is supposed to contain only a time, only a date, or both. The predefined formatting styles are specified by using the dateStyle and timeStyle attributes. These styles will use the locale specified by the parseLocale attribute. If the parseLocale attribute is missing, the formatting locale, which we talked about previously, is used as the parse locale.

If you want to use a different format for the date string, it is possible to do so by using a pattern. The pattern that is to be used to parse the string must be specified in the pattern attribute. If you define the pattern attribute, it must use the pattern syntax specified by java.text.SimpleDateFormat. The complete description of all of the available syntaxes can be found in the JavaDocs for that class. If the pattern attribute is defined, the type, dateStyle, and timeStyle attributes are all ignored.

When dealing with time, if the given time information does not specify a time zone, it is interpreted in the time zone determined by the algorithm we discussed earlier in this section.

Like all of the other actions that allow for a var, a value is stored in it. The var stores the result of the parse as a java.util.Date. If no var attribute is specified, the output is sent to the current JspWriter using java.util.Date.toString().

The <fmt:formatDate> can display the date, the time, or both. In this sample we'll concentrate on using a Date instance. There are five different values that can be used to specify the standard formats:

- Default
- Short
- Medium
- Long
- Full

The code in Example 6.6 shows the various combinations of formatting timestamps.

Example 6.6 When the Clock Strikes ...

```
<jsp:useBean id="now" class="java.util.Date" />
<table border="1">
      <tr><th>Format</th><th>Date</th><th>Time</th><th>Both</th><tr>
      <tr>
            <td>default</td>
            <td><fmt:formatDate type="date" value="${now}" /></td>
            <td><fmt:formatDate type="time" value="${now}" /></td>
            <td><fmt:formatDate type="both" value="${now}" /></td>
      </tr>
      <tr>
            <td>short</td>
            <td><fmt:formatDate dateStyle="short" type="date"
                                value="${now}" /></td>
            <td><fmt:formatDate timeStyle="short" type="time"
                                value="${now}" /></td>
            <td><fmt:formatDate dateStyle="short" timeStyle="short"
                                type="both" value="${now}" /></td>
      </tr>
      <tr>
            <td>medium</td>
            <td><fmt:formatDate dateStyle="medium" type="date"
                                value="${now}" /></td>
            <td><fmt:formatDate timeStyle="medium" type="time"
                                value="${now}" /></td>
            <td><fmt:formatDate dateStyle="medium"
             timeStyle="medium" type="both" value="${now}" /></td>
      </tr>
      <tr>
            <td>long</td>
```

```
            <td><fmt:formatDate dateStyle="long" type="date"
                                value="${now}" /></td>
            <td><fmt:formatDate timeStyle="long" type="time"
                                value="${now}" /></td>
            <td><fmt:formatDate dateStyle="long" timeStyle="long"
                                type="both" value="${now}" /></td>
      </tr>
      <tr>
            <td>full</td>
            <td><fmt:formatDate dateStyle="full" type="date"
                                value="${now}" /></td>
            <td><fmt:formatDate timeStyle="full" type="time"
                                value="${now}" /></td>
            <td><fmt:formatDate dateStyle="full" timeStyle="full"
                                type="both" value="${now}" /></td>
      </tr>
</table>
```

The results of these different formats are shown in Figure 6.9.

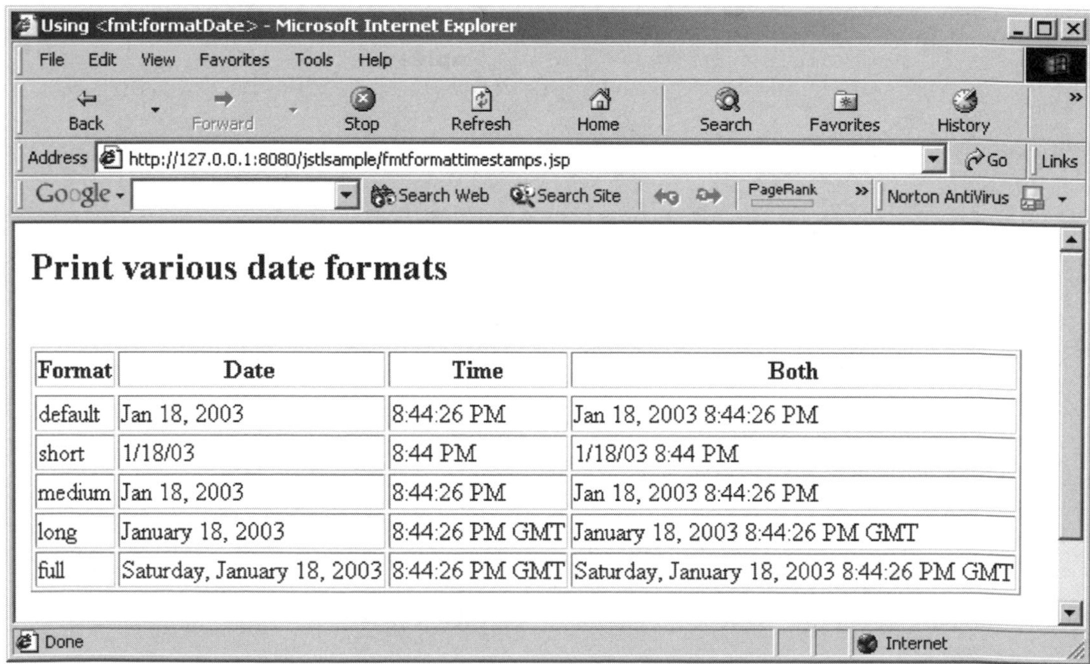

Figure 6.9: Date and Time format displays.

6.20.3 Customizing the Format

For most situations, the available format types used for displaying dates and times should suffice. However if you need to customize your format output, the `pattern` attribute allows you to do so. If a pattern is specified, the type, `dateStyle`, and `timeStyle` are ignored. Patterns use the syntax described by `java.text.SimpleDateFormat`. Table 6.5 shows the available syntax values as taken from the JavaDocs found at *http://java.sun.com/j2se/1.4/docs/api/index.html*. The letter specified in Table 6.5 can be used in either a long or short form. For example, M would be a single number, while MM would be a 2-digit number. MMM would be the short month name, while MMMM would be the long month name. The difference can be seen in the browser output shown in Figure 6.10. These format letter options in Table 6.5 can then be combined to form various output styles as shown in Table 6.6.

As we can see in the samples in Table 6.6, a pattern can contain text or punctuation that is passed through the pattern as literals. In order to insert a literal, you simply need to single quote the value you are interested in. If you need to print a single quote in the literal, then escape it by using two single quotes (' '). This is done instead of the attribute value itself that appears in the double quote. The browser output of the various sample formats is shown in Figure 6.11.

Letter	Date or time component	Examples
G	Era designator	AD
y	Year	2002; 02
M	Month in year	July; Jul; 07
w	Week in year	27
W	Week in month	2
D	Day in year	189
d	Day in month	11
F	Day of week in month	2
E	Day in week	Tuesday; Tue
a	Am/pm marker	PM
H	Hour in day (0–23)	0
k	Hour in day (1–24)	24
K	Hour in am/pm (0–11)	0
h	Hour in am/pm (1–12)	12
m	Minute in hour	30
s	Second in minute	55
S	Millisecond	978
z	Time zone	Pacific Standard Time; PST; GMT–08:00
Z	Time zone	–0800

Table 6.5: Available syntax for custom formatting.

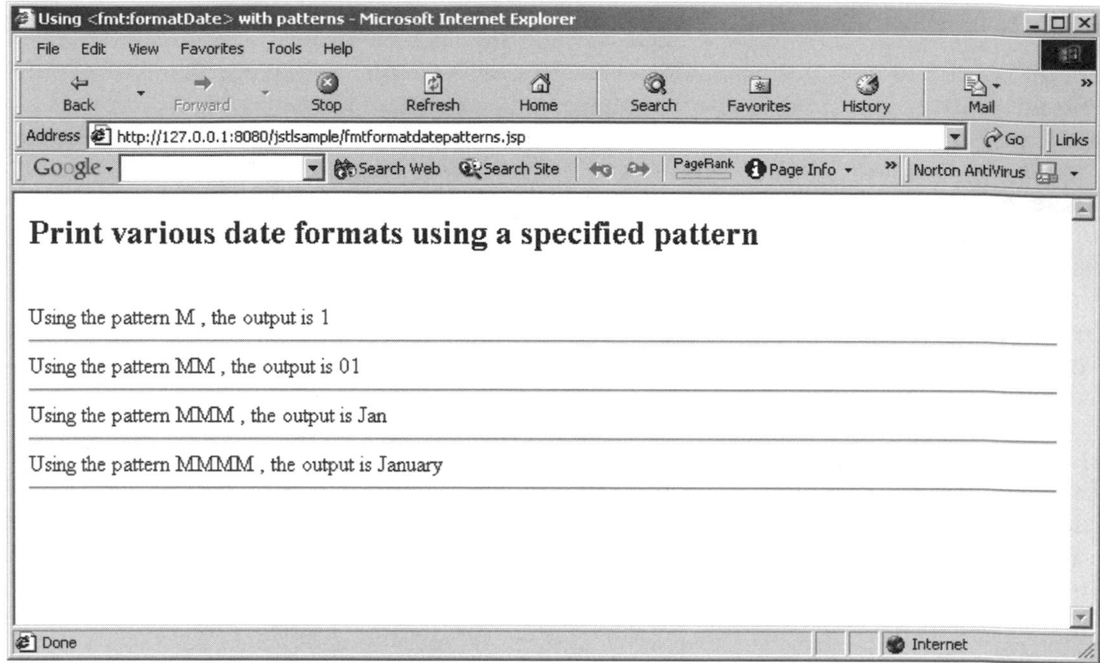

Figure 6.10: Difference in long and short format values.

Pattern
E-MM/dd/yy
E-MM/dd/yyyy
D/M/Y HH:mm:ss a
EEE d MMM yyyy hh 'o"clock' a, zzzz
yy.MM.dd G 'at' hh:mm z

Table 6.6: Creating and using custom patterns.

6.21 Using and Parsing Timestamps

While it is all well and good to have various ways to format timestamps that include all sorts of information, it is common to want to actually parse a timestamp or date. That is where `<fmt:parseDate>` comes in.

`<fmt:parseDate>` parses a string representation of dates and times. These timestamps were either formatted according to a specific locale or formatted using a custom pattern. `<fmt:parseDate>` will take a formatted date and create it in its native Java form.

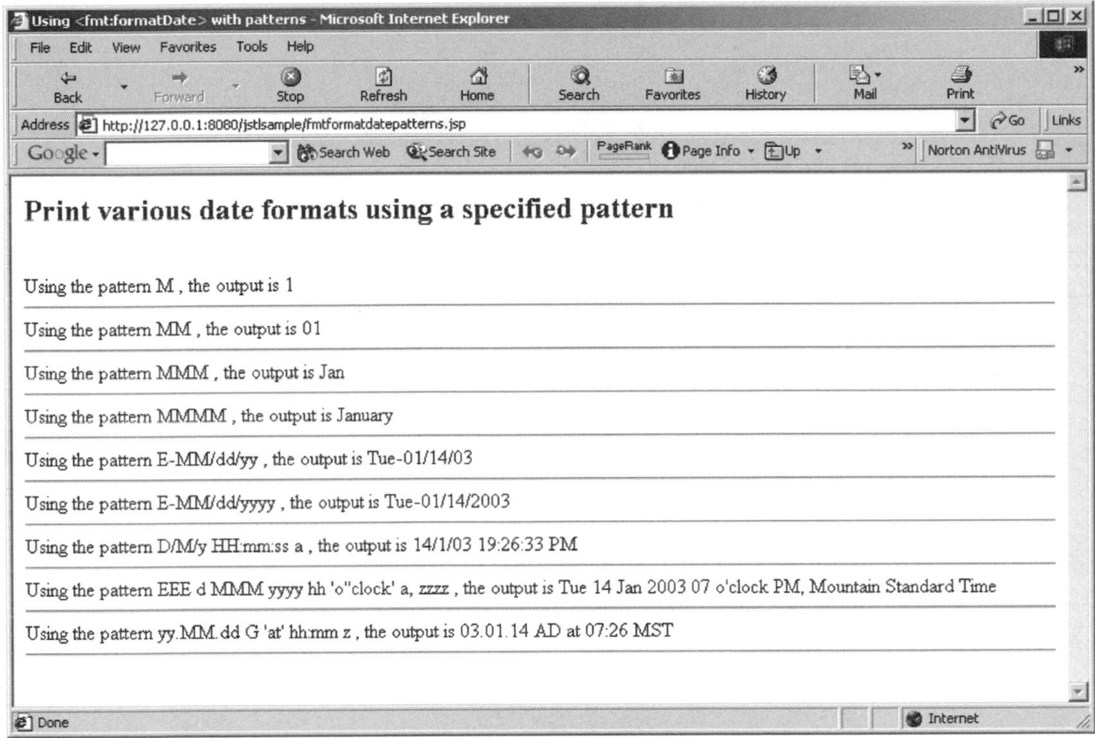

Figure 6.11: Browser output of various pattern options.

This is quite useful if you have a date (or time) that has been user-entered from an input form and which then needs to be converted into its Java form so that it can be used later or saved in a database.

The patterns syntax is the same as that we have already talked about, as covered in Table 6.5. For example, if we look at the code in Example 6.7, we can see that we are taking the value of an incoming parameter and then specifying the pattern. The `<fmt:parseDate>` then parses the value into the correct Java `Date` class format. If any parse error is thrown, we will catch it and just set the date to the current date. This class format is shown in the browser output shown in Figure 6.12.

Example 6.7 Parsing an Incoming Date

```
<c:catch var="error">
<fmt:parseDate var="pubDate" value="${param.pubDate}"
      pattern="MM/dd/yy" />
</c:catch>
<c:if test="${error != null}">
<jsp:useBean id="pubDate" class="java.util.Date" />
```

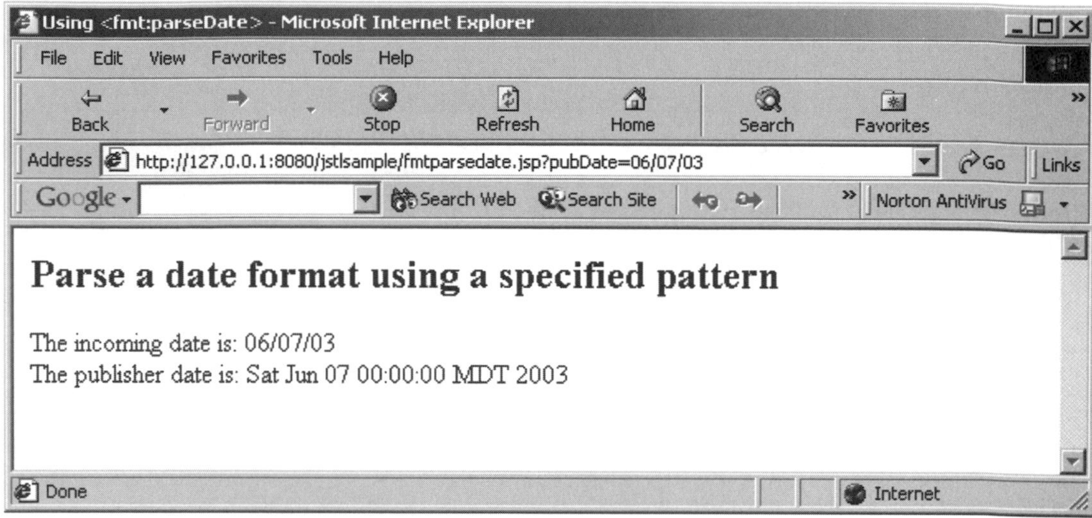

Figure 6.12: <fmt:parseDate> output.

```
</c:if>
The publisher date is: <c:out value="${pubDate}" />
```

By using the <fmt:parseDate> together with the <fmt:formatDate> it is possible to switch between date formats rather easily using code similar to that shown in Example 6.8.

Example 6.8 Changing Date Formats

```
<fmt:parseDate var="date" pattern="yyyy/MM/dd">2003/06/07
</fmt:parseDate>
<fmt:formatDate pattern="EEEE d MMMM yyyy" value="${date}"/>
```

6.22 Working with Numbers

Dates aren't the only things in applications that need parsing and formatting. Numbers such as currencies, percentages, scientific notations, and fixed-point representations are all locale-sensitive. However, they can be customized in their format. It might be sufficient just to let <c:out> take care of the display of numbers, but sometimes you want a little more control over the exact format so that columns line up on a web page, or only two

Attribute	Purpose
value	Numeric value if not defining value in body content
type	number|currency|percent (defaults to number)
pattern	A custom formatting pattern. Empty or null patterns are ignored
currencyCode	ISO-4217 currency code, used only when type is equal to currency
currencySymbol	Currency symbol, used only if type is equal to currency
groupingUsed	true|false (defaults to true) to indicate whether output should contain grouping separators
maxIntegerDigits	Maximum number of digits to show in the integer portion of formatted output
minIntegerDigits	Minimum number of digits to show in the integer portion of formatted output
maxFractionDigits	Maximum number of digits to show in a fractional portion of formatted output
minFractionDigits	Minimum number of digits to show in a fractional portion of formatted output
var	Exported scoped variable name that holds the formatted result as a String
scope	page|request|session|application (defaults to page scope). If scope is specified var must also be specified

Table 6.7: Attributes of <fmt:formatNumber> action.

values of a decimal number are displayed. There are any number of reasons that you want to format numbers. Let's look at what the actions have to offer, then we'll go through some usage samples.

6.22.1 <fmt:formatNumber> Action

The <fmt:formatNumber> action is used so that all numbers, currency, and percentages are represented correctly according to the current locale. The <fmt:formatNumber> action can be used without a body content by specifying the number in the value attribute. Alternatively, the value can be specified within the body content as the numeric value to be formatted. There is a whole host of attributes associated with this action as defined in Table 6.7.

When using this action, if it fails to determine a formatting locale, it uses Number.toString() as the output format. Also in the case of an exception occurring during the parsing of the value, the exception is caught and rethrown as a JspException. The message of the exception will contain the string value. The caught exception will provide the root cause of the exception.

When using the pattern attribute, the pattern symbols that can be used are those that are supported by the class java.text.DecimalFormat. For a complete list of these symbols, refer to the JavaDocs for that class.

If the numeric value is given as a string literal, it is first parsed into a java.lang.Number. If the string does not contain any decimal point, it is parsed using java.lang.Long.valueOf(). If there is a decimal point, java.lang.Double.valueOf() is used. The formatted result is output to the current JspWriter object. However, if the var attribute was specified, then the output is stored in the named scoped variable.

There are a number of attributes that are specific to formatting options. The groupingUsed attribute specifies whether the formatted output will contain any grouping separators. The same is true for how many digits or portions of a fractional should be displayed by using the various min/max attributes described in Table 6.7. When dealing with currency, the currency symbol of the formatting locale is used by default. However, this default can be overridden by using the currencySymbol or currencyCode attributes.

6.22.2 <fmt:parseNumber> Action

The <fmt:parseNumber> action takes a string representation of numbers, currencies, or percentages that have been formatted in a locale-specific, or custom, manner and parses the string correctly. Like the <fmt:formatNumber> action, the <fmt:parseNumber> can have its value specified in the value attribute or as the body content. Also like the <fmt:formatNumber> action, there are quite a few attributes that can be specified. The available attributes are defined in Table 6.8.

The numeric value to be parsed may be specified by using the value attribute. If value is not specified, it is read from the action's body content. The parse pattern to use may be specified with the pattern attribute. If the pattern attribute is not specified, then

Attribute	Description
value	String to be parsed
type	Specifies the type to use to parse the value attribute. Can be number|currency|percent. Defaults to number.
pattern	Custom formatting pattern used when parsing the string held in value.
parseLocale	A String or java.util.Locale that is to be used as the default formatting when parsing the string contained in value, or to which the pattern attribute (if specified) is applied to.
integerOnly	Specify whether just the integer portion of a value should be parsed.
var	An exported scoped variable that contains a parsed java.util.Number.
scope	Scope of var.

Table 6.8: Attributes of <fmt:parseNumber> action.

the appropriate pattern is looked up in the current locale. If a pattern string is specified using the pattern attribute, the syntax specified must be consistent with that defined by java.text.DecimalFormat. If looked up in a locale-dependent fashion, the parse pattern is determined via a combination of the type and parseLocale attributes. If the attribute pattern is null or empty, it is ignored. Depending on the value of the type attribute, the given numeric value is parsed as a number, currency, or a percentage.

The parse pattern for numbers, currencies, or percentages is determined by calling the appropriate method: getNumberInstance(), getCurrencyInstance(), or get PercentInstance(), in the java.text.NumberFormat class using the locale specified in the parseLocale attribute. If parseLocale is null or empty, it is treated as if it were missing. If parseLocale is missing, the current formatting locale is used as the parse locale.

When specifying a pattern, the formatting symbols in the pattern (such as decimal separator and grouping separator) are given by the parse locale. The integerOnly attribute specifies whether just the integer portion of the given value should be parsed.

As with the <fmt:formatNumber> action, if the var attribute is given, the parse result (which will be of type java.lang.Number) is stored in the named scoped variable. Otherwise it is output to the current JspWriter object using java.lang.Number.toString(). If the numeric string, whether defined in the value attribute or the body content, is null or empty, the scoped variable defined by attributes var and scope is removed. The reason for doing this is that it allows "empty" input to be distinguished from "invalid" input, which causes an exception.

Like <fmt:formatDate>, <fmt:formatNumber> can use a pattern. The pattern string used must follow the pattern syntax that is specified by the java.text.Decimal Format class. This syntax is taken from the JDK 1.4 javaDocs for the class and is shown in Table 6.9.

Let's take a closer look at the actions used to format numbers, along with some examples.

6.22.3 Formatting Numbers

There are quite a few attributes available to specify how to format numbers. You can either specify a value using the value attribute, or you can have the value defined in the <fmt:formatNumber> tag body. Using the tag body is helpful sometimes because you might have other custom actions that you have defined that need to do some type of processing on the value first. For example, we might have a custom action that looks up the current inventory of books given a specific author and returns that numeric value. We could make use of the action using <fmt:formatNumber> by doing the following:

```
<fmt:formatNumber>
    <jstlpg:currentInventory author="Spielman" />
<fmt:formatNumber>
```

Symbol	Location	Localized?	Meaning
0	Number	Yes	Digit
#	Number	Yes	Digit, zero shows as absent
.	Number	Yes	Decimal separator or monetary decimal separator
-	Number	Yes	Minus sign
,	Number	Yes	Grouping separator
E	Number	Yes	Separates mantissa and exponent in scientific notation. Need not be quoted in prefix or suffix.
;	Subpattern boundary	Yes	Separates positive and negative subpatterns
%	Prefix or suffix	Yes	Multiply by 100 and show as percentage.
\u2030	Prefix or suffix	Yes	Multiply by 1000 and show as per mille.
\u00A4	Prefix or suffix	No	Currency sign, replaced by currency symbol. If doubled, replaced by international currency symbol. If present in a pattern, the monetary decimal separator is used instead of the decimal separator.
'	Prefix or suffix	No	Used to quote special characters in a prefix or suffix, for example, “‘##’”formats 123 to “#123”. To create a single quote itself, use two in a row: “# o”clock”.

Table 6.9: Number pattern syntax.

This would use all of the default values of <fmt:formatNumber>, in addition to using the current locale. If we already had the value in a defined variable, we could also just specify it in the value attribute as in the next line and it would print to the current JspWriter:

```
<fmt:formatNumber value="${currentInventory}" />
```

But what if we want to use this formatted value somewhere else? We can easily store it away using the var attribute so that we can do so. This is shown in Example 6.9.

Example 6.9 Storing a Formatted Number

```
<fmt:formatNumber value="${currentInventory}" var="inventoryLevel" />
<c:if test="${currentInventory < 10}" >
Order your copy now. There are only
<c:out value="${inventoryLevel}" /> books left!
</c:if>
```

The benefit of doing the formatting this way instead of just using the <c:out> to print the number value arises because the locale being used by the browser will affect how formatting is done. This is all handled for you in the JSTL, so you don't have to worry about values being displayed out of character for the country they are being used in.

This is true whether we are talking about numbers, currency, or percentage values. In fact, if you are dealing with currency, the JSTL will actually massage the values into the appropriate format for the locale. For example, if we have a value given as 19.9512, we would want the value to read correctly for whatever currency is in question, right down to its being displayed with the right decimal places. Keep in mind that the JSTL isn't a currency converter, so when we are displaying a value, it's just that: a value. The value displayed has nothing to do with correctness. If $19.95 US is not the correct amount for translation from another currency, the JSTL won't catch those errors. Garbage in, garbage out. The code is shown in Example 6.10 and the screen shot is shown in Figure 6.13.

Example 6.10 Displaying Currency

```
<c:set var="amount" value="${19.9512}" />
The value <c:out value="${amount}" /> as it's displayed by various
countries:
<br/>
The currency in US is: <fmt:formatNumber value="${amount}"
                                          type="currency" />
<br/>
<fmt:setLocale value="EN_GB" />
The currency in Great Britain is: <fmt:formatNumber
  value="${amount}" type="currency" />
</fmt:setLocale>
```

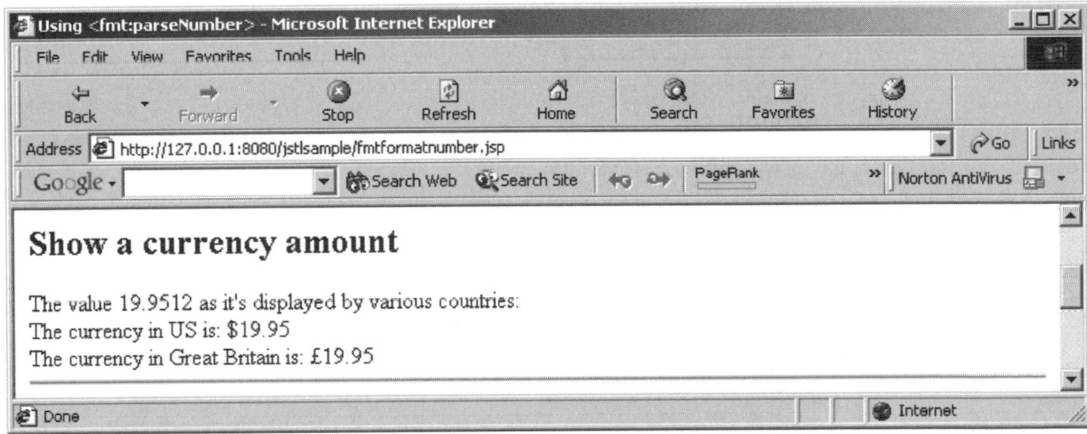

Figure 6.13: Displaying currency.

By using the various attributes available in this action, you can specify the minimum and maximum digits you want to display for both the integer and fraction portion of the number. You can also define if you want digits grouped together. This can make large numbers easier to read.

Let's look at a couple of different examples. For instance, take a random number like 299792458.[21] We can use this number and display it in any number of ways. Using

```
<fmt:formatNumber value="${speedOfLight}" maxIntegerDigits="7"
                  minIntegerDigits="3" />
```

we'd get 9,792,458 displayed. If we turned the grouping off as in

```
<fmt:formatNumber value="${speedOfLight}"
                  groupingUsed="false" />
```

we'd get an output of 299792458. If we reset our value as

```
<c:set var="speedOfLight" value="29979.2458" />
```

and specified

```
<fmt:formatNumber value="${speedOfLight}" maxIntegerDigits="5"
                  minIntegerDigits="1" maxFractionDigits
                  ="3" minFractionDigits="1"/>
```

we'd see an output of 29,979.246. Notice that the third digit of the fraction has been rounded up for us. In addition, if our minimum fraction amount was greater than the value we had, our fraction would be padded with zeros. Using the min/max variations can be very helpful when doing column displays, but keep in mind that you need to make sure your min and max numbers fit your application. You don't want to be displaying too much information for people, but at the same time you don't want important information chopped off. I know I wouldn't want my online banking program to have a maxIntegerDigit limit of 5 on my checking account just so the columns lined up nicely for me. I'd like a much more optimistic value, like 6 or 7. Figure 6.14 shows all of what we've just done in the browser for easy reading.

Aside from displaying currency or other attribute options, we can also create patterns that can be used to format numbers exactly as we'd like. Using the syntax in Table 6.9, we'll define a couple of patterns to get a sense of how they affect the display. This is shown in Figure 6.15. For more details about all of the available options that can be taken advantage of for formatting, consult the javaDoc for `java.text.DecimalFormat`.

---

[21] OK, so maybe it's not so random. Actually, it's the speed of light in vacuum, which is exactly 299,792,458 m/s (meters per second). And you thought you'd just be learning about the JSTL in this book...

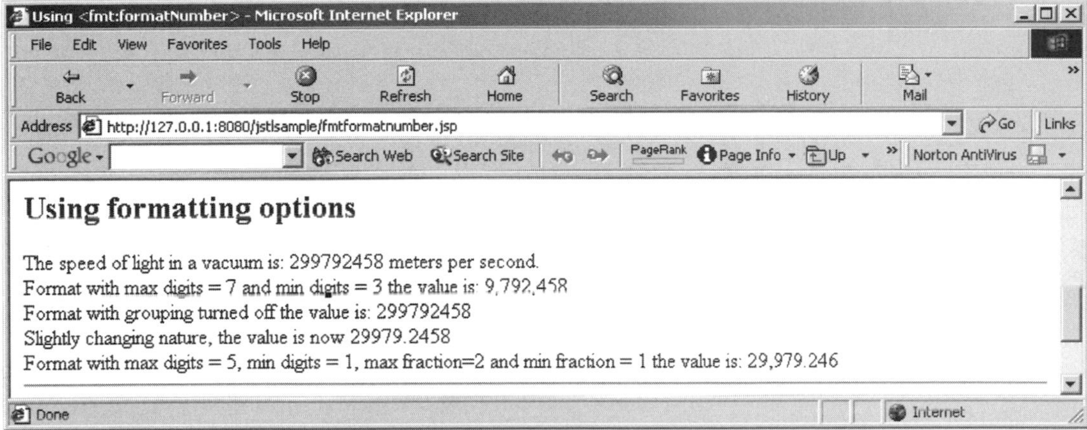

Figure 6.14: Using <fmt:formatNumber> attributes.

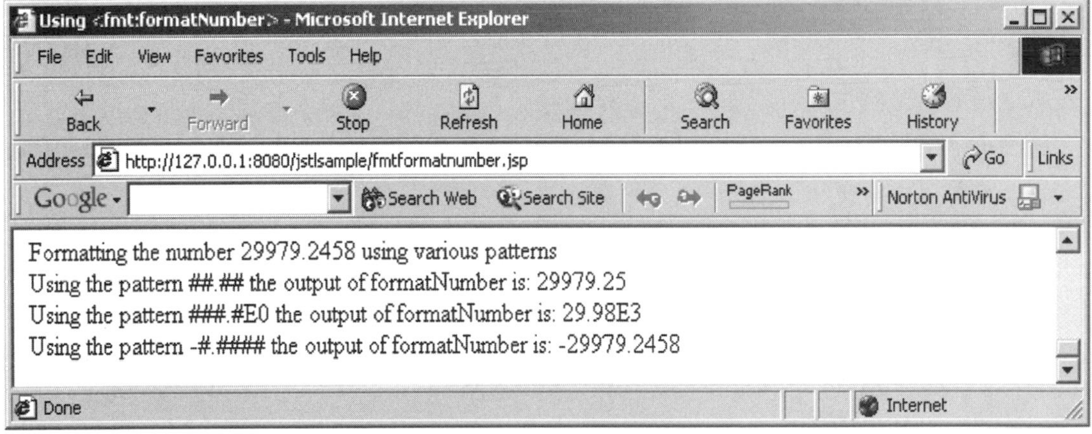

Figure 6.15: Display of "using" patterns.

6.22.4 Parsing Numbers

Just as with dates, we need the ability to parse numbers. Parsing numbers really follows the same principles and practices that we've already covered for dates. The difference is that we're using the patterns for numbers instead of the pattern syntax for dates. If you have forms or XML files that have data included in them, and you need to get a number from one format to another, you use the `<fmt:parseNumber>` action. Using `<fmt:parseNumber>`

we can get a value from a string representation to a numeric one. Having a string representation of a number is fairly common. This can happen if you have values that are coming from a database or from a user form as an input parameter. There might be calculations that you need to do and obviously you can't do them if the values are in string format.

The <fmt:parseNumber> works in a similar fashion to the <fmt:formatNumber>. The value we are interested in can be described by the value attribute or as the body of the action. <fmt:parseNumber> will use the notation that is appropriate for the default locale being used by the browser. This becomes valuable when dealing with user input so that, by default, the parse is based on how the user would likely enter the values. For example, if I have a form field that asks me to enter "How many feet above sea level is Denver, CO?" and I enter 5,280 as a value in my text box, and someone in France enters 5 280, they would both be parsed correctly by default. This is a key feature of the parsing actions provided in the JSTL as it eliminates the need for the page author to worry about dealing with the hair-pulling parsing code we've all written at some point in our life to make sure numbers and dates appeared in the correct format.

Using the various attributes available to <fmt:parseNumber> you can alter the way the parse is done. For example, using the integerOnly attribute set to true allows for any fractional part of a parse to be discarded. We might have an input parameter coming from a user detailing how many books they want to order. Well, if they put in 5.5, we don't want to ship them half a book. We can take care of this in the parse of the value to make sure that we only have whole numbers by doing

```
<fmt:parseNumber value="${currentOrder}" integerOnly="true" />
```

The value we got back would be 5.

Another useful area of the <fmt:parseNumber> action is that we can indicate what locale should be used for a parse, not necessarily the default. Having a specified locale is good when we're dealing with data values that might be coming from various countries. For example, if we know that each night we need to read an XML file generated from each of our distribution centers in four different countries, we can make sure that the parse Locale is always set to the country we are reading the data from so that we can import the information automatically.

We've already talked about how to use the decimal pattern syntax, so I won't spend time on it again here. Basically, you can define the various patterns that you want to use to parse the number. Of course, as in our previous Example 6.7, you want to have a <c:catch> around the parse in case an exception is thrown.

6.23 Encoding the Client Response

The last item to consider when doing I18N actions is how the response is returned to the client. The response needs to be encoded with the correct locale setting so that the browser renders it correctly. The responsibility for setting the response's locale lies with the I18N action. The only exception to this is if the localization context does not have a locale set.

The way the action sets the locale is by calling the ServletResponse.setLocale() and SerlvetResponse.setContentType() methods with the locale that is currently set in the localization context. These must be called before the ServletResponse.getWriter() is called because the value of the locale and charset affects the construction of the JspWriter.

There are a number of actions that can call the setLocale() method. When using the <fmt:setLocale> action, the setLocale() method is always called. Some of the other actions that might call it are

- <fmt:bundle>
- <fmt:setBundle>
- A <fmt:message> that establishes an I18N localization context
- Any formatting action that establishes a formatting locale on its own

Once sessions are enabled, and after an action has called ServletResponse.setLocale(), the action must determine the character encoding associated with the response locale (by calling ServletResponse.getCharacterEncoding()) and store it in the session scoped JSTL variable javax.servlet.jsp.jstl.fmt.request.charset. This attribute is used to set the response encoding to be the same as the request encoding. It is used by the <fmt:requestEncoding> action.

The <fmt:requestEncoding> action is used to set the request encoding to be the same as the encoding used for the response. This action may be used to set the request's character encoding in order to be able to correctly decode request parameter values whose encoding is different from ISO-8859-1, which is the default value. Primarily this action is needed because most browsers fail to follow the HTTP specification that includes a Content-Type header in their requests. For example if you had parameters coming in using UTF-8 encoding, you'd use the following code on the JSP before trying to access any of the parameters:

```
<fmt:requestEncoding value="UTF-8"/>
```

Otherwise the parameters would not be decoded correctly and would be displayed as garbage characters.

If the character encoding of the request parameters is not known in advance, the value attribute must not be specified. This will give the action a chance to resolve the charset. In this case, the <fmt:requestEncoding> action first checks if there is a charset defined in the request Content-Type header. If not, it uses the character encoding from the javax.servlet.jsp.jstl.fmt.request.charset scoped variable. This variable appears in session scope. If this scoped variable is not found, the default character encoding (ISO-8859-1) is used.

6.24 Summary

After completing this chapter you should feel like you can speak four languages fluently. Failing that, you should at least have a thorough understanding of all that is involved in creating internationalized applications.

We covered a lot of material in this chapter. You can now use all of the JSTL actions related to I18N and L10N so that your application can support whichever type of architecture it requires for your international clients.

chapter 7

SQL Tag Library Using the SQL Actions

The JSTL includes a number of actions that provide a mechanism for interacting with databases. The previous sentence should, at a very minimum, send up a red flag in your architectural visions. One might ask, "Do I really want to be able to perform SQL actions such as queries, updates, and transactions from my JSP? Isn't that business logic that belongs in the model?" The answer is yes. Yes, yes, yes. To follow a Model-View-Controller (MVC) architecture, which is the predominant design pattern used in building web applications today, you definitely want to keep your model information in your business logic. This means that you *don't* want it in your JSPs. Why then are these actions even provided in the JSTL? Good question and one that I've discussed with various members of the JSR-53 expert group. The reason is the "C" for community in the Java Community Process (JCP). The community has asked for it, the community has gotten it.

Many feel that for prototyping, small-scale, and/or very simple applications, or if you just don't have the engineering staff to implement a full MVC model, then the SQL actions might prove useful. While I can (barely) see the point being made for use of the SQL actions for prototyping or small-scale applications, I can't ever validate the argument that you just don't have the time to implement an MVC model correctly. If that is the one and only reason why you are choosing to use the SQL actions, then I suggest that you investigate using such frameworks as Struts which is part of the Jakarta projects and can be found at *http://jakarta.apache.org/struts/index.html*. Struts is an MVC framework that can be learned quickly and will provide a much cleaner architecture than having Model information located throughout your JSPs. For a complete discussion on Struts along with a sample application, refer to *The Struts Framework: Practical Guide for Java Programmers*, another title in the Morgan Kaufmann Practical Guide series.

If you are careful about how you code your SQL actions, it should be easy enough to pull out the code and put it into classes that represent the Model interaction at a later point. I am not going to go into the various design patterns that can be applied for doing business or integration tier access. But if you consider using the SQL actions in your application, it would be wise at least to familiarize yourself with such common patterns as Transfer Objects,[22] JDBC for Reading, Data Transfer Object (DTO) Factory, Data Transfer Hashmap, and Data Transfer Rowset. Doing so may help you avoid embedding the business logic/data access into your JSPs so deeply that you are left with a tangled mess.

With that said, I don't consider it an architectural flaw to have the SQL actions included in the JSTL. However, I do consider it an architectural flaw to use them in your application development. It is up to the page author and application architect to make sure that the design patterns are being adhered to correctly, if not for the maintenance issue of the application then for the practice of good engineering. However, since these actions are included in the JSTL, I must make sure you understand them and their features so that you can make an informed decision.

The JSTL SQL actions provide functionality that allows for:

- Making database queries
- Accessing query results
- Performing database modifications
- Database transactions

What all of the SQL actions have in common is that they work against a specific data source. Let's examine how the data source is set up and configured. We'll then go through the other configuration settings as well as the available interfaces. Then we'll a look at how to use the actions in situations where their use would be appropriate.

7.1 The Available <SQL> Actions

There are six actions provided in this tag library:

- `<sql:setDataSource>` for exporting a variable that defines a data source
- `<sql:query>` for querying to the database
- `<sql:update>` for updating the database
- `<sql:transaction>` for establishing a transaction context for doing queries and updates
- `<sql:param>` for setting parameter markers ("?") used in SQL statements.

[22]Value Objects are now called Transfer Objects (TOs) in Sun's core J2EE Patterns repository, while The Server Side website (*www.theserverside.com*) calls them Data Transfer Objects (DTOs).

- <sql:dateParam> for setting parameter markers ("?") of type java.util.Date in SQL statements.

Let's look at each action in more detail.

7.2 Working with the Data Source

SQL actions operate on a data source. A data source is an implementation of the javax.sql.DataSource interface and allows for the retrieval of a connection, or connections, to a specific database or data source. Most JDBC functionality is accomplished by providing the implementation of various interfaces. The database driver does this. Each driver vendor implements the core features of the JDBC functionality. This includes objects in the java.sql package such as Connection, Statement and ResultSet. Other interfaces in the javax.sql package might also be implemented, but it's up to the driver vendor to do so.

The Connection object acts as a factory for Statement objects. Statement objects are what gives you the ability to submit a SQL command to the database. Using the DataSource object, within the context of a java.sql.Connection object, the SQL statements are executed against the data source using the connection. The appropriate result set or return value is then returned. While most of this is handled under the covers for you in the SQL action implementation, I thought it would be good to give you a flavor for what is actually happening. If you want more details on how the innards of JDBC implementations work, there are lots of resources out there. One such reference is the *JDBC: Practical Guide for Java Programmers* (Morgan Kaufmann).

7.2.1 <sql:setDataSource>

The <sql:setDataSource> is used to export a data source either as a scoped variable or as the javax.servlet.jsp.jstl.sql.dataSource data source configuration variable. Using the var and scope attributes, the data source specified (either as a DataSource object or as a String) is exported. If no var is specified, the data source is exported in the javax.servlet.jsp.jstl.sql.dataSource configuration variable.

The data source may be specified by using the dataSource attribute. This can be specified as a DataSource object, as a Java Naming and Directory Interface (JNDI) relative path, or using a JDBC parameters string. If you don't want to use the dataSource attribute, it is also possible to specify the data source by using the four JDBC parameter attributes. All four of the parameters are just String types. These attributes are driver, url, user, and password. Using the JDBC attributes is just an easier way to configure the data source than specifying the values in the string syntax for the dataSource attribute. In Example 7.1 we see how to specify a data source using the JDBC parameters. We are making this data source available as an exported variable called datasource. This can then be used by other actions if they want to use this particular data source, as shown by the <sql:query> action.

Example 7.1 Setting a Data Source

```
<sql:setDataSource var="datasource"
                   driver="org.gjt.mm.mysql.driver"
                   url="jdbc:mysql://localhost/db"
                   user="guest"
                   password="guest"/>
<sql:query datasource="${datasource}"… />
```

7.3 Configuring a Data Source

There are two ways that a data source can be configured: through an attribute or through a configuration setting. Using the dataSource attribute of the SQL actions, it is possible to explicitly configure the data source for the action.

If all SQL actions are going to use the same data source, it is more convenient to set the data source by using the configuration setting javax.servlet.jsp.jstl.sql.dataSource. The constant Config.SQL_DATA_SOURCE can be used to refer to this configuration setting. The dataSource can be specified as either a String or javax.sql.DataSource. When using the configuration setting, there are two ways a data source can be specified as a string. The first way is through a JNDI relative path, assuming a container supporting JNDI. For example, with the absolute JNDI resource path java:comp/env/jdbc/myDatabase, the JNDI relative path to the data source resource would simply be jdbc/myDatabase, given that java:comp/env is the standard JNDI root for a J2EE application.

The second way is by specifying the parameters needed by the JDBC Driver Manager class, using the syntax url[,[driver][,[user][,password]]]. For example,

```
jdbc:mysql://localhost/,org.gjt.mm.mysql.Driver
```

In this case, the database doesn't require a user name or password. It's probably not the way you would want a production database, but to keep our sample simple it's fine. If the "," or "\" character occurs in any of the JDBC parameters, it can be escaped by a preceding "\".

The JDBC java.sql.DriverManager class provides a way to manage all drivers, but it isn't very efficient. It is best to use the DriverManager during prototyping. Which, come to think of it, is really the only time you should be using the SQL actions anyway. Remember that you are better off using a DataSource object that provides connection management features because connection management is one of the most expensive areas of performance when dealing with the database.

7.4 Using a Data Source

Now that we've seen how to configure a data source, let's take a look at how it actually gets used with the various SQL actions. The actions that use the data source to access a database are the <sql:query>, <sql:update>, and <sql:transaction>.

A reference to the data source is obtained according to the following algorithm. This algorithm will be implemented by the application vendor supporting the JSTL. However, I feel that it's important to understand how it works so that you know what you can expect when dealing with data sources settings.

First, if the datasource attribute is specified in the action itself, then use that. Otherwise, get the configuration setting associated with javax.servlet.jsp.jstl.sql.dataSource using the method find() in the Config class. If the value found is not null, then use it. Keep in mind that the value of the configuration setting can be defined as either a DataSource object or a String. If it's a DataSource object, then this is the data source that is used by the action. Otherwise there is still some work to be done. For a String value, it is assumed that it is a JNDI relative path. The data source is retrieved from the container's JNDI naming context by concatenating the specified relative path to the J2EE defined root. The J2EE defined root is java:comp/env/.

If the JNDI lookup fails, then it is assumed that the string specifies JDBC parameters. This is the syntax we looked at in Example 7.1 that defines the URL, driver, username, and password. If a driver is specified then make sure that the driver is loaded. The data source is then accessed by the named URL through the DriverManager class. Empty strings are used if no user or password is specified. If we get to this point and still don't have a data source, then we are out of luck and an exception is thrown. If a data source isn't specified in either the attribute or the configuration variable, then an exception is thrown. You can't say we didn't try.

We should gain a performance advantage when dealing with data sources from the application vendor's implementations. An implementation does not need to create new objects each time a SQL action is called. It may reuse objects that it previously created for identical arguments.

7.5 Maxrows Configuration Setting

Working with result sets can be time consuming. If you have a very large result set being returned from a query, it's possible that your users can be sitting at their browsers twiddling their thumbs, so it's common to limit the number of rows returned on a query. This prevents using unnecessary resources on the server box, but more importantly it allows you to tune your application more efficiently so that your users don't surf to another site.

The maximum number of rows to be included in a query result is specified by the variable named javax.servlet.jsp.jstl.sql.maxRows. This variable can be referenced by using the constant Config.SQL_MAX_ROWS. The value of this variable is wrapped in an

Integer object that must be greater than or equal to −1. The maxRows can be set from the Config class or from the deployment descriptor. If the maximum number of rows is not specified or is −1, it means that there is no limit on the result set. If you are not using the max rows, you'd best know for sure that you are not going to be returning thousands of records. You will find your memory consumption to be extremely high if you are. Having runaway queries definitely leads to some very unhappy users, not to mention the DBA.

7.6 Configuring and Using a Data Source

The data source needs to be configured somewhere when doing any type of database access. Typically this is handled in the backend Java code so that a JSP author doesn't really need to worry about it. However, if the data access is moved into the JSP, you must have a way to set the data source appropriately so that the various database accesses take place against the correct data source. Using the <sql:setDataSource> is one way to accomplish this. The other way is to have a default data source setup using the configuration setting. The configuration setting can be defined in the web.xml file or it can be set using the Config.set() method. Example 7.2 shows how to set the configuration in the web.xml file. This sample is using the MySQL database and drivers. If you are using a different database, you will have to take a look at the documentation and determine the URL, driver, and appropriate username/password to use.

Example 7.2 Setting the Data Source in the web.xml

```
<context-param>
      <param-name>javax.servlet.jsp.jstl.sql.dataSource
      </param-name>
      <param-value>
           jdbc:mysql://localhost/jstlbook,org.gjt.mm.mysql.Driver
      </param-value>
</context-param>
```

If the dataSource is set in the web.xml file, then it will apply to all SQL actions that need to reference a data source. It is possible to override the default data source by using a var with <sql:setDataSource> and setting it for a specific scope. As you can see, there are a number of ways to set up the data source that you want to use with your actions.

While it is fairly easy to set up data sources to various databases and use the appropriate one in your actions, you'll want to be aware of the performance issues. It is standard practice when writing database access business logic that you implement (or use someone else's implementation of) a connection pool. A connection pool allows for a small number of connections to be open to a database at the same time and then shares the connections among numerous clients. Using a connection pool decreases the amount of time spent establishing the connection. Connection establishment is one of the highest performance hits there is in application development.

When using <sql:setDataSource>, no connection pooling takes place. This means that each and every time you set a data source, a new connection is established with the database. This is more than likely not something that you want in your high-speed application. But, for that matter, if you are concerned with the application performance, then it probably means that your application should not be using the SQL actions in the JSPs to start with; rather you should be implementing a more standard MVC model application.

To use <sql:setDataSource> we can either use the datasource attribute to access an already defined data source, or use the JDBC required parameters. The JDBC parameters include a required URL, a driver, username, and password. If you're using the datasource attribute and you are working with a J2EE container that supports JNDI, you can use the JNDI name like jdbc/jstlbook. The code shown in Example 7.2 can be described using the <sql:setDataSource> as shown in Example 7.3. It is possible then to access the data source using the named var described in the <sql:setDataSource> action from any other action that requires it. Accessing the named var is demonstrated with the <sql:update> action.

Example 7.3 Setting and Using a Data Source with <sql:setDataSource>

```
<sql:setDataSource var="datasource"
                   scope="application"
                   driver="org.gjt.mm.mysql.Driver"
                   url="jdbc:mysql://localhost/jstlbook"/>

<sql:update dataSource="${datasource}" sql="
 CREATE TABLE IF NOT EXISTS books (title VARCHAR(75),
                                   author VARCHAR(25),
                                   edition INTEGER,
                                   pubdate TIMESTAMP(8))">
</sql:update>
```

7.7 How to Modify Data

Before you can do anything interesting with data, there must *be* data. Using the <sql:update> action it's possible to create, update, and delete data. I want to stress (again) that it is not recommended to do data modifications directly from a JSP file. This type of functionality usually rests in the hands of a Java programmer who is supplying a JavaBean to the JSP author. The JavaBean accesses the business logic methods that takes care of doing the data manipulation. In the circumstances where you absolutely want to do data modifications from your JSP, <sql:update> is your action.

7.7.1 <sql:update> Action

The <sql:update> action is used to execute SQL insert, update, or delete statements. It is also possible to perform a SQL statement that returns nothing, like a DDL statement. The SQL statement can be specified either by using the sql attribute or by providing the statement in the action's body content. Like <sql:query>, <sql:update> can have parameter markers within the SQL statement. The parameter values are then provided with the <sql:param> action. The connection to the database is handled the same way that it is handled for <sql:query>. If the datasource attribute is specified for the action, then the <sql:update> cannot be nested within a <sql:transaction>.

Using the var attribute that we are familiar with by now, a scoped variable can be specified to store the result of the <sql:update> action. The scope attribute is only used when a var attribute is specified. The result is a java.lang.Integer and will be the number of rows that were affected by the update. Zero is returned if no rows were affected and for any SQL statement that returns nothing (such as SQL DDL statements). This is the same behavior you would expect if you used the executeUpdate() method of the JDBC class Statement.

Let's take a look at how the <sql:update> action would be used. In Example 7.4, we specify a datasource as well as request scoped variable called updateResult. The value of updateResult will be how many rows were affected on the execution of this update. In this case, the value of updateResult will be 1.

Example 7.4 Using <sql:update>

```
<sql:update dataSource="$(datasource)" var="updateResult"
          scope="request">
     UPDATE book SET Title = 'JSTL First Edition' WHERE
     author = 'Spielman'
</sql:update>
```

If no datasource attribute is specified, then you use the one that is currently set by the configuration setting or that was set by a <sql:setDataSource> action. If a data source has not been correctly set by one of the appropriate methods, you will get an exception stack trace that looks a lot like Figure 7.1.

If you are using a specific data source for the <sql:update> action, you cannot have the action nested within a <sql:transaction>. This makes sense because you can't have transactions spanning multiple data sources. We've seen an example of how to use the <sql:update> action using a CREATE in Example 7.2, so let's see what else we can do with

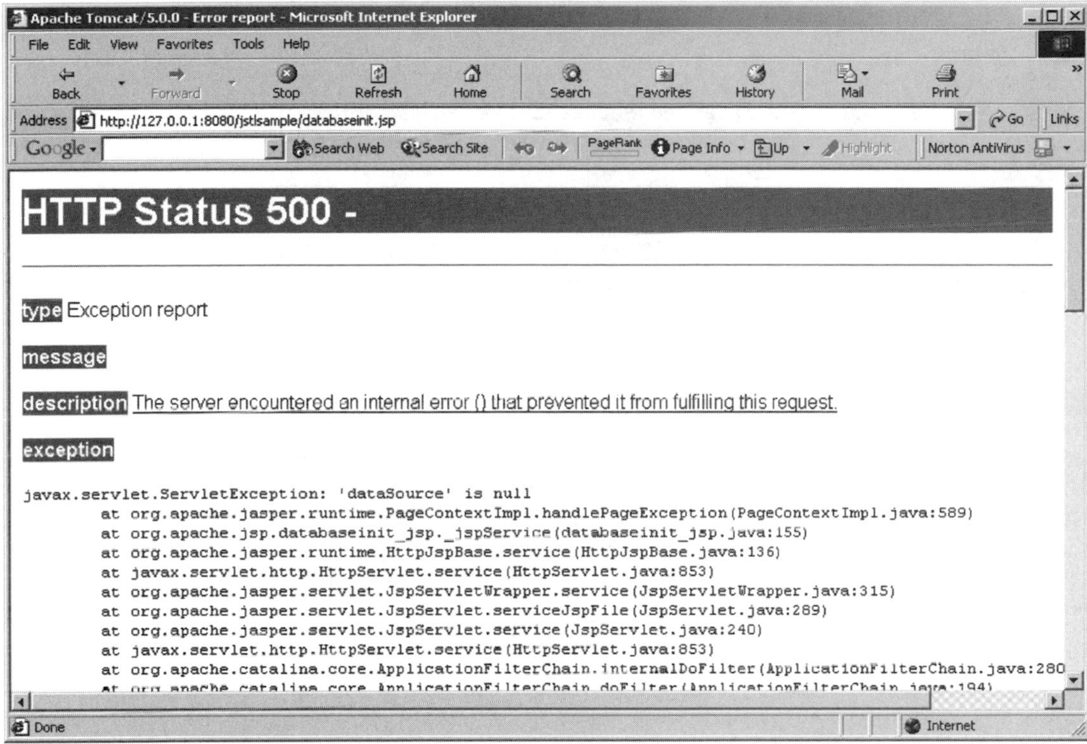

Figure 7.1: Lacking a data source.

<sql:update>. There are two points of interest that are worth mentioning: using the var and how to actually pass parameters to SQL statements.

7.7.2 How to Use var with <sql:update>

When doing any type of data modification, a value is returned that indicates how many rows in the data source were affected. The CREATE sample would return a 0 because no rows were actually affected; however, an INSERT, DELETE, or UPDATE might cause 0 or more rows to be affected. Having the value of affected rows can be quite useful if you are trying to determine logic further down in your JSP based on the results of the data modification. For example, if we inserted a row as shown in Example 7.5, we would get a value of 1 back and could then test for a successful insert.

Example 7.5 Inserting Data Using var

```
<sql:update var="result" sql="INSERT INTO books (title, author,
  edition, pubdate) values('JSTL: Practical Guide for Java
```

```
  Programmers','Spielman',1,'12/1/03')">
</sql:update>
<c:if test="${result == 1}" >
          Your data was inserted successfully!
</c:if>
```

While an INSERT might only affect 1 row, a DELETE or UPDATE might affect many rows. Using the var value can help you tailor your JSP if you want to display messages accordingly.

7.8 Interfaces and Classes

There are two interfaces (Result and SQLExecutionTag) and one class (ResultSupport) provided in the JSTL for the SQL actions. These are used in the implementation of various actions found in the SQL tag library. If you are writing your own custom actions, you might be interested in them. I want to cover these interfaces and the class so that we can talk about the SQL actions that make use of result sets. Let's take an initial look at what each has to offer.

7.8.1 Result Interface

The Result interface is found in the javax.servlet.jsp.jstl.sql package. This interface represents the result of a <sql:query> action. It provides access to the following information in the query results:

- The result rows
- The column names
- The number of rows in the result
- An indication whether the rows returned represent the complete result or just a subset that is limited by a maximum row setting

Table 7.1 gives a description of the available methods and the return value for each one.

7.8.2 SQLExecutionTag Interface

This interface allows the tag handlers implementing it to receive values for parameter markers ("?") in their SQL statements. This interface is found in the javax.servlet.jsp.jstl.sql package. The SQLExecutionTag interface is exposed so that new custom parameter actions that you might write may retrieve their parameters from

Method	Description	Return value
getRows()	Returns the result of the query as an array of SortedMap objects. Each item of the array represents a specific row in the query result.	java.util. SortedMap[]
getRowsByIndex()	Returns the result of the query as an array of arrays. The first array dimension represents a specific row in the query result. The array elements for each row are: Object instances of the Java type corresponding to the mapping between column types and Java types defined by the JDBC specification when the ResultSet.getObject() method is used.	Object[][]
getColumnNames()	The names of the columns in the result. The order of the names in the array matches the order in which columns are returned in method getRowsByIndex().	String[]
getRowCount()	The number of rows in the result.	int
isLimitedByMaxRows()	True if the query was limited by a maximum row setting.	boolean

Table 7.1: Result interface method description.

Method	Description	Return value
addSQLParameter(Object value)	Adds a PreparedStatement parameter value.	void

Table 7.2: SQLExecutionTag interface method descriptions.

any source and process them before substituting them for a parameter marker in the SQL statement of the enclosing SQLExecutionTag action. This interface is implemented by both <sql:query> and <sql:update>.

The addSQLParameter() method of this interface is called by nested parameter actions (such as <sql:param>) to substitute PreparedStatement parameter values for "?" parameter markers in the SQL statement of the enclosing SQLExecutionTag action. When implementing this interface, you must keep track of the index of the parameter values being added. The methods available in the SQLExectionTag are shown in Table 7.2.

7.8.3 ResultSupport Class

The ResultSupport class is found in the javax.servlet.jsp.jstl.sql package. This is a support class that allows for the creation of javax.servlet.jsp.jstl.sql.Result objects from source java.sql.ResultSet objects. Working with Result objects is much easier for a page author because it allows for access and manipulation of data from a SQL query. There are two possible ways to call the toResult() method:

- public static Result toResult(java.sql.ResultSet rs) to take a ResultSet and convert it to a Result.
- public static Result toResult(java.sql.ResultSet rs, int maxRows), which will convert maxRows of a ResultSet to a Result.

7.9 Finding What You Need with <sql:query>

The <sql:update> allows you to make updates, but sometimes you just want to get data. The <sql:query> action takes care of this for you. The attributes are similar to those that we've already talked about for <sql:update>. The same logic applies for datasource, sql, var, and scope, but there are two additional attributes specific to the <sql:query>. These are maxRows and startRow. MaxRows is another configuration setting, like datasource. Using the maxRows setting prevents JSP authors from writing runaway queries. We've all, on one occasion or another, had the pleasure of watching a database grind to its knees, or watched the memory on a machine go down the tubes. Usually this is because of a query that was only supposed to return 10 rows, but which is now somehow returning 10,000 rows. The maxRows will prevent these types of poorly conceived queries from happening. If using the configuration setting, you can set it up in the web.xml as shown in Example 7.6.

Example 7.6 Setting maxRows in web.xml

```
<context-param>
      <param-name>javax.servlet.jsp.jstl.sql.maxRows</param-name>
      <param-value>100</param-value>
</context-param>
```

If you specify the maxRows attribute to the <sql:query>, it will override any setting in the web.xml. The query results will return only up to the number of maxRows specified. Using a positive integer to specify startRow, the value tells the query where to start storing results. Using a zero-based index (like most of Java), a startRow value of 1 is actually the second element in the result. Using startRow can be quite helpful when paging through large result sets. If the startRow value is greater then the size of the result set, then nothing will be returned from the query.

While it is not required to use the maxRows and the startRow together, it can be helpful to do so. This combination gives you more control over what gets returned in your result set. The code in Example 7.7 shows how to use both values.

If we had a result set of 8 rows, only 5 would be returned, starting at index 1. Therefore, we would get rows 1–5, but not row 0. Keep in mind that if the startRow is higher then the actual number of rows in the result set, you will get an empty result set. We are including the SQL statement as part of the body content, but it could just as well have been defined in the sql attribute of the action.

Example 7.7 Combining maxRows and startRow

```
<sql:query var="bookList" dataSource="${datasource}"
          maxRows="5" startRow="1">
     SELECT * FROM books WHERE title LIKE 'J%' ORDER BY author
</sql:query>
```

7.9.1 <sql:query> Action

No mystery here, the <sql:query> action is used to query a database. There are a number of attributes that are used with this action. It is possible to specify a data source by using the dataSource attribute. If present, it will override the default data source using the algorithm we talked about in "Configuring a Data Source", Section 7.3. If the dataSource is null after the algorithm, then a JspException is thrown. If a dataSource is specified, then the <sql:query> action must be specified inside of a <sql:transaction> action. We will talk about the <sql:transaction> in a minute.

A single result set is returned from a query. If the query produces no results, an empty Result object (of size zero) is returned. This would be the case for a SQL statement that contained an INSERT, DELETE, UPDATE, or any SQL statement that returns nothing such as a SQL DDL statement. Returning an object of size zero is consistent with the way return values are handled by the executeUpdate() method of the JDBC Statement class. This result set contains rows of data if there are results. The data is then stored in a scoped variable that is defined by the var and scope attributes. The default scope is page.

Obviously, there must be a way to specify the SQL query to be used. This can be done by using the sql attribute, or by including the SQL statement in the action's body content. The code in Example 7.8 and that in Example 7.9 do exactly the same thing.

Example 7.8 SQL Defined in Attribute

```
<sql:query sql="SELECT * FROM books WHERE title = 'JSTL' ORDER BY author"
          var="titles" dataSource="${datasource}" >
</sql:query>
```

Example 7.9 SQL in Body Content

```
<sql:query var="titles" dataSource="${datasource}" >
SELECT * FROM books WHERE title = 'JSTL' ORDER BY author
</sql:query>
```

7.10 Passing Parameters to SQL Statements

When doing queries or data modification, the chances are pretty high that you are going to want to pass some parameters to the SQL statements. JSTL handles this with the <sql:param> action. <sql:param> can be nested in a <sql:update> or a <sql:query> action.

A query can contain parameter markers. These markers are indicated by using a "?" in the query. Using parameter markers identifies JDBC PreparedStatement parameters. The way to supply parameters is by using a nested <sql:param> parameter action. One parameter action is required for each parameter in the SQL statement. The actual mechanism used for this parametric replacement is the implementation of the SQL ExecutionTag interface. If we wanted to have the title as a parameter to the query, we could do so as shown in Example 7.10. Just note that you might need to escape characters properly in the query if required. This is done using the "\" (backslash, without the quotes) before the character you need to escape.

Example 7.10 Supply a Parameter in a Query

```
<sql:query sql="SELECT * FROM books WHERE title = ? ORDER BY author"
         var="titles" dataSource="${datasource}" >
     <sql:param value="${titleSelected}"/>

</sql:query>
```

We have already talked about the MaxRows configuration setting. Let's see how it is used in the <sql:query> action along with the maxRows attribute. If the maxRows attribute is specified, then that value takes precedence over the value specified in the configuration setting. It is commonplace that the maxRows and startRow attribute are used together. The startRow is used to specify the index of the first row to be included in the Result object returned by the action. We then specify maxRows of 5 and a startRow of 7 in Example 7.11.

Example 7.11 Query Using maxRows and startRow

```
<sql:query sql="SELECT * FROM books WHERE title = 'JSTL' ORDER BY
               author" var="titles" dataSource="${datasource}"
```

```
        maxRows="5"
        startRow="7" >
</sql:query>
```

The returned Result object will start with the row at index 7. The rows 0 through 6 that were contained in the result set by the original query will be skipped over. All remaining rows of the original query will be included, up to the number specified by the maxRows value. Note that if maxRows is not specified as an attribute, or as a configuration setting configured, or is equal to –1, then all rows are returned from the database. The Result object would contain the rows startRow + maxRows.

If you are using startRow, keep in mind that you probably want to make sure that the order of rows remains consistent. The best way to do this is to use an order by clause in your SQL statement. Otherwise, not all Relational Database Management System (RDBMS) implementations are the same and you might get different results on different databases.

Let's go into a more detailed example. Say that you have a search form with a text box called "title". You want to use the title as a parameter to a query. Such code for a form is shown in Example 7.12. The HTML included is just for better formatting in the browser.

Example 7.12 Simple Form with Text Box

```
<form action="doquery.jsp" method="post">
<table>
<tr>
<td>book title:<td><td><input type="text" name="title" value="" />
</td>
</tr>
<tr>
<td></td><td><input type="submit" value="Perform Search" /></td>
</tr>
</table>
</form>
```

When we submit this form, it will be sent to the doquery.jsp. This file will take the parameter and use it to perform a query and then display the results. The contents of doquery.jsp are shown in Example 7.13. There is quite a bit going on here, so let's step through it as it's a good taste of putting together everything that we've learned so far.

First, remember that we get to this page as a result of a post being done from the form. So a request parameter called "title" will be present as one of the form fields. We create a catch statement, just in case something goes wrong in our query, and then perform a SELECT statement using the parameter. The "?" in a SQL statement is a placeholder for a parameter value. The "?" will be replaced by the value provided by the <sql:param> action. In this sample, there is only one parameter, but it's possible to have many parameters. Each "?" in a SQL statement must have a corresponding <sql:param>. Each parameter must be specified in the same order as the SQL statement. If I had put "JSTL" in the search text box, the actual query would end up looking like:

```
SELECT * FROM books WHERE title LIKE 'JSTL' ORDER BY author
```

A key feature of the <sql:param> to be pointed out here is that the action takes care of handling escaping characters. If the parameter value has quotes, backslashes, or any other special characters like "&" or angle brackets, they will be handled correctly by the <sql:param>. Using <sql:param>, taking care of character escaping is just one less thing to worry about.

After the query is performed, we access the result set from the bookList variable. We check to see if there are any results to process by comparing the rowCount metadata value to 0. If there are any rows, we'll proceed to list out and format each row in the result set so that we can display the results of the search to the user.

Example 7.13 doquery.jsp Source

```
<c:catch var="sqlError">
      <sql:query var="bookList" >
            SELECT * FROM books WHERE title LIKE ? ORDER BY author
            <sql:param value="${param.title}" />
      </sql:query>
</c:catch>
<c:choose>
<c:when test="${not empty sqlError}" >
A SQL error has occurred.
</c:when>
<c:otherwise>
<h2>Listing all books that start with
    <c:out value="${param.title}" />, ordered by author</h2>
<br>

<c:if test="${bookList.rowCount == 0}" >
      <c:out value="No matches found" />
</c:if>
      <table>
      <th>Title</th>
      <th>Author</th>
      <c:forEach var="book" items="${bookList.rows}">
            <tr>
                  <td><c:out value="${book.title}" /></td>
```

```
                <td><c:out value="${book.author}" /></td>
            </tr>
        </c:forEach>
        </table>
        </c:otherwise>
</c:choose>
```

7.10.1 Dealing with Date Parameters

When using parameters, handling dates is slightly different so that databases can do comparisons based on date values. The <sql:dateParam> is used specifically for dealing with date parameters, but works just like <sql:param>. <sql:dateParam> is used for parameters that are of type java.util.Date. The value must be specified using the value attribute. There is also a type attribute to indicate whether this is a timestamp, date, or time value. The default value for the type attribute is timestamp. The action will convert the provided java.util.Date instance to the correct instance depending on the type attribute value. This would be a java.sql.Date, java.sql.Time, or java.sql.Timestamp.

A value and type are specified in the attributes. The type is used because a date can be represented in three different ways: as just a time (3:20 a.m.), as just a date (07/04/2003), or as a timestamp (07/04/2003 3:20 a.m.), which includes the entire time and date. We saw how to format dates and times using the <fmt:formatDate> action in the I18N chapter. However, to keep this sample easy to follow, let's just assume that our date is formatted correctly.

Without duplicating all of the code shown in Example 7.13, the date parameter passed in from a form text field can now be used in the query. This is shown in Example 7.14.

Example 7.14 Using the <sql:dateParam> in a Query

```
<sql:query var="bookList" >
      SELECT * FROM books WHERE title LIKE ? AND pubdate > ? ORDER
      BY author
      <sql:param value="${param.title}" />
      <sql:dateParam value="${param.pubdate}" />
</sql:query>
```

7.11 Working with Result Sets

Throughout the various samples in this book, we've accessed a result set. Usually we've looped through a result set pulling out column values from a particular row. Let's talk about the structure of the result sets and different ways to access information you might be interested in. When you store a result in a scoped variable, there are properties and metadata available that can be used in various ways.

7.11.1 Accessing Rows and Columns

There are two ways to access information for each row. One is by using the variable rows and using the column name to get the information in each row. The other is by using rowsByIndex, which uses a column index value to get at the information. Example 7.15 shows how to get data by using the rows collection along with column names. In this sample, we have a result set called booklist. We are creating our own table header names because we know what columns we want to display. Using the <c:forEach>, we loop through the rows collection. For every item in the collection, we access the row data by using the var book. Each column in the row is accessed by the name of the column.

Example 7.15 Getting at the Row Data Using the Rows Collection

```
<table>
<tr>
<th>Title</th>
<th>Author</th>
<th>Publication Date</th>
</tr>
<c:forEach var="book" items="${bookList.rows}">
      <tr>
            <td><c:out value="${book.title}" /></td>
            <td><c:out value="${book.author}" /></td>
            <td><fmt:formatDate value="${book.pubdate}" type="date"/></td>
      </tr>
</c:forEach>
</table>
```

The browser output is shown in Figure 7.2.

In Example 7.16 we get the same information, only in a more dynamic fashion. By using the columnNames and rowsByIndex collections, we are able to build a table on the fly that contains the result set. This is very useful if you don't know exactly what your column names are. If the query is performed based on different criteria that a user selects, the number of columns and the column names might change from query to query. The code in Example 7.16 shows exactly how to do this.

There are a couple of things to note in this sample. First, you'll notice that the output shown in Figure 7.3 has the column names as they appear in the database. So you need to be aware of how your columns are named if you are planning on making them pretty for user viewing. By looping through the result set using rowsByIndex, we can now

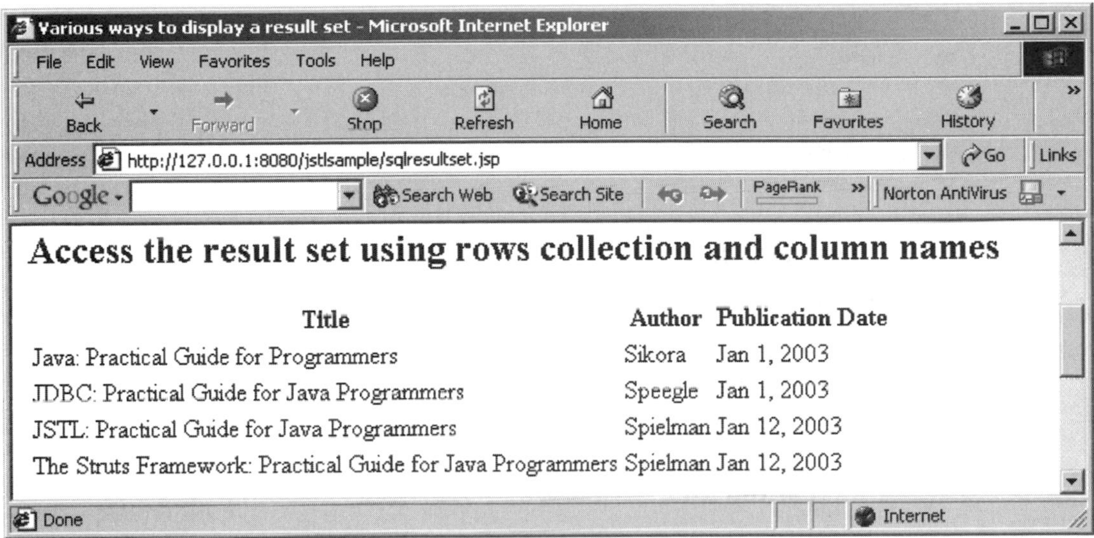

Figure 7.2: Accessing a result set using rows and column names.

use a nested <c:forEach> loop to iterate over each column in the row. This is a fairly generic way to work with result sets without having to be worried about names and types of columns.

Example 7.16 Getting at the Row Data Using the columnNames and rowsByIndex Collection

```
<table>

      <tr>
      <c:forEach items="${bookList.columnNames}" var="columnName">
            <th><c:out value="${columnName}"/></th>
      </c:forEach>
      </tr>

      <c:forEach var="book" items="${bookList.rowsByIndex}">
      <tr>
            <c:forEach var="columnValue" items="${book}" >
                  <td><c:out value="${columnValue}"/></td>
            </c:forEach>
      </tr>
</c:forEach>
</table>
```

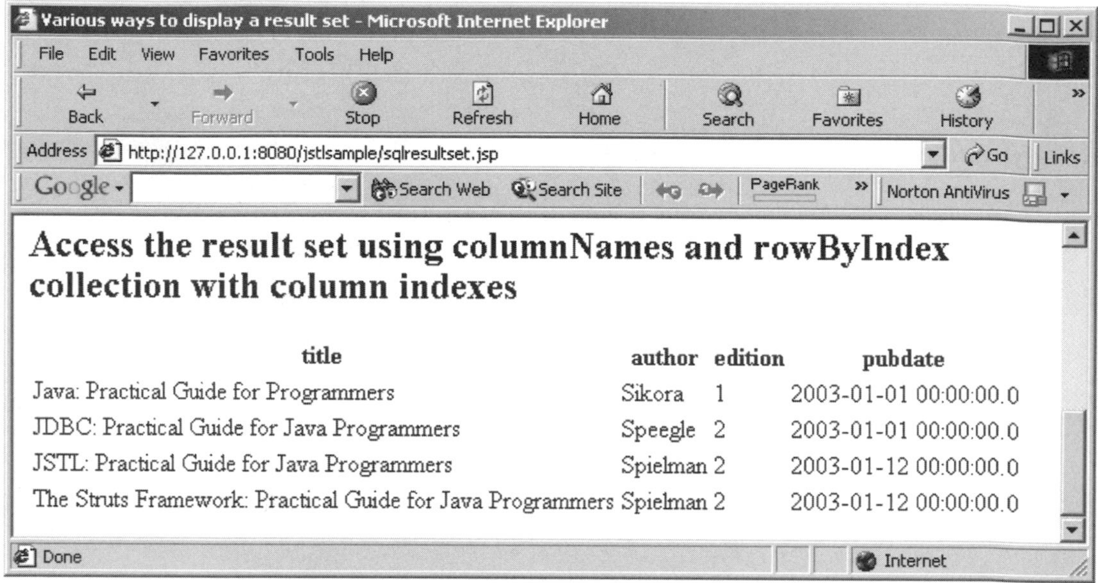

Figure 7.3: Browser output using columnNames and rowsByIndex collections.

7.11.2 Using Result Set Metadata

Aside from the different ways to access data in the result set, there are two metadata values associated with a result set. The `rowCount` value is an `Integer` that can be used to find out how many rows are in the result set. The `limitedByMaxRows` is a `boolean` used to determine whether or not the rows in the result set were limited because the `maxRows` configuration setting (or `maxRows` attribute) was reached. If the total number of rows returned in the result set does not exceed the `maxRows` setting, then the value will be `false`. Otherwise, it will be set to `true`.

If the value is `true`, it might indicate that you need to get more of the result set. You can possibly get more of the result set by using the `startRow` attribute on the query, or maybe by asking the user to try and make their query more specific if the query is being built dynamically. Example 7.17 shows how these variables would be accessed and the accompanying browser output is shown in Figure 7.4.

Example 7.17 Using Metadata

```
The rowCount metadata value is <c:out value="${bookList.rowCount}" />
<br>
The boolean limitedByMaxRows is equal to:
  <c:out value="${bookList.limitedByMaxRows}" />
```

Figure 7.4: Displaying metadata values.

7.12 Dealing with Transactions

So far we have seen relatively simple database samples. A query here, an insert there. In the real world, there are many instances of database interaction that require a bit more thought. When dealing with database interaction that requires certain steps to happen in a certain order, you're typically dealing with transaction material. A transaction is a set of steps that all have to be completed successfully in a unit. Otherwise, none of the steps should succeed. If any one of the steps in a transaction fails, then something called a rollback is performed on the previous steps done up to that point. If all of the steps complete successfully, then a commit is done on the entire transaction and all of the changes made to the database are saved. Handling transaction management, rollbacks, and commits is not a trivial matter. If this is not done correctly you can easily end up having bad data in your database, which is something no one really looks forward to. JSTL provides just about the easiest way I've seen to handle transactions. Wrapping `<sql:query>` and/or `<sql:update>` in a `<sql:transaction>` action is about all there is to it.

7.12.1 Words of Caution

I must make this comment concerning transactions. JSTL makes it easy enough to implement transactions. However, the truth of the matter is that if you have such a need to implement transactions, more than likely it should be in the business tier code, not in the presentation tier. Granted, you could still be using <sql:transaction> in a prototype application, but I strongly suspect that if you are finding yourself doing transactions in a prototype, there is more development in place than simple prototyping. I encourage you to consider the ramifications of doing such transaction processing within the presentation tier. These include blurring of the tier divisions for engineering efforts, code that will ultimately be harder to maintain, and flat out breaking of the MVC model.

7.13 <sql:transaction> Action

The <sql:transaction> action is used to group nested <sql:query> and <sql:update> actions so that they are all performed as a single transaction. The isolation level of the transaction is defined by using the `isolation` attribute. The attribute values are those defined by `java.sql.Connection`. The transaction isolation levels are used to prevent situations from happening between concurrent transactions. Let's briefly describe the various situations that can occur and then correlate what each isolation level allows for. The three types of situations that can occur are:

- Dirty reads
- Nonrepeatable reads
- Phantom reads

A dirty read occurs when a transaction reads data written by a concurrent uncommitted transaction. For example, one transaction is writing some data to the database. The second is then reading that data, but the first rolls the transaction back. The second transaction has read data that doesn't exist.

A nonrepeatable read occurs when a transaction re-reads data it has previously read and finds that the data has been modified by another transaction that was committed since the initial read.

A phantom read occurs when a transaction re-executes a query with the same search criteria and a different result set is returned. This can happen because another transaction might have already done a commit that changed the result set.

The four isolation levels and the corresponding behaviors are described in Table 7.3. You need to evaluate what your application is doing to determine which is the correct isolation level to use.

7.14 How to Use <sql:transaction>

It is possible to use as many <sql:query> and <sql:update> actions within a transaction as you like. If any one of the actions fails, then all of the SQL actions will be rolled back in the database. This, of course, is assuming that the database you are using supports

Value	Dirty read	Nonrepeatable read	Phantom read
read_committed	Prevented	Allowed	Allowed
read_uncommitted	Allowed	Allowed	Allowed
repeatable_read	Allowed	Allowed	Allowed
serializable	Prevented	Prevented	Prevented

Table 7.3: Transaction isolation levels

transactions. Not all do, and you will need to check your database documentation to make sure that transactions are supported. When talking about performing a rollback, notice that I mentioned that only SQL actions would be rolled back. It is possible to include other actions within a <sql:transaction>, but any effects that those actions might have on scoped variables or writing output to the JspWriter will not be changed once they have occurred. So it's possible to have a rather strange-looking page output if you include <c:out> or other actions within the <sql:transaction> and the transaction fails. This is a subtle point, but an important one to keep in mind.

In Example 7.18 we have a <sql:transaction> that performs both an update and a query. This is a similar example to the one we've already talked about when dealing with result sets. Now however, we are indicating that if the update or the query fails, you should rollback any changes so they are not committed. The use of the isolation attribute gives the JSP author more control over how independent transactions need to be. In this example, I'm not indicating the dataSource attribute in the <sql:transaction>. Doing it this way causes the default data source to be used that is either set by the configuration setting or by a <sql:setDataSource> action. All SQL actions will use the data source of the <sql:transaction>. So even though it's possible to specify a data source to both <sql:update> and <sql:query>, doing so when those actions are nested within a transaction will cause a compilation error that will resemble Figure 7.6. We can see in Figure 7.5 that the update occurred correctly in the database because the edition of the JSTL book has been changed to 2.

Example 7.18 Using <sql:transaction>

```
<sql:transaction isolation="serializable">
      <sql:update>
            UPDATE books SET edition="2" WHERE author="Spielman"
      </sql:update>
      <sql:query var="bookList" >
            SELECT * FROM books ORDER BY author
      </sql:query>
</sql:transaction>
```

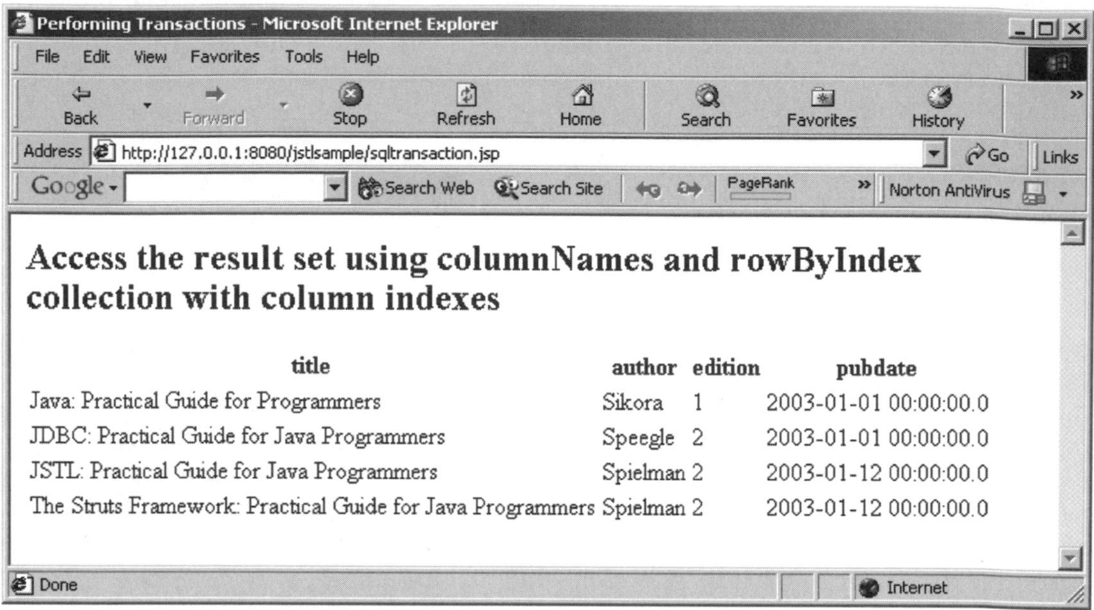

Figure 7.5: Results of a successful transaction.

When using the `<sql:transaction>` action, if the DBMS set as the data source does not support transactions, then an exception will be thrown. The DBMS support for transactions is determined by the tag handler for the `<sql:transaction>` by making a `Connection.getTransactionIsolation()` method call against the data source in the `doStartTag()` of the action. For this particular action, it is important to understand how the tag handler implementation is done because when you are dealing with transactions it is possible that rollbacks might be necessary.

The `doEndTag()` method will call the `Connection.commit()` on the transaction, while the `doCatch()` will cause a `Connection.rollback()` to happen. If all goes well with the completed transaction, then the `doFinally()` method is called. This will restore the transaction level if it was changed from the DBMS default, restore the autocommit mode, and close the connection.

If you are using JTA[23] user transactions with a `<sql:transaction>`, beware. The behavior of the action is undefined within that context.

---

[23]JTA specifies standard Java interfaces between a transaction manager and the parties involved in a distributed transaction system. For more information visit *http://java.sun.com/products/jta*.

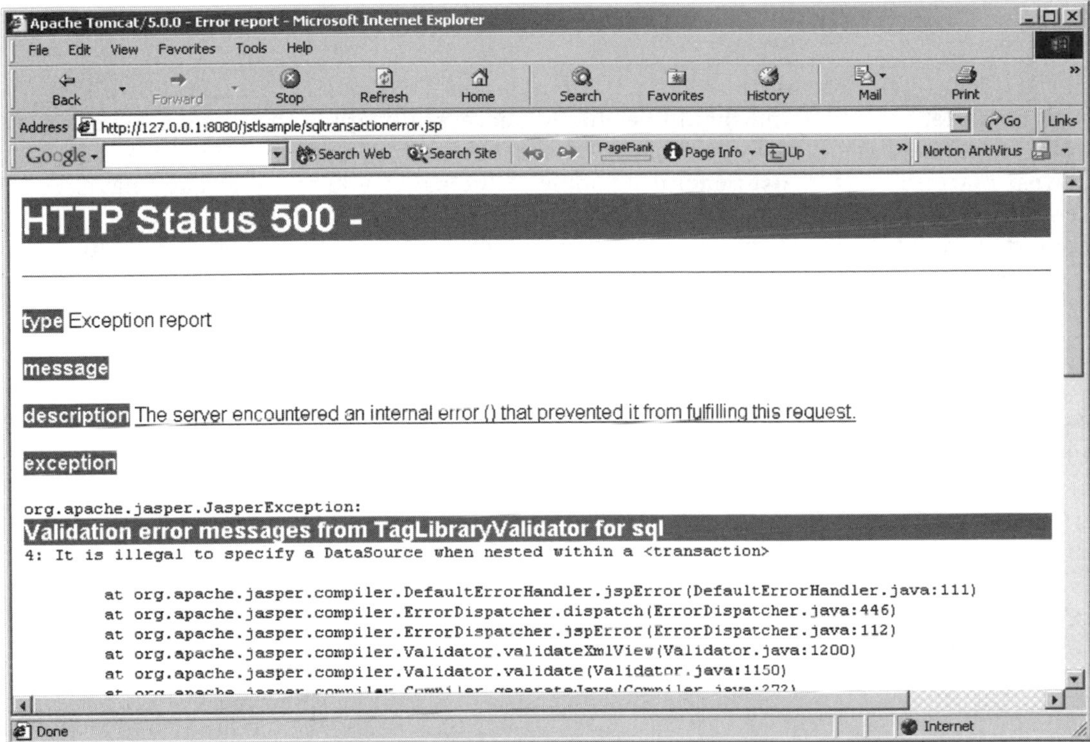

Figure 7.6: Using dataSource in nested SQL actions is a no-no.

7.15 Summary

In this chapter on the SQL actions, we found some of the reasons why we would and would not want to use the provided actions. These actions are useful for prototype or simple applications. However, having direct access from your JSPs to your database breaks the MVC model. You want to be aware of the implications of breaking the MVC and be careful not to do so.

We looked at the various features of this tag library, including how to set up data sources as well as the available public interfaces and classes. These actions can be used for accessing, updating, and deleting data. It is also possible to use transactions as long as the database you are using supports transactions. We walked through each of the available actions and looked at various samples for using them.

7.16 Conclusion

At this point, you should have a full appreciation for the JSTL. You've got all of the actions under your belt and should be able to successfully apply their usage to your page authoring. There are so many projects out there that have JSP code that can utilize the JSTL; a great place to start is just refactoring some of the pages you might already have. You'll see how easy and efficient it is using the JSTL compared to debugging through scriptlet code that might be scattered throughout the pages. I hope that this book has helped you get a head start on everything you need to know to get rolling.

chapter 8

JSTL Quick Reference

The purpose of the JSTL quick reference is to help you look up syntax, actions, and attribute values or find the answer to simple questions you might have while in active development. It is not meant to be an in-depth description of the features. For details, refer to the chapter that covers the area you are interested in.

The following conventions are used throughout this section. "A" represents variable A, which also might be referred to as varA in some samples. "B" represents variable B, which also might be referred to as varB in some samples. For any action that has a scope attribute, the default scope is page. This information is based on the contents of the JSTL 1.0 final release specification.

8.1 Expression Language Syntax

- The expression language can only be used in attribute values.
- Invoke by using the syntax `${expr}`, where expr is a valid expression as defined by the expression language.
- Expressions are evaluated within quotes.

  Example usage: `<c:out value="${A + B}" />`

8.1.1 Literals

<table>
<tr><th>Literal</th><th>Syntax</th><th>Examples</th></tr>
<tr><td>Boolean</td><td>'true' | 'false'</td><td>true</td></tr>
<tr><td>Integer</td><td>["+","-"] ["1"-"9"] (["0"-"9"])*</td><td>+10 -45</td></tr>
<tr><td>Floating point</td><td>(["+","-"])? (["0"-"9"])+ "."
(["0"-"9"])* (["e","E"]
(["+","-"])? (["0"-"9"])+)?
| (["+","-"])? "." (["0"-"9"])+
(["e","E"] (["+","-"])?
(["0"-"9"])+)? | (["+","-"])?
(["0"-"9"])+ ["e","E"]
(["+","-"])? (["0"-"9"])+</td><td>10.20 -10.20 +1.7E+10</td></tr>
<tr><td>String</td><td>String with single or double quotes.
Double quote escaped with \",
single quote escaped as \' , backslash
escaped as \\. '([^'\]|\'|\\)*' |
"([^'\]|\'|\\)*"</td><td>"Sue\'s Blog"</td></tr>
<tr><td>Null</td><td>'null'</td><td>null</td></tr>
</table>

8.1.2 "[ ]" and "." Operators

The EL follows ECMAScript for the usage of the "." and "[ ]" operators for property access when working with collections.

- The ".", also called the dot operator, retrieves a named property by effectively calling the `getProperty()` method on that property.

  Example: `${book.title}` translates into `book.getTitle()`.

- The "[ ]" operator lets you retrieve named, numbered, or indexed properties.

  Example: `${books[0]}` retrieves the first item in the collection called `books`.

8.1.3 Arithmetic Operators

Operation	Symbol	Operator type	Rules applied	Example
Addition	+	Binary	A + B 1. If A and B are null, return 0 2. If A or B is Float, Double, or a String containing ".", "e", or	${varA + varB}

			"E", coerce both A and B to Double and apply operator 3. Otherwise coerce both A and B to Long and apply operator 4. If operator results in exception, error	
Subtraction	–	Binary	A - B 1. If A and B are null, return 0 2. If A or B is Float, Double, or a String containing ".", "e", or "E", coerce both A and B to Double and apply operator 3. Otherwise coerce both A and B to Long and apply operator 4. If operator results in exception, error	${varA - varB}
Multiplication	*	Binary	A * B 1. If A and B are null, return 0 2. If A or B is Float, Double, or a String containing ".", "e", or "E", coerce both A and B to Double and apply operator 3. Otherwise coerce both A and B to Long and apply operator 4. If operator results in exception, error	${varA * varB}
Division	/ and div	Binary	A / B 1. If A and B are null, return 0 2. Coerce both A and B to Double and apply operator 3. If operator results in exception, error	${varA / varB} or ${varA div varB}
Module	% and mod	Binary	A % B 1. If A and B are null, return 0 2. If A or B is Float, Double, or a String containing ".", "e", or "E", coerce both A and B to Double and apply operator	${varA % varB} or ${varA mod varB}

Operation	Symbol	Operator type	Rules applied	Example
			3. Otherwise coerce both A and B to Long and apply operator 4. If operator results in exception, error	
Minus	–	Unary	If A is null, return 0 1. If A is a String and A contains “.”, “e”, or “E”, coerce to a Double and apply operator 2. Otherwise, coerce to a Long and apply operator 3. If operator results in exception, error 4. If A is Byte, Short, Integer, Long, Float, Double, retain type, apply operator. If operator results in exception, error, otherwise, error	${-varA}

8.1.4 Relational Operators

Operator	Rules applied	Example
“==” and “eq” “!=” and “ne”	1. If A==B, apply operator 2. If A is null or B is null, return false for ==, true for != 3. If A or B is Float or Double, coerce both A and B to Double apply operator	${varA == varB} ${varA eq varB} ${varA != varB} ${varA ne varB}
“?”<” and “lt” “>” and “gt” “<=” and “le” “>=” and “ge”	1. If A==B, if operator is <=, le, >=, or ge, return true, otherwise return false 2. If A is null or B is null, return false 3. If A or B is Float or Double, coerce both A and B to Double and apply operator 4. If A or B is Byte, Short, Character, Integer, Long, coerce both A and B to Long and apply operator	${varA < varB} ${varA lt varB} ${varA > varB} ${varA gt varB} ${varA <= varB} ${varA le varB} ${varA >= varB} ${varA ge varB}

5. If A or B is String, coerce both A and B to String, compare lexically. If A is Comparable if A.compareTo(B) throws exception error, otherwise use result of A.compareTo(B)
6. If B is Comparable if B.compareTo(A) throws exception error otherwise use result of B.compareTo(A)
7. If A or B is Byte, Short, Character, Integer, Long, coerce both A and B to Long, apply operator
8. If A or B is Boolean, coerce both A and B to Boolean, apply operator
9. If A or B is String, coerce both A and B to String, compare lexically
10. Otherwise, if an error occurs while calling A.equals(B), error.
11. Otherwise, apply operator to result of A.equals(B)

8.1.5 Logical Operators

<table>
<tr><th>Operator</th><th>Operator type</th><th>Rules applied</th><th>Example</th></tr>
<tr><td>&& and and</td><td>Binary</td><td>Coerce both A and B to Boolean, apply operator</td><td>${varA && varB}
${varA and varB}</td></tr>
<tr><td>|| and or</td><td>Binary</td><td>Note: The operator stops as soon as expression can be determined, i.e., A and B and C and D—if B is false, then only A and B is evaluated.</td><td>${varA || varB}
${varA or varB}</td></tr>
<tr><td>! and not</td><td>Unary</td><td>Coerce A to Boolean, apply operator</td><td>${!varA}
${not varA}</td></tr>
</table>

8.1.6 Empty Operator

The empty operator is a prefix operator that can be used to determine if a value is null or empty.

Rules applied to evaluate empty A:

1. If A is null, return true.
2. Otherwise, if A is the empty string, then return true.
3. Otherwise, if A is an empty array, then return true.
4. Otherwise, if A is an empty Map, return true.
5. Otherwise, if A is an empty List, return true.
6. Otherwise return false.

Examples:

```
${empty varA}

<c:if test="${!empty param.name}" var="result" >
```

8.1.7 Operator Precedence

Highest-to-lowest, left-to-right. Parentheses can be used to change precedence, as in "${(a *(b +c))}"

- [] .
- () - (unary) not ! empty
- */div % mod
- + - (binary)
- < > <= >= lt gt le ge
- == != eq ne
- && and
- || or

8.1.8 Reserved Words

The following words are reserved for the language and should not be used as identifiers without being quoted.

```
and  eq  gt  true  instanceof  or  ne  le  false  empty  not
lt  ge  null  div  mod
```

8.1.9 Coercion Rules

Note: The order of the contents of each table represents the order in which the rules are applied. These rules are taken from the JSTL 1.0 specification.

If A is:	Return
a String	A
null	" "
A.toString() throws exception	Error
A.toString()	A.toString()
a primitive type	a String, that is '" "+A'

Table 8.1: Coerce A to String.

If A is:	Return
null or " "	0
Character, convert to short, and then apply the following rules	
a Boolean	Error
Number type N	A
Number with less precision than N	Coerce quietly, do not throw an error that the number was less precise
Number with greater precision than N	Coerce quietly, do not throw an error that the number was more precise
String, and new N.valueOf(A) throws exception	Error
String, and N.valueOf(A) does not throw exception	Return it
Otherwise	Error

Table 8.2: Coerce A to primitive Number type N.

If A is:	Return
null or " "	(char) 0
Character	A
Boolean	Error
Number with less precision than short	Coerce quietly and do not throw an error—return (char) A
Number with greater precision than short	Coerce quietly and do not throw an error—return (char) A
String	A.charAt (0)
Otherwise	Error

Table 8.3: Coerce A to Character.

If A is:	Return
null or " "	False
A is Boolean	A
A is String and Boolean.valueOf(A) throws exception	Error
String	Boolean.valueOf(A)
Otherwise	Error

Table 8.4: Coerce A to Boolean.

If A is:	Return
null	null
A primitive type, return an appropriate object with equivalent value, as follows:	
Assignable to T	Coerce quietly
An int	New Integer(A)
A Float	New Float(A)
A String, and T has no PropertyEditor	
Is null	Null
Otherwise	Error
String and T's PropertyEditor throws exception	
""	Null
Otherwise	Error
Otherwise apply T's PropertyEditor	
Otherwise	Error

Table 8.5: Coerce A to any other type T.

8.1.10 Accessing Named Variables

The EL evaluates an identifier by looking up its value as an attribute, according to the behavior of `PageContext.findAttribute(String)`.

For example: `${product}`.

This expression will look for the attribute named "product", searching the page, request, session, and application scopes, and will return its value. If the attribute is not found, `null` is returned. An identifier that matches one of the implicit objects described in the next section will return that implicit object instead of an attribute value.

8.1.11 Implicit Objects

The EL defines a set of implicit objects. When an expression references one of these objects by name, the appropriate object is returned instead of the corresponding attribute.

For example: `${pageContext}` returns the PageContext object, even if there is an existing pageContext attribute containing some other value.

Name	Description	Example
pageContext	The PageContext object	${pageContext}
pageScope	A Map that maps page-scoped attribute names to their values	${pageScope.varA}—a page-scoped attribute called varA, null if not found
requestScope	A Map that maps request-scoped attribute names to their values	${requestScope.varA}—a request-scoped attribute called varA, null if not found
sessionScope	A Map that maps session-scoped attribute names to their values	${sessionScope.varA}—a session-scoped attribute called varA, null if not found
applicationScope	A Map that maps application-scoped attribute names to their values	${applicationScope.varA}—an application-scoped attribute called varA, null if not found
param	A Map that maps parameter names to a single String parameter value. This value is obtained by calling ServletRequest.getParameter(String name)	${param.books}—the String value of the books parameter, null if not found
paramValues	A Map that maps parameter names to a String[] of all values for that parameter. This value is obtained by calling ServletRequest.getParameterValues(String name)	${paramValues.books}—a String[] containing all of the values of the books parameter, null if not found
header	A Map that maps header names to a single String header value. This value is obtained by calling ServletRequest.getHeader(String name)	${header['Accept-Language']}—the String value of the Accept-Language header, null if not found
headerValues	A Map that maps header names to a String[] of all values for that header. The values are obtained by calling ServletRequest.getHeaders(String)	${headerValues['Accept-Language']}—a String[] containing all of the values of the AcceptLanaguage header, null if not found

Name	Description	Example
cookie	A Map that maps cookie names to a single Cookie object. Cookies are retrieved according to the semantics of httpServlet Request.getCookies(). Note: If the same name is shared by multiple cookies, an implementation must use the first one encountered in the array of Cookie objects returned by the getCookies() method. However, users of the cookie implicit object must be aware that the ordering of cookies is currently unspecified in the Servlet specification.	${cookie.lastLoginTime}
initParam	A Map that maps context initialization parameter names to their String parameter value. The values are obtained by calling ServletContext. getInitParameter (String name)	${initParam.serverName}

8.2 Configuration Settings

Configuration settings can be used to set values for various variables that are used by some JSTL actions. They can be set in the web.xml file or by a specific action as indicated.

Example web.xml snippet using a configuration setting:

```
<context-param>
        <param-name>
              javax.servlet.jsp.jstl.fmt.locale
        </param-name>
        <param-value>
              en
        </param-value>
</context-param>
```

The javax.servlet.jsp.jstl.core.Config class is used for setting, retrieving, and removing configuration settings. The various configuration settings are described in the following tables.

Locale	
Description	Specifies the locale to be used by the I18N-capable formatting actions. This disables browser-based locales. A String value is interpreted as defined in action <fmt:setLocale>
Variable name	`javax.servlet.jsp.jstl.fmt.locale`
Java Constant	`Config.FMT_LOCALE`
Type	String or `java.util.Locale`
Set by	`<fmt:setLocale>`
Used by	`<fmt:bundle>`, `<fmt:setBundle>`, `<fmt:message>`, `<fmt:formatNumber>`, `<fmt:parseNumber>`, `<fmt:formatDate>`, `<fmt:parseDate>`

Fallback Locale	
Description	Specifies the fallback locale to be used by the I18N-capable formatting actions if none of the preferred match any of the available locales. A String value is interpreted as defined in action <fmt:setLocale>
Variable name	`javax.servlet.jsp.jstl.fmt.fallbackLocale`
Java Constant	`Config.FMT_FALLBACK_LOCALE`
Type	String or `java.util.Locale`
Set by	none
Used by	`<fmt:bundle>`, `<fmt:setBundle>`, `<fmt:message>`, `<fmt:formatNumber>`, `<fmt:parseNumber>`, `<fmt:formatDate>`, `<fmt:parseDate>`

I18N Localization Context	
Description	Specifies the default I18N localization context to be used by the I18N-capable formatting actions. A String value is interpreted as a resource bundle basename.
Variable name	`javax.servlet.jsp.jstl.fmt.localizationContext`
Java Constant	`Config.FMT_LOCALIZATION_CONTEXT`
Type	String or `javax.servlet.jsp.jstl.fmt.LocalizationContext`
Set by	`<fmt:setBundle>`
Used by	`<fmt:message>`, `<fmt:formatNumber>`, `<fmt:parseNumber>`, `<fmt:formatDate>`, `<fmt:parseDate>`

TimeZone	
Description	Specifies the application's default time zone. A String value is interpreted as defined in action <fmt:timeZone>
Variable name	`javax.servlet.jsp.jstl.fmt.timeZone`
Java Constant	`Config.FMT_TIMEZONE`
Type	`String or java.util.TimeZone`
Set by	`<fmt:setTimeZone>`
Used by	`<fmt:formatDate>, <fmt:parseDate>`

DataSource	
Description	The data source to be accessed by the SQL actions. It can be specified as a string representing either a JNDI relative path or a JDBC parameters string or as a `javax.sql.DataSource` object.
Variable name	`javax.servlet.jsp.jstl.sql.dataSource`
Java Constant	`Config.SQL_DATA_SOURCE`
Type	`String or javax.sql.DataSource`
Set by	`<sql:setDataSource>, Deployment Descriptor, Config class`
Used by	`<sql:query>, <sql:update>, <sql:transaction>`

MaxRows	
Description	The maximum number of rows to be included in a query result. If the maximum number of rows is not specified, or is −1, it means that no limit is enforced on the maximum number of rows. Value must be >= −1.
Variable name	`javax.servlet.jsp.jstl.sql.maxRows`
Java Constant	`Config.SQL_MAX_ROWS`
Type	`Integer`
Set by	`Deployment Descriptor, Config class`
Used by	`<sql:query>`

8.3 Core Tag Library

The following actions are contained in the Core tag library.

8.3.1 Tag Library URI

```
<%@ taglib uri="http://java.sun.com/jstl/core" prefix="c" %>
```

8.3.2 General Purpose Actions

<c:out>

Description	Evaluates an expression and outputs the result of the evaluation to the current JspWriter object.
Usage Example	`<c:out value="Reference Samples" escapeXml-"false" default="Samples"/>`

Attributes

Name	Description	Type	Required	Dynamic
value	Expression to be evaluated	Object	✔	✔
escapeXml	Determines whether characters <, >, &, ', " in the resulting string should be converted to their corres-ponding character entity codes. Default value is true.	boolean	✖	✔
default	Default value if the resulting value is null.	Object	✖	✔

<c:set>

Description	Sets the value of a scoped variable or a property of a target object.
Usage Example	`<c:set value="<b>Test Data </b>" var="myData"/>`

Attributes

Name	Description	Type	Required	Dynamic
value	Expression to be evaluated.	Object	✔	✔
var	Name of the exported scoped variable to hold the value specified in the action. The type of the scoped variable is whatever type the value expression evaluates to.	String	✔	✖
scope	Scope for `var`.	String	✖	✖
target	Target object whose property will be set. Must evaluate to a JavaBeans object with setter property `property`, or to a `java.util.Map` object.	Object	✔ (when not using var)	✔

Name	Description	Type	Required	Dynamic
property	Name of the property to be set in the target object.	String	✔ (when using target)	✔

<c:remove>				
Description	Removes a scoped variable.			
Usage Example	`<c:remove var="myVar" />`			
Attributes				
Name	**Description**	**Type**	**Required**	**Dynamic**
var	Name of the scoped variable to be removed.	String	✔	✖
scope	Scope for var.	String	✖	✖

<c:catch>				
Description	Catches a java.lang.Throwable thrown by any of its nested actions.			

Usage Example	`<c:catch var="error">`
	`nested actions`
	`</c:catch>`			

Attributes				
Name	**Description**	**Type**	**Required**	**Dynamic**
var	Name of the exported scoped variable for the exception thrown from a nested action. The type of the scoped variable is the type of the exception thrown.	String	✖	✖

8.3.3 Conditional Actions

<c:if>	
Description	Evaluates its body content if the expression specified with the `test` attribute is true.

Usage Example	With body content
	`<c:if test="${varA < 5}" >`
	`Do something`
	`</c:if>`
	
	Without body content
	`<c:if test="${varA < 5}" var="result" />`

Attributes				
Name	**Description**	**Type**	**Required**	**Dynamic**
test	The test condition that determines whether or not the body content should be processed.	String	✔	✔
var	Name of the exported scoped variable for the resulting value of the test condition. The type of the scoped variable is `Boolean`.	String	✔ (when not providing body content)	✖
scope	Scope for `var`.	String	✖	✖

<c:choose>				
Description	Provides the context for mutually exclusive conditional execution.			

Usage Example	`<c:choose>`
	body content (<when> and <otherwise> subtags)
	`</c:choose>`			

Attributes				
Name	**Description**	**Type**	**Required**	**Dynamic**
none				

<c:when>				
Description	Represents an alternative within a <c:choose> action.			

Usage Example	`<c:when test="`*`${varA < 5}`*`">`
	body content
	`</c:when>`			

Attributes				
Name	**Description**	**Type**	**Required**	**Dynamic**
test	The test condition that determines whether or not the body content should be processed.	boolean	✔	✔

<c:otherwise>				
Description	Represents the last alternative within a <c:choose> action.			

Usage Example	`<c:otherwise>`
	`body content`
	`</c:otherwise>`			

Attributes				
Name	**Description**	**Type**	**Required**	**Dynamic**
none				

8.3.4 Iterator Actions

<c:foreach>				
Description	Repeats its nested body content over a collection of objects, or repeats it a fixed number of times.			

Usage Example	`Iterating over a collection of objects`
	
	`<c:forEach var="book" items="${bookList.rows}"`
	`begin='0' end='2'>`
	`body content`
	`</c:forEach>`
	`Iterating over a fixed number of items`
	`<c:forEach begin="1" end="${totalSize - 1}" >`
	`body content`
	`</c:forEach>`			

Attributes				
Name	**Description**	**Type**	**Required**	**Dynamic**
var	Name of the exported scoped variable for the current item of the iteration. This scoped variable has nested visibility. Its type depends on the object of the underlying collection.	String	✖	✖
varStatus	Name of the exported scoped variable for the status of the iteration. Object exported is of type javax.servlet.jsp.jstl.core. LoopTagStatus. This scoped variable has nested visibility.	String	✖	✖

items	Collection of items to iterate over.	J2SE Collection type	✖	✔
begin	If items specified: Iteration begins at the item located at the specified index. First item of the collection has index 0. If items not specified: Iteration begins with index set at the value specified.	int	✖	✔
end	If items specified: Iteration ends at the item located at the specified index (inclusive). If items not specified: Iteration ends when index reaches the value specified.	int	✖	✔
step	Iteration will only process every step item of the collection, starting with the first one.	int	✖	✔

<c:forToken>				
Description	Iterates over tokens, separated by the supplied delimiters.			

Usage Example	`<c:forTokens var="token" items="${tokens}"`
	`delims="," >`
	`body content`
	`</c:forTokens>`			

Attributes				
Name	**Description**	**Type**	**Required**	**Dynamic**
var	Name of the exported scoped variable for the current item of the iteration. This scoped variable has nested visibility.	String	✖	✖
varStatus	Name of the exported scoped variable for the status of the iteration. Object exported is of	String	✖	✖

Name	Description	Type	Required	Dynamic
	Type `javax.servlet.jsp.jstl.core.LoopTagStatus`. This scoped variable has nested visibility.			
items	String of tokens to iterate over	String	✔	✔
delims	The set of delimiters (the characters that separate the tokens in the string).	String	✔	✔
begin	Iteration begins at the token located at the specified index. First token has index 0.	int	✖	✔
end	Iteration ends at the token located at the specified index (inclusive).	int	✖	✔
step	Iteration will only process every step token of the string, starting with the first one.	int	✖	✔

8.3.5 URL Related Actions

<c:import>				
Description	Imports the content of a URL-based resource.			

Usage Example	Resource content inline or exported as a String object
	`<c:import url="/header.jsp" var="header" >`
	` optional body content for <c:param> subtags`
	`</c:import>`
	Resource content exported as a Reader object
	`<c:import url="/authors.xml"`
	`          varReader="reader">`
	`  body content where varReader is consumed by`
	`  another action`
	`</c:import>`			

Attributes				
Name	**Description**	**Type**	**Required**	**Dynamic**
url	The URL of the resource to import.	String	✔	✔
context	Name of the context when accessing a relative URL resource that belongs to a foreign context.	String	✖	✔

var	Name of the exported scoped variable for the resource's content. The type of the scoped variable is String.	String	✖	✖
scope	Scope for var.	String	✖	✖
charEncoding	Character encoding of the content at the input resource.	String	✖	✔
varReader	Name of the exported scoped variable for the resource's content. The type of the scoped variable is Reader.	String	✖ (Required only if content exported as a Reader Object)	✖

<c:url>

Description	Builds a URL with the proper rewriting rules applied.
Usage Example	`<c:url var="homePage" scope="session" value="http://www.switchbacksoftware.com" />`

Attributes

Name	Description	Type	Required	Dynamic
value	URL to be processed.	String	✔	✔
context	Name of the context when specifying a relative URL resource that belongs to a foreign context.	String	✖	✔
var	Name of the exported scoped variable for the processed URL. The type of the scoped variable is String.	String	✖	✖
scope	Scope for var.	String	✖	✖

<c:redirect>

Description	Sends an HTTP redirect to the client.
Usage Example	`<c:redirect url="http://www.mkp.com" />`

Attributes

Name	Description	Type	Required	Dynamic
url	The URL of the resource to redirect to.	String	✔	✔
context	Name of the context when redirecting to a relative URL resource that belongs to a foreign context.	String	✖	✔

<table>
<tr><th colspan="5"><c:param></th></tr>
<tr><td>Description</td><td colspan="4">Adds request parameters to a URL. Nested action of <c:import>, <c:url>, <c:redirect>.</td></tr>
<tr><td>Usage Example</td><td colspan="4"><pre><c:import url="/header.jsp" >
 <c:param name="title"
        value="Import action Samples" />
</c:import></pre></td></tr>
<tr><th colspan="5">Attributes</th></tr>
<tr><th>Name</th><th>Description</th><th>Type</th><th>Required</th><th>Dynamic</th></tr>
<tr><td>name</td><td>Name of the query string parameter.</td><td>String</td><td>✔</td><td>✔</td></tr>
<tr><td>value</td><td>Value of the parameter.</td><td>String</td><td>✔</td><td>✔</td></tr>
</table>

8.4 XML Tag Library

These are the actions contained in the XML tag library.

8.4.1 Tag Library URI

```
<%@ taglib uri="http://java.sun.com/jstl/xml" prefix="x" %>
```

8.4.2 XML Core Actions

<table>
<tr><th colspan="5"><c:parse></th></tr>
<tr><td>Description</td><td colspan="4">Parses an XML document.</td></tr>
<tr><td>Usage Example</td><td colspan="4">XML provided in body content<pre><x:parse var="doc">
  <person>
       <firstname>Sue</firstname>
       <lastname>Spielman</lastname>
  </person>
</x:parse></pre>XML provided from imported variable<pre><c:import var="xmlfile" url="/people.xml" />
<x:parse var="doc" xml="${xmlfile}" /></pre></td></tr>
<tr><th colspan="5">Attributes</th></tr>
<tr><th>Name</th><th>Description</th><th>Type</th><th>Required</th><th>Dynamic</th></tr>
<tr><td>xml</td><td>Source XML document to be parsed.</td><td>String</td><td>✔ (only if content not provided in body content)</td><td>✔</td></tr>
</table>

systemId	The system identifier (URI) for parsing the XML document.	String	✖	✔
filter	Filter to be applied to the source document.	`org.xml.sax.XMLFilter`	✖	✔
var	Name of the exported scoped variable for the parsed XML document. The type of the scoped variable is implementation dependent.	String	✖	✖
scope	Scope for var.	String	✖	✖
varDom	Name of the exported scoped variable for the parsed XML document. The type of the scoped variable is `org.w3c.dom.Document`.	String	✖	✖
scopeDom	Scope for `varDom`.	String	✖	✖

<x:out>

Description	Evaluates an XPath expression and outputs the result of the evaluation to the current `JspWriter` object.
Usage Example	`<x:out select="$doc/person/firstname" />`

Attributes

Name	Description	Type	Required	Dynamic
select	XPath expression to be evaluated.	String	✔	✔
escapeXml	Determines whether characters <, >, &, ', " in the resulting string should be converted to their corresponding character entity codes. Default value is true.	boolean	✖	✔

<x:set>

Description	Evaluates an XPath expression and stores the result into a scoped variable.
Usage Example	`<x:set var="name" select="$doc/person" scope="request" />`

Attributes				
Name	**Description**	**Type**	**Required**	**Dynamic**
select	XPath expression to be evaluated.	String	✔	✖
var	Name of the exported scoped variable to hold the value specified in the action. The type of the scoped variable is whatever type the value expression evaluates to.	String	✔	✖
scope	Scope for `var`.	String	✖	✖

8.4.3 XML Flow Control

<x:if>	
Description	Evaluates the XPath expression specified in the select attribute and renders its body content if the expression evaluates to true.

Usage Example	With body content
	`<x:if select="$doc/catalog">`
	`  process body content`
	`</x:if>`
	
	Without body content
	`<c:if select="$doc/catalog" var="result" />`

Attributes				
Name	**Description**	**Type**	**Required**	**Dynamic**
select	The test condition that tells whether or not the body content should be processed.	String	✔	✖
var	Name of the exported scoped variable for the resulting value of the test condition. The type of the scoped variable is `Boolean`.	String	✔ (when not providing body content)	✖
scope	Scope for var.	String	✖	✖

<x:choose>	
Description	Provides the context for mutually exclusive conditional execution.

Usage Example	`<x:choose>`
	body content (<x:when> and <x:otherwise> subtags)
	`</x:choose>`

Attributes				
Name	**Description**	**Type**	**Required**	**Dynamic**
none				

<x:when>	
Description	Represents an alternative within a <x:choose> action.

Usage Example	`<x:when select="$doc/catalog/book/edition=1">`
	`body content`
	`</x:when>`

Attributes				
Name	**Description**	**Type**	**Required**	**Dynamic**
select	The test condition that tells whether or not the body content should be processed.	boolean	✔	✔

<x:otherwise>	
Description	Represents the last alternative within a <x:choose> action.

Usage Example	`<x:otherwise>`
	`body content`
	`</x:otherwise>`

Attributes				
Name	**Description**	**Type**	**Required**	**Dynamic**
none				

8.4.4 Iterator Actions

<x:foreach>	
Description	Evaluates the given XPath expression and repeats its nested body content over the result, setting the context node to each element in the iteration.

Usage Example	`<x:forEach select="$doc/catalog//book" />`
	`body content`
	`</x:forEach>`

Attributes				
Name	**Description**	**Type**	**Required**	**Dynamic**
var	Name of the exported scoped variable for the current item of the iteration. This scoped	String	✖	✖

Name	Description	Type	Required	Dynamic
	variable has nested visibility. Its type depends on the result of the XPath expression in the select attribute.			
select	XPath expression to be evaluated.	String	✔	✖

8.4.5 Transformation Actions

<x:transform>

Description	Applies an XSLT stylesheet transformation to an XML document.

Usage Example	`<c:import var="xmlfile" url="/catalog.xml" />`
	`<c:import var="xslfile" url="/catalog.xsl" />`
	
	`<x:parse var="doc" xml="${xmlfile}" />`
	`<x:transform xml="${xmlfile}" xslt="${xslfile}" />`

Attributes

Name	Description	Type	Required	Dynamic
xml	Source XML document to be transformed. (If exported by <x:set>, it must correspond to a well-formed XML document, not a partial document.)	`String`, `Reader`, `javax.xml.transform.Source`, `org.w3c.dom.Document`, or object exported by `<x:parse>`, `<x:set>`.	✔ (unless XML provided in body content	✔
xslt	Transformation stylesheet as a String, Reader, or Source object.	`String`, `Reader`, or Source object.	✔	✔
xmlSystemId	The system identifier (URI) for parsing the XML document.	String	✖	✔
xsltSystemId	The system identifier (URI) for parsing the XSL style sheet.	String	✖	✔
var	Name of the exported scoped variable for the transformed XML document. The type of the scoped variable is `org.w3c.dom.Document`.	String	✖	✖

scope result	Scope for var. Object that captures or processes the transformation result.	String javax.xml.transform. Result	✖ ✖	✖ ✔

<x:param>				
Description	Set transformation parameters. Nested action of <x:transform>.			

Usage Example	`<x:transform xml="${xmlfile}" xslt="${xslfile}" >`
	` <x:param name="publisher" value="New Publisher" />`
	`</x:transform>`			

Attributes				
Name	**Description**	**Type**	**Required**	**Dynamic**
name	Name of the transformation parameter.	String	✔	✔
value	Value of the parameter.	String	✔	✔

8.5 SQL Tag Library

These are the actions provided in the SQL tag library.

8.5.1 Tag Library URI

```
<%@ taglib uri="http://java.sun.com/jstl/sql" prefix="sql" %>
```

8.5.2 Actions

<sql:query>	
Description	Queries a database.

Usage Example	With body content
	`<sql:query var="bookList" >`
	`      SELECT * FROM books WHERE title LIKE 'J%'`
	`      ORDER BY author`
	` </sql:query>`
	Without body content
	`<sql:query var="bookList"`
	`      sql=" SELECT * FROM books WHERE title LIKE`
	`      'J%' ORDER BY`
	`      author " />`

Attributes				
Name	**Description**	**Type**	**Required**	**Dynamic**
sql	SQL query statement.	String	✔ (if body content not provided)	✔
dataSource	Data source associated with the database to query. A String value represents a relative path to a JNDI resource or the parameters for the DriverManager class.	javax.sql.DataSource or String	✖	✔
maxRows	The maximum number of rows to be included in the query result. If not specified, or set to −1, no limit on the maximum number of rows is enforced.	int	✖	✔
startRow	The returned Result object includes the rows starting at the specified index. The first row of the original query result set is at index 0. If not specified, rows are included starting from the first row at index 0.	int	✖	✔
var	Name of the exported scoped variable for the query result. The type of the scoped variable is javax.servlet.jsp.jstl.sql.Result	String	✔	✖
scope	Scope of var.	String	✖	✖

<sql:update>	
Description	Executes an SQL INSERT, UPDATE, or DELETE statement. In addition, SQL statements that return nothing, such as SQL DDL statements, can be executed.
Usage Example	see below

```
<sql:update dataSource="${datasource}" sql="
  CREATE TABLE IF NOT EXISTS books (title
        VARCHAR(25),author VARCHAR(25),edition
        INTEGER,pubdate TIMESTAMP(8))">

</sql:update>
```

Attributes				
Name	**Description**	**Type**	**Required**	**Dynamic**
sql	SQL update statement.	String	✔	✔
dataSource	Data source associated with the database to query. A `String` value represents a relative path to a JNDI resource or the parameters for the `DriverManager` class.	`javax.sql.DataSource` or `String`	✖	✔
var	Name of the exported scoped variable for the result of the database update. The type of the scoped variable is `java.lang.Integer`.	String	✖	✖
scope	Scope of `var`.	String	✖	✖

<sql:transactions>	
Description	Establishes a transaction context for <sql:query> and <sql:update> subtags.
Usage Example	(see below)

```
<sql:transaction isolation="serializable">
  <sql:update >
       UPDATE books SET edition="2" WHERE
       author="Spielman"
  </sql:update>
  <sql:query var="bookList" >
       SELECT * FROM books ORDER BY author
  </sql:query>
</sql:transaction>
```

Attributes				
Name	**Description**	**Type**	**Required**	**Dynamic**
isolation	Transaction isolation level. If not specified, it is the isolation level the DataSource has been configured with.	String	✖	✔
dataSource	Data source associated with the database to query. A `String` value represents a relative path to a JNDI resource or the parameters for the `DriverManager` class.	`javax.sql.DataSource` or `String`	✖	✔

<sql:setDataSource>	
Description	Exports a data source either as a scoped variable or as the data source configuration variable (javax.servlet.jsp.jstl.sql.dataSource).

Usage Example	`<sql:setDataSource var="datasource"`
	`scope="application"`
	`driver="org.gjt.mm.mysql.Driver"`
	`url="jdbc:mysql://localhost/jstlbook"/>`

Attributes

Name	Description	Type	Required	Dynamic
dataSource	Data source associated with the database to query. A String value represents a relative path to a JNDI resource or the parameters for the DriverManager class.	javax.sql.DataSource or String	✔ (if specifying only a data source)	✔
driver	JDBC parameter: driver class name.	String	✖	✔
url	JDBC parameter: URL associated with the database.	String	✔ (if no dataSource specified)	✔
user	JDBC parameter: database user on whose behalf the connection to the database is being made.	String	✖	✔
password	JDBC parameter: user password	String	✖	✔
var	Name of the exported scoped variable for the data source specified. Type can be String or DataSource.	String	✖	✖
scope	If var is specified, scope of the exported variable. Otherwise, scope of the data source configuration variable.	String	✖	✖

<sql:param>	
Description	Sets the values of parameter markers ("?") in a SQL statement. Subtag of SQLExecutionTag actions such as <sql:query> and <sql:update>.

Usage Example	`<sql:query var="bookList" >`
	`SELECT * FROM books WHERE title LIKE ? ORDER BY author`
	`<sql:param value="${searchParam}"/>`
	`</sql:query>`

Attributes				
Name	**Description**	**Type**	**Required**	**Dynamic**
value	Value of the parameter.	Object	✔ (if no body content specified)	✔

<sql:dateParam>	
Description	Sets the values of parameter markers ("?") in a SQL statement for values of type `java.util.Date`. Subtag of SQLExecutionTag actions, such as <sql:query> and <sql:update>.

Usage Example	`<sql:query var="bookList" >`
	`SELECT * FROM books WHERE pubdate > ? ORDER BY author`
	`<sql:dateParam value="${param.pubdate}" />`
	`</sql:query>`

Attributes				
Name	**Description**	**Type**	**Required**	**Dynamic**
value	Parameter value for DATE, TIME, or TIMESTAMP column in a database table.	`java.util.Date`	✔	✔
Type	One of "date", "time" or "timestamp".	String	✔	✔

8.6 I18N Tag Library

These are the tags contained in the I18N tab library.

8.6.1 Tag Library URI

```
<%@ taglib uri="http://java.sun.com/jstl/fmt" prefix="fmt" %>
```

8.6.2 Internationalization Actions

<fmt:setLocale>	
Description	Stores the specified locale in the `javax.servlet.jsp.jstl.fmt.locale` configuration variable.
Usage Example	`<fmt:setLocale value="${param.currentLocale}" />`

Attributes				
Name	**Description**	**Type**	**Required**	**Dynamic**
value	A String value is interpreted as the printable representation of a locale, which must contain a two-letter (lower-case) language code (as defined by ISO-639), and may contain a two-letter (upper-case) country code (as defined by ISO-3166). Language and country codes must be separated by hyphen ('-') or underscore ('_').	`String` or `java.util.Locale`	✔	✔
variant	Vendor- or browser-specific variant. Reference the javadocs on `java.util.Locale` for more information on variants.	`String`	✖	✔
scope	Scope of the *locale* configuration variable.	`String`	✖	✖

<fmt:bundle>				
Description	Creates an I18N localization context to be used by its body content.			
Usage Example	`<fmt:bundle basename="resources.jstlpgtz" >`			
Attributes				
Name	**Description**	**Type**	**Required**	**Dynamic**
basename	Resource bundle base name. This is the bundle's fully-qualified resource name, which has the same form as a fully-qualified class name, that is, it uses "." as the package component separator and does not have any file type (such as ".class" or ".properties") suffix.	`String`	✔	✔
prefix	Prefix to be prepended to the value of the message key of any nested <fmt:message> action.	`String`	✖	✔

<fmt:setBundle>				
Description	Creates an I18N localization context and stores it in the scoped variable or the `javax.servlet.jsp.jstl.fmt.localization Context` configuration variable.			
Usage Example	`<fmt:setBundle basename="resources.jstlpgtz" />`			
Attributes				
Name	**Description**	**Type**	**Required**	**Dynamic**
basename	Resource bundle base name. This is the bundle's fully-qualified resource name, which has the same form as a fully-qualified class name, that is, it uses "." as the package component separator and does not have any file type (such as ".class" or ".properties") suffix.	`String`	✔	✔
var	Name of the exported scoped variable which stores the I18N localization context of type `javax.servlet.jsp.jstl.fmt.LocalizationContext`	`String`	✖	✖
scope	Scope of var or the localization context configuration variable.	`String`	✖	✖

<fmt:message>				
Description	Looks up a localized message in a resource bundle.			
Usage Example	`<fmt:message key="hello" />`			
Attributes				
Name	**Description**	**Type**	**Required**	**Dynamic**
key	Message key to be looked up.	`String`	✔	✔
bundle	Localization context in whose resource bundle the message key is looked up.	`LocalizationContext`	✖	✔
var	Name of the exported scoped variable which stores the I18N localization context of type `javax.servlet.jsp.jstl.fmt.LocalizationContext`	`String`	✖	✖

Name	Description	Type	Required	Dynamic
scope	Scope of var or the localization context configuration variable.	String	✖	✖

<fmt:param>				
Description	Supplies a single parameter for parametric replacement to a containing <fmt:message>.			

Usage Example	`<fmt:message key="hellopersonal" >`
	`<fmt:param value="${param.username}"/>`
	`</fmt:message >`			

Attributes				
Name	**Description**	**Type**	**Required**	**Dynamic**
value	Argument used for parametric replacement.	Object	✔ (if no body content specified)	✔

<fmt:requestEncoding>				
Description	Sets the request's character encoding.			
Usage Example	`<fmt:requestEncoding value="UTF-8" />`			
Attributes				
Name	**Description**	**Type**	**Required**	**Dynamic**
value	Name of character encoding to be applied when decoding request parameters.	String	✔ (if no body content specified)	✔

<fmt:timezone>	
Description	Specifies the time zone in which time information is to be formatted or parsed in its body content.
Usage Example	`<fmt:timeZone value="${param.currentTimeZone}" >`

Attributes				
Name	**Description**	**Type**	**Required**	**Dynamic**
value	The time zone. A String value is interpreted as a time zone ID. This may be one of the time zone IDs supported by the Java platform (such as "America/Los_Angeles") or a custom time zone ID (such as "GMT-8"). See java.util.TimeZone for more information on supported time zone formats.	String or java.util.TimeZone	✔	✔

<fmt:setTimeZone>	
Description	Creates an I18N localization context and stores it in the scoped variable or the javax.servlet.jsp.jstl.fmt.localizationContext configuration variable.
Usage Example	<fmt:setTimeZone value="${param.currentTimeZone}" scope="application"/>

Attributes				
Name	**Description**	**Type**	**Required**	**Dynamic**
value	The time zone. A String value is interpreted as a time zone ID. This may be one of the time zone IDs supported by the Java platform (such as "America/Los_Angeles") or a custom time zone ID (such as "GMT-8"). See java.util.TimeZone for more information on supported time zone formats.	String or java.util.TimeZone	✔	✔
var	Name of the exported scoped variable which stores the time zone of type java.util.TimeZone.	String	✖	✖
scope	Scope of var or the time zone configuration variable.	String	✖	✖

8.6.3 Formatting Actions

<fmt:formatNumber>				
Description	Formats a numeric value in a locale-sensitive or customized manner as a number, currency, or percentage.			
Usage Example	`<fmt:formatNumber value="${speedOfLight}" pattern= "##.##" />`			
Attributes				
Name	**Description**	**Type**	**Required**	**Dynamic**
value	Numeric value to be formatted.	`String` or `Number`	✔	✔
type	Specifies whether the value is to be formatted as number, currency, or percentage	`String`	✖	✔
pattern	Custom formatting pattern.	`String`	✖	✔
currencyCode	ISO 4217 currency code. Applied only when formatting currencies (i.e. if type is equal to "currency"); ignored otherwise.	`String`	✖	✔
currencySymbol	Currency symbol. Applied only when formatting currencies (i.e. if type is equal to "currency"); ignored otherwise.	`String`	✖	✔
groupingUsed	Specifies whether the formatted output will contain any grouping separators.	`boolean`	✖	✔
maxIntegerDigits	Maximum number of digits in the integer portion of the formatted output.	`int`	✖	✔
minIntegerDigit	Minimum number of digits in the integer portion of the formatted output.	`int`	✖	✔
maxFractionDigits	Maximum number of digits in the fractional portion of the formatted output.	`int`	✖	✔
minFractionDigits	Minimum number of digits in the fractional portion of the formatted output.	`int`	✖	✔
var	Name of the exported scoped variable which stores the formatted result as a `String`.	`String`	✖	✖
scope	Scope of var or the time zone configuration variable.	`String`	✖	✖

<fmt:parseNumber>	
Description	Parses the string representation of numbers, currencies, and percentages that were formatted in a locale-sensitive or customized manner.
Usage Example	`<fmt:parseNumber value="${currentOrder}" integerOnly="true" />`

Attributes

Name	Description	Type	Required	Dynamic
value	String to be parsed	String	✔ (if value not specified in body content)	✔
type	Specifies whether the string in the value attribute should be parsed as a number, currency, or percentage.	String	✖	✔
pattern	Custom formatting pattern that determines how the string in the value attribute is to be parsed.	String	✖	✔
parseLocale	Locale whose default formatting pattern (for numbers, currencies, or percentages, respectively) is to be used during the parse operation, or to which the pattern specified via the pattern attribute (if present) is applied.	String or java.util. Locale	✖	✔
integerOnly	Specifies whether just the integer portion of the given value should be parsed.	boolean	✖	✔
var	Name of the exported scoped variable which stores the parsed result (of type java.lang.Number).	String	✖	✖
scope	Scope of var or the time zone configuration variable.	String	✖	✖

<fmt:formatDate>	
Description	Allows the formatting of dates and times in a locale-sensitive or customized manner.
Usage Example	`<fmt:formatDate dateStyle="short" type="date" value="${now}" />`

Attributes				
Name	**Description**	**Type**	**Required**	**Dynamic**
value	Date and/or time to be formatted.	`java.util.Date`	✔	✔
type	Specifies whether the time, the date, or both the time and date components of the given date are to be formatted.	`String`	✖	✔
dateStyle	Predefined formatting style for dates. Follows the semantics defined in class `java.text.DateFormat`. Applied only when formatting a date or both a date and time (i.e. if `type` is missing or is equal to “date” or “both”); ignored otherwise.	`String`	✖	✔
timeStyle	Predefined formatting style for times. Follows the semantics defined in class `java.text.DateFormat`. Applied only when formatting a time or both a date and time (i.e. if `type` is equal to “time” or “both”); ignored otherwise.	`String`	✖	✔
pattern	Custom formatting style for dates and times.	`String`	✖	✔
timeZone	Time zone in which to represent the formatted time.	`String` or `java.util.TimeZone`	✖	✔
var	Name of the exported scoped variable which stores the formatted result as `String`.	`String`	✖	✖
scope	Scope of `var` or the time zone configuration variable.	`String`	✖	✖

<fmt:parseDate>				
Description	Parses the string representation of dates and times that were formatted in a locale-sensitive or customized manner.			
Usage Example	`<fmt:parseDate var="pubDate" value="${param.pubDate}" pattern="MM/dd/yy" />`			
Attributes				
Name	**Description**	**Type**	**Required**	**Dynamic**
value	Date string to be parsed.	`String`	✔ (if value not supplied in body content)	✔
type	Specifies whether the date string in the value attribute is supposed to contain a time, a date, or both.	`String`	✖	✔
dateStyle	Predefined formatting style for days which determines how the date component of the date string is to be parsed. Applied only when formatting a date or both a date and time (i.e. if type is missing or is equal to “date” or “both”); ignored otherwise.	`String`	✖	✔
timeStyle	Predefined formatting style for times which determines how the time component in the date string is to be parsed. Applied only when formatting a time or both a date and time (i.e. if type is equal to “time” or “both”); ignored otherwise.	`String`	✖	✔
pattern	Custom formatting pattern which determines how the date string is to be parsed.	`String`	✖	✔
timeZone	Time zone in which to represent the date string.	`String` or `java.util.TimeZone`	✖	✔

Name	Description	Type	Required	Dynamic
parseLocale	Locale whose predefined formatting styles for dates and times are to be used during the parse operation, or to which the pattern specified via the pattern attribute (if present) is applied.	String or java.util.Locale	✖	✔
var	Name of the exported scoped variable in which the parsing result (of type java.util.Date) is stored.	String	✖	✖
scope	Scope of var or the time zone configuration variable.	String	✖	✖

Index